# eNTERPRISE mATHEMATICS

## For GCSE and Standard Grade

### Y11 HIGHER

Edited by David Hobbs
University of Exeter

HEINEMANN
EDUCATIONAL

## To the teacher

The *Enterprising Mathematics Course* covers the National Curriculum at Key Stage 4 and is written in accordance with the Statutory requirements and in the spirit of the Non-Statutory Guidance. It adopts a context-based approach, encouraging cross-curricular links and exploration within mathematics itself.

The books have been written in a style that encourages active learning and teaching. For this reason the material is intended to be worked through with discussion in the classroom and guidance from teachers. No single book can be right for all classes, and teachers will need to use their judgement in supplementing and omitting pages as appropriate.

Further guidance in using the materials is provided in the Teaching Guide which accompanies this book. The Teaching Guide includes photocopiable pages of data, etc. together with photocopiable *Help sheets* for use at key points.

## To the student

This book has been written to help you understand that mathematics is about much more than just 'doing sums'. *Enterprising Mathematics* shows how mathematics is needed in other subjects at school or college and in the world around you . Mathematical ideas are developed through five themes:

- Environment    • Leisure and Recreation    • Design    • Science
- Business and Commerce

*Enterprising Mathematics* encourages you to do mathematics for yourself. On most pages you will find at least one 'box' containing suggestions for something extra for you to do:

### You could . . .

- These boxes contain ideas for you to develop yourself. They are all suitable for coursework.

There are also whole pages headed *Further activities* which provide more ideas for you to develop.

### For discussion

- To understand mathematical ideas you need to *talk* about them with your teacher and with other students.

Also the first page of each chapter provides a focus for an initial discussion.

### Find out

- These draw your attention to particular words or ideas which it is worth knowing more about.

There are also similar boxes headed **Did you know?** We hope you will enjoy these and want to talk about them with others.

### You will need the CASH FLOW sheet.

Ask your teacher for this sheet.

There will not be enough time to do all the things that are suggested in this book, and a choice will have to be made. You may need to discuss this with your teacher.

The ideas that you develop as you use this book are important. Working with your own ideas can be far more satisfying than working with other people's. *Enterprising Mathematics* encourages an active response from you. We hope you will enjoy using this book.

# Environment

# Leisure and Recreation

# Design

# Population growth

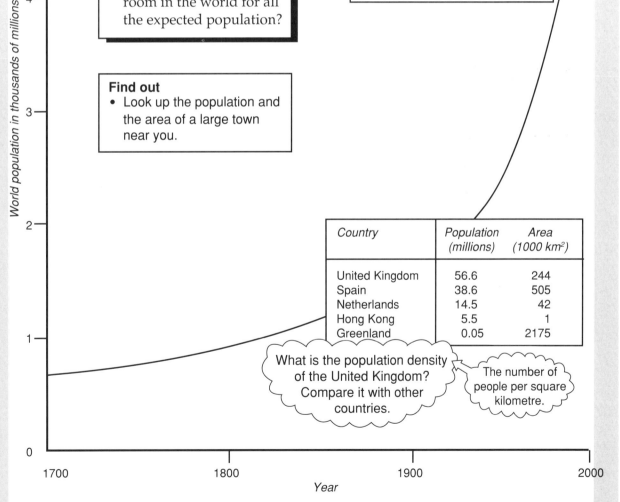

**Did you know?**
- The world population is expected to exceed 6 000 million by the end of this century and 10 000 million by the end of the next.
- The total land area of the world is about 135 million km² (but that includes 14 million km² for Antarctica).

**You could ...**
- Group several people together. Measure the space they take up and then estimate the space needed for a million people.
- Try to estimate the actual space really needed to support a million people.

**For discussion**
- Will there be enough room in the world for all the expected population?

**Find out**
- Look up the population and the area of a large town near you.

| Country | Population (millions) | Area (1000 km²) |
| --- | --- | --- |
| United Kingdom | 56.6 | 244 |
| Spain | 38.6 | 505 |
| Netherlands | 14.5 | 42 |
| Hong Kong | 5.5 | 1 |
| Greenland | 0.05 | 2175 |

What is the population density of the United Kingdom? Compare it with other countries.

The number of people per square kilometre.

*World population in thousands of millions* (y-axis: 0 to 6)

*Year* (x-axis: 1700 to 2000)

# A : The changing population

Here is some information about the population of the United Kingdom gathered in the censuses this century.

|  | Numbers in thousands | | |
| --- | --- | --- | --- |
| Year | Total | Males | Females |
| 1901 | 38 237 | 18 492 | 19 745 |
| 1911 | 42 082 | 20 357 | 21 725 |
| 1921 | 44 027 | 21 033 | 22 994 |
| 1931 | 46 038 | 22 060 | 23 978 |
| 1951 | 50 225 | 24 118 | 26 107 |
| 1961 | 52 709 | 25 481 | 27 228 |
| 1971 | 55 515 | 26 952 | 28 562 |
| 1981 | 55 848 | 27 104 | 28 742 |
| 1991 | 55 496 | 26 907 | 28 589 |

Source: Annual Abstract of Statistics 1992

There was no census taken in 1941. Why not?

**A1** (a) Plot a graph to show how the total population has changed.
(b) When was the population growing fastest?
(c) What population would you predict for 2001?

**A2** (a) What has been the increase in population since 1901?
(b) How many times greater was the 1991 population than the 1901 population?
(c) What was the percentage increase in the population from 1901 to 1991?

**A3** Calculate the fraction of males in each census. Comment on how it has changed.

**A4** The table on the right shows the population of Great Britain classified according to ethnic types.
Find the percentage for each type to 1 decimal place.

|  | Total (thousands) |
| --- | --- |
| White | 51 689 |
| West Indian/ African | 597 |
| Asian | 1356 |
| Other | 671 |

Source : Labour Force Surveys
Office of Population Censuses and Surveys

**A5** The table shows the age distribution in two towns in the 1991 census.

|  | 0 – 4 | 5 – 17 | 18 – 29 | 30 – 44 | 45 – Pensionable age | Pensionable age and over |
| --- | --- | --- | --- | --- | --- | --- |
| Luton | 14 592 | 30 557 | 37 252 | 36 050 | 30 214 | 23 003 |
| Worthing | 5384 | 12 500 | 15 192 | 17 885 | 16 346 | 28 847 |

Calculate the percentages in each age group.
Compare the age structures of the two towns.

# B : The age structure of the population

There are about 56 million people in the UK. Some are dependent on others.
For example
- pensions have to be provided for women over the age of 60
  and men over the age of 65.
- education is provided for the young.

Such things have to be financed by the working population. But in the 1970s the birth rate declined. So early in the 21st century there will be a shortage of working people to provide that finance.
Thus the age structure of the population is important.

**B1** The pyramid diagrams below show the age structure of Great Britain in 1961 and of Mexico in 1979. Comment on them.

### Population of Great Britain 1961          Population of Mexico 1979

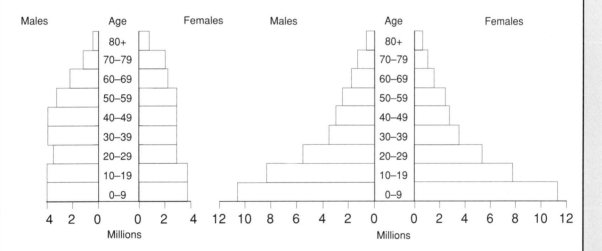

**B2** The table on the sheet AGE STRUCTURE shows the age distribution of the estimated resident population of the UK in 1987.
The pyramid diagram below it refers to 1901.
Using a coloured pen draw a pyramid diagram for 1987 on top of the 1901 diagram.
Make some comments comparing the two pyramid diagrams.

**B3** In 1987 what percentages of the population consisted of
(a) males over 64,
(b) females over 64,
(c) people of pensionable age?

**B4** Estimate the percentage of the population who were below the age of 16 in 1987.

## What is the average age of the population?

One form of average is the **mean average** : add up the ages of the people
and divide by the number of people.
Since the information on the sheet AGE STRUCTURE has been grouped it is
not possible to find the exact mean.  The best that can be done is to find
an approximate mean using mid-interval ages:

| Age | Mid-interval age | Number of people |
| --- | --- | --- |
| 0–4 | 2 | 3642 |
| 5–9 | 7 | 3467 |

Then the total age of the 0–4 age group is taken as 3642 × 2 which is 7284,
the total age of the 5–9 age group is taken as 3467 × 7 which is 24 269,
and so on.

**B5**   In the table on the sheet  write the mid-interval ages in the space next to the Age
column.
You can use the fourth column for the results of the multiplications or you can add
them up as you go using the memory of your calculator.
Divide the total by 56 764 to find the approximate mean average.

**B6**   Find the approximate mean ages of
(a) the males      (b)  the females.
Compare them.

You could use a
computer program.

A second form of average is the **median average** : the half-way item when the
numbers are arranged in increasing order.
Again the best that can be done is to find an approximation.  A convenient method, and
one which gives other useful information too,  is to make a **cumulative frequency** table
and graph.

**B7**   Complete the column headed *Number
of people* in the cumulative table on
the sheet. Then on graph paper plot a
cumulative graph. The start of it is
shown on the right.
From the graph read off an
approximation for the median age of
the whole population.
Compare it with the approximate
mean age (see B5).

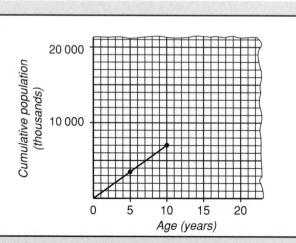

The graph can also be used to find the age above which, or below which, any fraction of the population lies. For example, to find the age above which a quarter of the population lies read across and down from $\frac{3}{4} \times 56\,764$ which is 42573.

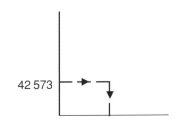

42 573

*Check that this gives about 56.*

56 is called the **upper quartile**.

**B8** Find the lower quartile (that is, the age below which a quarter of the population lies).

The difference between the quartiles, that is *upper quartile – lower quartile*, is called the **inter-quartile range**.

**B9** Check that the inter-quartile range is about 37.

The inter-quartile range gives a measure of the age-spread of the central 50% of the distribution. The greater the inter-quartile range, the more spread out is the central 50%.

**B10** Complete the table on the Age structure sheet for males and females. Plot cumulative graphs on the same sheet and find the medians, the quartiles and the inter-quartile ranges. Comment.

**Find out**
- In 1985 the life expectancy for males in England and Wales was 71.8 years and for females was 77.7 years.
  Look up the latest figures.

The Guinness Book of Records is a useful source of population data.

**You could . . .**
- Obtain the latest figures for the age structure of the UK population and compare them with the 1987 figures by finding the mean, median and inter-quartile range.

# C : How do populations grow?

In order to plan needs for the future it is necessary for the Government to make estimates of the population in 5 years' time, 10 years' time, etc.  Various **mathematical models** can be made to predict the future population.  Here are three simple ones.

### Model 1

Assume that the population grows by the same amount each year.

For example, take the present population of Great Britain as 55 million, and suppose it grows by 2 million each year.

In 1 year's time the population would be 55 + 2 million,
in 2 years' time the population would be 55 + 2 × 2 million,
in 3 years' time the population would be 55 + 2 × 3 million,

and so on.

---

**C1**   What would the population be in   **(i)** 5 years' time,   **(ii)** 10 years' time?
Give a formula for the population in *t* years' time.

**C2**   When would the population reach   **(i)** 85 million   **(ii)** 100 million
**(iii)** *N* million?

---

The graph shows how the population grows according to this model.  This is a **linear** model – the graph is a straight line.

The equation of the graph is

$$P = 55 + 2t$$

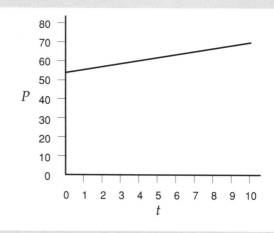

---

**C3**   The population of Kenya is about 20 million.
Suppose it grows by 1.5 million each year.

(a)  What would its population be in   (i)   1 year's time,
(ii)   2 years' time,
(iii)  10 years' time?
Give a formula for the population in *t* years' time.

(b)  When would the population reach   (i)   50 million,
(ii)   *N* million?

(c)   Draw a graph to show how the population increases.

## Model 2

Another model of growth can be made by assuming that the population increases by the same **fraction** each year – by 3% say.

This gives a different type of growth because the actual increase is not constant as in **Model 1**: it depends on the size of the population.

When the growth rate is 3% the population is **multiplied** by 1.03 each year.

Suppose the current population is 55 million and it grows by 3% each year.

In 1 year's time it would be $55 \times 1.03$ million.

In 2 years' time it would be $(55 \times 1.03) \times 1.03$ million
which is $55 \times 1.03^2$ million.

In 3 years' time it would be $55 \times 1.03^3$ million.

And so on.

> **Reminder**
>
> **To increase 55 by 3%**
>
> 3% is 3 hundredths, 0.03 as a decimal
>
> The new population is
> $$55 + (55 \times 0.03)$$
> This is the same as
> $$55 \times (1 + 0.03)$$
> which is
> $$55 \times 1.03$$
>
> The multiplying factor is 1.03

**C4** (a) Calculate the population after 1, 2, 3, 4 years.

(b) When would the population reach 70 million?

(c) What is the population ($P$ million) at time $t$ years?

(d) Plot a graph. Label it with its equation: $P = \ldots \ldots$

(e) Make two comments comparing the graph with the graph in Model 1.

> **For discussion**
> - Is a growth rate of 4% per year the same as 2% per half year?
> - What is the growth rate per month?

**C5** What is the multiplier for a growth rate of 1% per year? Find how a population of 55 million would grow with a growth rate of 1% per year.

Show it on the same graph as for C4 and label it with its equation.

**C6** Kenya is one of the fastest growing countries in the world with a growth rate of about 4% per year. Its population in 1980 was about 17 million. Make a prediction of its population in the year 2000.

**C7** Brazil had a population of about 136 million in 1985 with a growth rate of 2.26% per year. The United States had a population of about 239 million in 1985 with a growth rate of 0.89% per year. Estimate when both countries will have the same population.

> Try this computer program:
>
> ```
> 10   INPUT "Starting population "P
> 20   INPUT "Growth rate (%) "R
> 30   INPUT "Number of years " N
> 40   Y = 0
> 50   REPEAT
> 60     PRINT Y"    "P
> 70     P = P*(1 + R/100)
> 80     Y = Y + 1
> 90   UNTIL Y = N + 1
> ```
>
> You might wish to improve the program.

**C8** A population of 20 million is declining at 3% each year.
What is the multiplier each year?
Find the population  (i)  in 1 year's time
                     (ii) in 2 years' time.
Give a formula for the population in $t$ years' time.

> **BACTERIA IN FOOD LEFT AT ROOM TEMPERATURE DOUBLE EVERY 20 MINUTES**

**C9**   Suppose that initially 1 bacterium was present.
   (a)   (i)   How many bacteria would there be one hour later?
         (ii)  How long would it take for there to be 1000 bacteria?
         (iii) After $n$ lots of 20 minutes how many bacteria would there be?
         (iv)  How many bacteria would there be at time $t$ hours?

   (b)   What is the percentage increase every 20 minutes?

   (c)   (i)   The population of bacteria is multiplied by 2 every 20 minutes. By what is it multiplied every 10 minutes?
         (ii)  What is the percentage increase every 10 minutes?
         (iii) What is the percentage increase every 1 minute?

**C10**  A population of bacteria is tripled every 15 minutes.
   (a)   What is the percentage increase every 15 minutes?
   (b)   What is the multiplier every 5 minutes?
   (c)   What is the percentage increase every 5 minutes?

**C11**  A population of bacteria increases by 15% every hour.
   (a)   What is the multiplier per hour?
   (b)   What is the multiplier per day?
   (c)   What is the percentage increase per day?

---

**C12**  A lake is to be stocked with 1000 fish.
It is expected that the number of fish will increase by 20% every year.
At the end of each year some fish will be removed.
If 100 are removed, the number of fish at the end of the first year will be
$$1000 \times 1.2 \ - \ 100$$
which is 1100.

Continue the calculation for three more years assuming 100 fish are removed each year.

The process can be represented algebraically by
$$f_{n+1} = f_n \times 1.2 \ - \ c$$

where $f_n$ is the number of fish at the end of year $n$, and $c$ is the number removed each year.

Try other numbers for $c$ and comment on your results.

Try other growth rates.

Write a computer program?

## Model 3

Fortunately populations do not grow as in Models 1 and 2! As the population increases, the growth rate usually slows down, possibly due to a shortage of resources – food, living space, etc. So instead of a yearly growth rate of 3%, say, the growth rate $r$ % might be

$$3 \times ( \quad ) \%$$

> Something which decreases as
> $P$ increases.

A possibility for putting in the bracket is $1 - P/80$, say. As $P$ increases, $1 - P/80$ decreases and so the growth rate slows down. When $P$ is 80, $1 - P/80$ is 0 and so growth ceases. The maximum population size is therefore 80.

---

**C13** The *multiplier* for a growth rate of $r$% is $1 + r/100$.
Check that the multiplier can be written as $1 + 0.03(1 - P/80)$.

---

Suppose the initial population is 55 million.
Taking $P$ as 55 gives a multiplier of 1.009375 and so the population at the end of the first year is $55 \times 1.009375$ million, which is 55.515625 million.
In the second year the multiplier is $1 + 0.03(1 - 55.515625/80)$.

---

**C14** Check that this comes to 1.009181641 and that the population at the end of year 2 is 56.025 million (to 3 decimal places).

**C15** Continue the process to find the population at the end of the third year.

---

The repeated calculations get tedious and so it is sensible to use a computer program.

- Try inputs as above taking N as 20, 50, 100, 150, etc. What happens to the population?

- Try other growth rates.

- Try other values of M.

- Can you make the population decrease?

```
10    INPUT P
20    INPUT R
30    INPUT M
40    INPUT N
50    T = 1
60    REPEAT
70    P = P*(1 + R/100 - R/100*P/M)
80    PRINT T"    "INT(P*1000 + 0.5)/1000
90    T = T + 1
100   UNTIL T = N + 1
```

> M is 80 in the example above

> Number of years

- Compare Model 3 with Model 2 by including another column in the printout.

  Suggestions:  add to line 50  : Q = P
  add to line 70  : Q = Q*(1 + R/100)
  add to line 80  : "    "INT(Q*1000 + 0.5)/1000

- Draw some graphs.

# Now try these . . .

1. The table shows the population of England and Wales in the censuses this century.
   (a) Has there been much change in the fraction of the population which is female?
   (b) Plot a graph to show how the total population has changed.
   (c) How many times greater was the 1991 population than the 1901 population?
   (d) What was the percentage increase in the population from 1901 to 1991?

| Year | Population in thousands | |
| | Males | Females |
| --- | --- | --- |
| 1901 | 15 729 | 16 799 |
| 1911 | 17 446 | 18 625 |
| 1921 | 18 075 | 19 811 |
| 1931 | 19 133 | 20 819 |
| 1951 | 21 016 | 22 742 |
| 1961 | 22 304 | 23 801 |
| 1971 | 23 683 | 25 067 |
| 1981 | 23 873 | 25 281 |
| 1991 | 23 272 | 24 676 |

2. The table shows the age structure of the male and female population of England and Wales in 1971.
   (a) Find estimates for the mean average ages of the males and females.
   (b) Draw cumulative frequency graphs for males and females and find
       (i) the median average ages,
       (ii) the lower quartiles,
       (iii) the upper quartiles,
       (iv) the inter-quartile ranges.
   (c) Comment on your results.

| | Population in millions | |
| | Males | Females |
| --- | --- | --- |
| 0–9 | 4.7 | 4.5 |
| 10–19 | 4.1 | 3.9 |
| 20–29 | 4.0 | 3.9 |
| 30–39 | 3.3 | 3.2 |
| 40–49 | 3.4 | 3.5 |
| 50–59 | 3.2 | 3.4 |
| 60–69 | 2.7 | 3.2 |
| 70–79 | 1.2 | 2.1 |
| 80 and over | 0.4 | 0.9 |

3. (a) The population of a country is 30 million in 1980.
   It grows by 1.5 million per year.
   Write down a formula for the population $n$ years later.
   (b) The population of another country is also 30 million in 1980.
   It grows by 3.5% per year.
   Write down a formula for the population $n$ years later.
   (c) Find approximately how long after 1980 the two populations become the same size again.
   (d) On the same axes sketch graphs to show how the populations grow.

# Mapping the earth

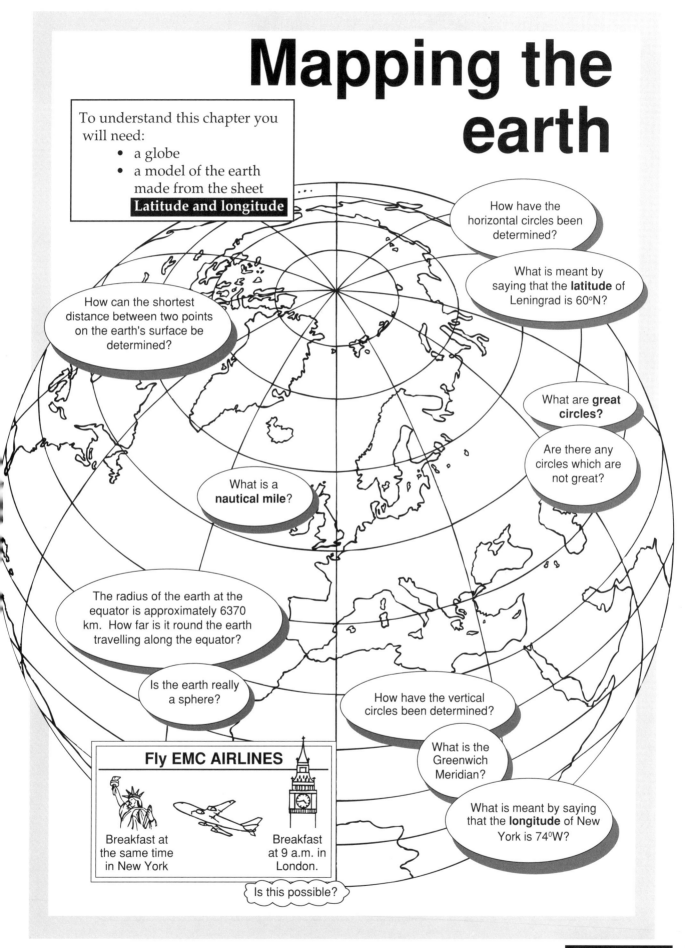

To understand this chapter you will need:
- a globe
- a model of the earth made from the sheet **Latitude and longitude**

How have the horizontal circles been determined?

What is meant by saying that the **latitude** of Leningrad is 60°N?

How can the shortest distance between two points on the earth's surface be determined?

What are **great circles?**

Are there any circles which are not great?

What is a **nautical mile**?

The radius of the earth at the equator is approximately 6370 km. How far is it round the earth travelling along the equator?

Is the earth really a sphere?

How have the vertical circles been determined?

What is the Greenwich Meridian?

What is meant by saying that the **longitude** of New York is 74°W?

**Fly EMC AIRLINES**

Breakfast at the same time in New York

Breakfast at 9 a.m. in London.

Is this possible?

# A: Finding distances on the earth's surface

*In the examples on this page distances are found between places on or close to the equator.*

> The latitudes and longitudes in this section are given to the nearest degree unless otherwise stated.

Kampala (Uganda) and Quito (Ecuador) are both very close to the equator.
The longitude of Kampala is 32°E, and of Quito is 78°W.
Here is how to find the distance between them.

> O is the centre of the earth.

**1**  Draw a diagram showing a section through the earth at the equator.
Mark roughly the positions of Kampala and Quito.

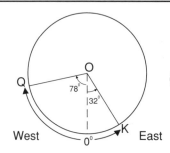

> Remember all the angles of longitude are measured East or West from the Greenwich meridian (0°).

**2**  Find the angle QOK:
$$\angle QOK = 78° + 32° = 110°$$

**3**  The distance between K and Q is
$\frac{110}{360}$ of the distance round the equator,

which is approximately $\frac{110}{360} \times 40\,000$ km    to the nearest hundred

$$= 12\,200 \text{ km}$$

> The distance round the equator is
> $2\pi \times$ radius
> $= 2\pi \times 6370$ km
> $= 40\,000$ km (to the nearest hundred).

---

**A1**  Baker Island (Pacific Ocean) and Pontianak (Borneo) are both almost on the equator. The longitude of Baker Island is 176°E and of Pontianak is 109°E. Find the distance between them.

> Notice that they are both **east**.

**A2**  Macapa (Brazil) is very close to the equator and has a longitude of 51°W. Find its distance from Kampala.

**A3**  Find the distance from Baker Island to Quito.
(Which distance? The shorter distance.)

**A4**  What is the distance from Quito to Macapa along the equator?
(There is a quick way of doing this one. Can you find it?)

*In the examples on this page distances are found between points with the **same longitude**.*

Hong Kong and Perth (Australia) are both approximately on the same circle of longitude. The latitude of Hong Kong is $22^0$N and of Perth is $32^0$S.

Here is how to find the distance between them.

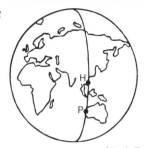

① Draw a diagram showing a 'vertical' section of the earth through the circle of longitude on which Hong Kong and Perth are located. Mark approximately the positions of Hong Kong and Perth.

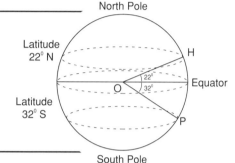

North Pole

Latitude $22^0$ N

H

$22^0$
O $32^0$ Equator

Latitude $32^0$ S

P

South Pole

② Find the angle POH:
  ∟ POH = $32^0$ + $22^0$ = $54^0$

> Perth is $32^0$ **South** of the equator.
> Hong Kong is $22^0$ **North** of the equator.

③ The distance between P and H is $\frac{54}{360}$ of the distance round the earth,

  which is approximately $\frac{54}{360} \times 40\,000$ km

  = 6000 km

> to the nearest hundred

> **Assumption**
> All sections of the earth through the poles are circles with the same radius, 6370 km.
> So the circumference of the circle of longitude is the same as the distance round the equator.

**A5** Moscow and Nairobi are both approximately on the same circle of longitude. Moscow has a latitude of $56^0$N. Nairobi has a latitude of $1^0$S. Find the distance between them.

> Note that they are both **North** of the equator.

**A6** Glasgow and Madrid have approximately the same longitude. The latitude of Glasgow is $55^0$ 53'N and of Madrid is $40^0$24'N. Find the distance between them.

> There are 60 minutes (60') in $1^0$.

**A7** Washington is at ($39^0$N, $77^0$W). Lima is at ($12^0$S, $77^0$W). Find the distance between them.

**For discussion**
• An explorer walked 10 km north, 10 km east and 10 km south. The explorer was then back at the starting point. Where on the earth's surface could the starting point have been?

> There is more than one possible place.

*In the examples on this page distances are found between points with the **same latitude.***

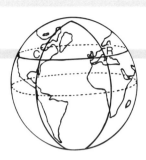

Rome and Chicago are approximately on the same circle of latitude, 42⁰N. Rome has a longitude of $12\frac{1}{2}$ ⁰E, and Chicago has a longitude of 88⁰W. Here is how to find the distance between them.

**1** Draw a diagram showing the circle of latitude through Rome and Chicago. Mark approximately the positions of Rome and Chicago.

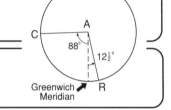

**2** Find the angle CAR:
$$\llcorner CAR = 88^0 + 12\tfrac{1}{2}^0 = 100\tfrac{1}{2}^0$$

*A is the centre of the circle of latitude.*

**3** The distance between R and C is $\frac{100.5}{360}$ of the distance round the circle of latitude.

**4** *But what is the distance round the circle of latitude?*

Draw a diagram showing a section of the earth through the poles. Mark in a point P at a latitude of 42⁰.

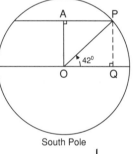

First, find the radius of the circle of latitude:
$$AP = OQ = OP \times \cos 42^0$$
$$= 6370 \times \cos 42^0 \text{ km}$$
$$= 4734 \text{ km}$$

*More accuracy than is really justified is given here. The final answer is given to the nearest hundred.*

*Or from triangle OAP*
$$AP = OP \cos 42^0$$

Then, the distance round the circle of latitude is
$2\pi \times 4734 = 29\,700$ km (to the nearest hundred).

**5** Put **3** and **4** together:
The distance between R and C is $\frac{100.5}{360} \times 29\,700 = 8300$ km  *to the nearest hundred*

**A8** Halifax (Nova Scotia) and Bucharest are approximately on the same circle of latitude, $44\frac{1}{2}$ ⁰N. What is the radius of this circle of latitude? Halifax has a longitude of $63\frac{1}{2}$ ⁰W, and Bucharest has a longitude of 26⁰E. Find the distance between them.

**A9** Birmingham and Berlin are approximately on the same circle of latitude, $52\frac{1}{2}$ ⁰N. The longitude of Birmingham is 1⁰50'W, and of Berlin is 13⁰ 24'E. Find the distance between them.

**A10** Sydney is at (34⁰S, 151⁰E) and Cape Town at (34⁰S, 18⁰E). Find the distance between them.

# B : Time and place

We all know that when it is daytime on one half of the world, it is night-time on the other half.
Day moves into night (and night into day) because the earth is turning.
How fast is it turning, and what difference does it make?

**The earth does 1 full turn on its axis in 24 hours. A full turn is $360^0$. So in 1 hour the earth turns through $15^0$.**

Because the earth is turning (which way?), the sun appears first (*rises*) in the east and then, several hours later, disappears (*sets*) in the west.

At any place on the earth, noon (midday) is defined as the moment when the sun is exactly due south of that place. All other times of day are worked out from noon.

So as you move east or west your time changes!

**Find out**
- What are time zones?
- How do sundials work?
- How can the fact that the shadows are shortest when the sun is exactly south of your position be used to deduce your longitude?

*When it is 9 a.m. in London what time would it be in Washington, USA, which is on longitude $77^0$W?*

London is on $0^0$ longitude. So Washington is $77^0$ west of London.
$77^0$ is about 5 hours of time ($77 \div 15 \approx 5$).
Is Washington ahead of, or behind, London in time?
As Washington is to the west, it must see the sun *after* London and so it is *behind* in time.
When it is 9 a.m. in London the time in Washington is therefore about 4 a.m. ($9 - 5 = 4$).

**Did you know?**
- Between Land's End and Yarmouth there is a time difference of almost 29 minutes.
- Russia has the greatest time difference of any country, 10 hours.

**B1** When the time is 0700 in London about what time would it be in Buenos Aires ($58^0$W)?

**B2** When it is midnight in London about what time would it be in Brisbane ($153^0$E)?

**B3** Nadia lives in London. She received a telephone call at 4 a.m. from a friend in Bombay. What time was it in Bombay? (The longitude of Bombay is $73^0$E.)

**B4** What is the difference in time between
(a) San Francisco ($122^0$W) and Washington ($77^0$W)
(b) Berlin ($13^0$E) and Baghdad ($44^0$E)
(c) New York ($75^0$W) and Delhi ($77^0$E)?

**B5** Pierre works in Marseilles ($5^0$E). He urgently needs to contact an office in Hong Kong ($114^0$E) when it opens at 0800. What time should he phone from Marseilles?

**B6** How fast do you need to go for time to stand still?

# C : Making maps

You will need a globe and an atlas which contains various representations of the earth.

- *Find maps on which*
  *(a) circles of **latitude** are shown as straight lines,*
  *(b) circles of **longitude** are shown as straight lines.*
- *Can the shortest distance between two points on the earth's surface be found by drawing a straight line on a map?*
- *Look at Greenland on various maps. Look at it on the globe. Comment.*

**Did you know?**
- Australia has three times the area of Greenland.
- South America has about two and a half times the area of Australia.
- Antarctica has about twice the area of Australia.

Maps can easily be taken for granted. But the problem of representing accurately the surface of the earth on a flat piece of paper is an impossible one. A piece of paper cannot be fitted onto a sphere without crumpling it up or having gaps! Ways of making maps have therefore been devised which are not accurate in *all* respects but which are accurate in *some* respects. Various *projections* are used to make maps.
*Compare the two projections on this page. Comment on their differences.*

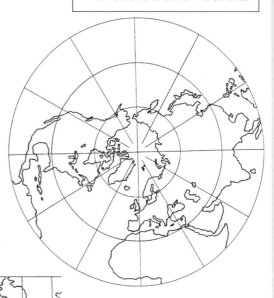

*Polar zenithal projection*

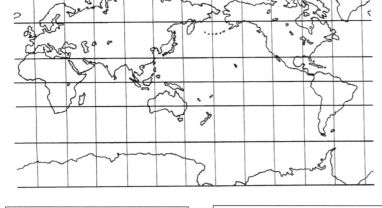

*Mercator's projection*

**Find out**
- Find out about other map projections – for example, conical projection.
- Find out about the Peters atlas.

**For discussion**
- Imagine two lines on the earth's surface at right angles to the equator. Are they parallel?

- The angles of a triangle add up to $180^0$.

Do parallel lines meet?

Is it actually possible to draw parallel lines?

Do they?

## A cylindrical projection

Imagine a sheet of paper wrapped around a model of the earth.
Each point P on the earth's surface can be mapped onto a point P' on the paper cylinder by going across from the vertical axis. The paper is then unfolded. Circles of latitude become horizontal straight lines, and circles of longitude become vertical straight lines.

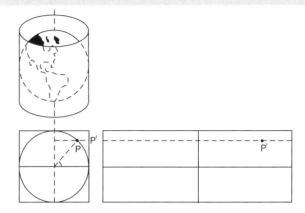

**C1** Suppose the diameter of the sphere is 8 cm.
Show that the length of the paper is about 25.1 cm.
Draw the rectangle full-size on a sheet of A4 paper.
Mark in lines for the equator and for the Greenwich meridian.

**C2** The point P has latitude $t°$ and longitude $g°$.
Explain why the distance of P' above the equator is
$4 \times \sin t°$ cm, and the distance from the Greenwich meridian is
$\frac{g}{360} \times 25.1$ cm.
Use these results to mark in some lines of latitude and longitude. Also mark in the positions of some cities.

**Did you know?**
- Mercator's projection is based on a cylinder but lines are drawn from the centre of the earth to map points onto the cylinder. Because this gives rise to problems near the poles, the method is modified by altering the spacing of the lines of latitude.
  An advantage of Mercator's projection is that a straight line on the map corresponds to a course on the earth with a constant compass bearing. This makes it useful for navigational purposes.

## A zenithal projection

This projection is made by projecting from the centre of the earth onto a tangent plane.
Circles of latitude project onto circles.
Circles of longitude project onto straight lines.

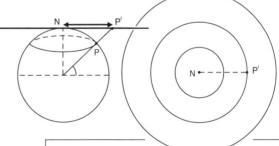

**C3** Suppose again that the sphere has a diameter of 8 cm.
Show that a circle at latitude $t°$ maps onto a circle of radius $\frac{4}{\tan t°}$ cm.

**C4** Draw some circles corresponding to various circles of latitude.
Draw some lines of longitude.
Mark in some cities.

**Did you know?**
- Not only do circles of longitude map to straight lines, but so do all great circles. This means that the shortest distance between two points on the earth's surface appears as a straight line on the map. This is a useful feature for navigation by ships and planes. A disadvantage is that points near the edge of the hemisphere appear too far out. Distances, angles and areas are therefore distorted.

Can you explain why?

# Now try these . . .

1. The diameter of the earth is approximately 12 740 km.
   What is the distance round the earth, to the nearest hundred km, at the equator?

2. Rome and Chicago are approximately on the same circle of latitude. Explain why the shortest route between them is not along the circle of latitude.

3. What are the latitudes and longitudes of the points at the other ends of the earth's diameter from
   (a) Kampala ($0^0$N, $32^0$E)
   (b) London ($51.5^0$N, $0^0$E)
   (c) Sydney ($34^0$S, $151^0$E)?

4. When it is 12 noon in London what time is it in
   (a) New York $75^0$W
   (b) Hong Kong $114^0$E?

5. Find the shortest distances between these places:
   (a) Mbandaka (Zaire) $18^0$E and Padang (Sumatra) $100^0$E, both almost on the equator
   (b) London $51^030'$N and Accra $5^030'$N, both almost on the same circle of longitude
   (c) Belfast ($55^0$N, $6^0$W) and Tangier ($36^0$N, $6^0$W)
   (d) Stockholm ($59^0$N, $18^0$E) and Cape Town ($34^0$S, $18^0$E)
   (e) Peking ($40^0$N, $116^0$E) and Philadelphia ($40^0$N, $75^0$W)
   (f) Tehran ($35^045'$N, $51^030'$E) and Tokyo ($35^045'$N, $139^045'$E)

6. What is the radius of the circle of latitude which forms the Arctic circle ($66.5^0$N)?
   What is its circumference?
   What would be the change of longitude in travelling 1000 km along the Arctic circle?

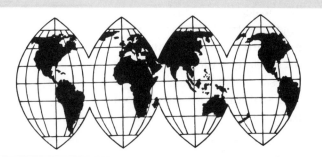

7. A nautical mile is defined as the distance along the circumference of a great circle (such as the equator) while moving through an angle of one-sixtieth of a degree (1 minute). Find the length of a nautical mile in metres.

# What's the probability?

## Come to the
## School Fair

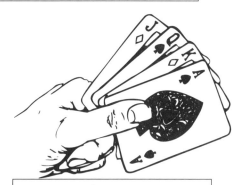

**10p a go!**
Pick two cards from two reds and two blacks. If they are the same colour you get your money back and another 10p!

**10p a go!**
Throw two dice.
If the difference between their scores is 3 or more, you get your money back and another 10p!

## Roll a 10p

If when the 10p stops it does not cross a line, you keep your 10p and we also give you another one.

**£1 a go!**
Throw six dice.
Get 6 sixes -
and win a car!

### You could . . .

- Try out the games to see if they will make money.
- Devise similar games of your own

# A : For discussion

### • How often does the letter *e* occur?

| Number of letters | 100 | 200 | 300 | 400 | 500 | 600 | 700 | 800 | 900 | 1000 | 1100 | 1200 | 1300 | 1400 | 1500 | 1600 | 1700 | 1800 | 1900 | 2000 |
|---|---|---|---|---|---|---|---|---|---|---|---|---|---|---|---|---|---|---|---|---|
| Number of e's so far | 9 | 21 | 36 | 50 | 62 | 71 | 83 | 96 | 108 | 114 | 124 | 143 | 156 | 172 | 187 | 198 | 209 | 220 | 227 | 235 |
| Fraction of e's | 0.09 | 0.105 | 0.12 | | | | | | | | | | | | | | | | | |

From **The Return of the Native** by Thomas Hardy

### • How likely is it that the next car which passes is a Ford?

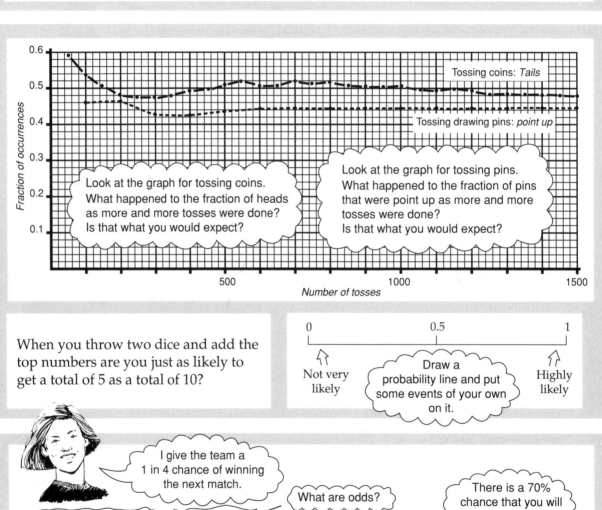

When you throw two dice and add the top numbers are you just as likely to get a total of 5 as a total of 10?

Draw a probability line and put some events of your own on it.

I give the team a 1 in 4 chance of winning the next match.

What are odds?

What are the probabilities for each horse?

What is the total probability?

There is a 70% chance that you will get rain tomorrow.

If you put £1 on each horse would you be certain of winning something?

**3.45 Coronation Stakes**

Chimes of Freedom ------------ 7 - 1
Hasbah ------------------------- 9 - 2
Heart of Joy -------------------- Evens
Mai Oui ------------------------- 10 - 1
Model Village ------------------- 20 - 1
Pharoah's Delight -------------- 7 - 2
Water Well --------------------- 33 - 1

# B : Finding probabilities without collecting data

Sometimes probabilities can be written down without having to collect data. They can be found from a list of the possible outcomes using ideas of "fairness" or symmetry.

For example

 1 When a coin is tossed there are two possible outcomes:
   *tail (T)*      *head (H)*
For a fair coin these are equally likely, so the probability of each outcome is $\frac{1}{2}$.
This means that in the long run you would expect to get a head on about $\frac{1}{2}$ of the occasions when the coin is tossed.

2 When two coins are tossed there are four possible outcomes:
   *TT*   *TH*   *HT*   *HH*
For fair coins these outcomes are all equally likely.
So the probability of getting 2 heads, for example is $\frac{1}{4}$.

 3 When a die is thrown there are six possible outcomes
   *1*   *2*   *3*   *4*   *5*   *6*
Since the die is symmetrical these 6 outcomes are all equally likely and so the probability of getting a 2, say, is $\frac{1}{6}$. The probability of not getting a 2 is $\frac{5}{6}$. In the long run you would get a *2* on about 1 throw in every 6 and *not a 2* on about 5 throws in every 6.

4 When a drawing pin is tossed there are two possible outcomes:
   *point up*      *point down*
**But** these are not equally likely.
So the probability of *point-up* is not $\frac{1}{2}$.
The probability of *point-up* would have to be found by experiment.

Experiments suggest that point down is more likely.

So in order to find probabilities in this way you need to list the possible outcomes, making sure that they are all equally-likely on the grounds of "fairness" or symmetry.
Then the probability of a particular event occurring is

$$\frac{\text{the number of outcomes in which the event occurs}}{\text{the total number of outcomes}}$$

**B1**   When 2 coins are tossed what is the probability of getting
(a) two heads      (b) a head and a tail      (c) both coins the same?
If you tossed the 2 coins 1000 times, about how many times would you expect to get *at least one* head?

**B2**   When a die is thrown what is the probability of getting
(a) an even number      (b) an odd number?
If you tossed the die 600 times, about how many times would you expect to get either a 5 or a 6?

**B3**   A coin and a die are thrown together.  List all the possible outcomes (be systematic!).
What is the probability of  (a)  a head and a 4    (b)  a tail and either a 5 or a 6?

**B4**   A bag contains 10 identical beads: 3 are red, 5 are green and 2 are yellow.
A bead is selected at random.  What is the  probability of getting
(a)   a red bead        (b)   a bead which is not yellow?

**B5**   A bag contains 15 beads, some of them blue and some white.  A bead is selected at
random, its colour is noted and it is then replaced.  This is done 200 times with these
results:
blue 83                white 117
How many beads of each colour would you expect there to be in the bag?

**B6**   The probability that an event occurs is $\frac{2}{5}$.
What is the probability that it does *not* occur?

**B7**
> **Only 10p a go!**
> Toss 3 coins. If they are
> all the same we give you
> 30p.

(a)   Write down the possible outcomes when 3 coins are tossed.
(b)   In 100 tosses of the 3 coins how many times would you
expect to get all 3 coins the same?
How much would the stall expect to pay out?
What would the expected profit be for 100 tosses of the 3
coins? What would the expected profit be per go?

**B8**
> **Only 10p a go!**
> Toss 2 coins.  If you get
> 2 heads we give you 30p.

> Would you get the same result
> if you worked it out from 200
> goes, say?

Work out the expected
profit per go.

**You could . . .**
- Devise a game throwing
a coin and a die (see B3).
Work out the expected
profit per go.

## For discussion
- A French mathematician, d'Alembert (1717 – 1783),
once claimed that the probability of getting 2 heads
when 2 coins are tossed is $\frac{1}{3}$ because there are 3
outcomes: both heads, both tails and one of each.
Criticise his argument.

- Does tossing one coin twice lead to the same
outcomes and probabilities as tossing two coins?

- "When two dice are thrown and  the
total found, there are 11 possible
totals from 2 to 12.
So the probability of getting a total of
3 is $\frac{1}{11}$."

Do you agree?

- A student asked people to
choose a number at random
from 1 to 9.  The student
expected the nine numbers
to be equally likely.
Do you agree?
Try it out.

> Suppose instead you
> asked them to choose
> from a set of cards
> (face down) numbered
> 1 to 9. How do the
> results compare?

# C : A probability pattern

When 2 coins are tossed there are 4 possible outcomes.

TT  TH  HT  HH

So there is

1 way to get 0 heads
2 ways to get 1 head
1 way to get 2 heads

| Number of heads | 0 | 1 | 2 |
|---|---|---|---|
| Number of ways | 1 | 2 | 1 |

When 3 coins are tossed there are 8 possible outcomes. You have listed them in B7. Check that you agree with the table on the right.

*Why are there 8?*

| Number of heads | 0 | 1 | 2 | 3 |
|---|---|---|---|---|
| Number of ways | 1 | 3 | 3 | 1 |

Now make a list of the possible outcomes for 4 coins. Draw up a table to show the number of ways of getting the various numbers of heads.

*How many outcomes are there in total?*

Could you have completed the table without having to list the possible outcomes?

*Is there a pattern?*

*Suggestion: Write the numbers out like this*

1   1          one coin

1   2   1      two coins

1   3   3   1  three coins

*What are the totals for each line?*

Without listing all the possible outcomes find the number of ways for the various numbers of heads when tossing

6 coins, 7 coins, . . . , 10 coins.

Is the probability of getting 3 heads with 4 coins the same as the probability of getting 6 heads with 8 coins?

Draw a bar chart to show the probabilities of the various numbers of heads when 10 coins are tossed.

Use your knowledge of the probabilities to invent some coin tossing games. For example, toss 5 coins. You win if . . .

Assume that the probability that a baby is a girl is $\frac{1}{2}$. In 1000 families with 5 children each, how many would you expect to have 0 girls, 1 girl, etc? For families of 4 children would you expect 2 of each to be the most common?

*Try it for other family sizes too.*

What would the expected profit be when 32 marbles are rolled?

10p
a marble

30p 20p 0 0 20p 30p

# D : Combined events

As you might have seen when two dice are thrown and the top numbers are added together, the totals are not all equally likely. Here is a way to work out the probabilities for the various totals.

The diagram shows the 36 possible outcomes. All of these outcomes are equally likely. To distinguish between the dice one is blue and one is red. Two outcomes have been marked to show a total of 5.

*Score on red die*

*Score on blue die*

|   | 1 | 2 | 3 | 4 | 5 | 6 |
|---|---|---|---|---|---|---|
| 1 |   |   |   | 5 |   |   |
| 2 |   |   |   |   |   |   |
| 3 |   |   |   |   |   |   |
| 4 | 5 |   |   |   |   |   |
| 5 |   |   |   |   |   |   |
| 6 |   |   |   |   |   |   |

*Note that 1 on the blue and 4 on the red is different from 4 on the blue and 1 on the red.*

*Does throwing a single die twice lead to the same outcomes as throwing two dice?*

> **D1**   Copy the diagram and complete it to show the totals.

*How many outcomes give a total of 5? What is the probability of a total of 5?*

*What is the probability of getting a double?*

*both top numbers the same.*

*What is the probability that the score on the red die is greater than the score on the blue die?*

*What is the probability of a total of at least 8?*

*What is the probability of at least one six?*

*What is the probability of just one six?*

*Is it true that the probability of either a double or a total of 5 is the same as (the probability of a double) + (the probability of a total of 5)? And is it true when 5 is replaced by 6? Explain and give some more examples.*

> **D2**   Draw up a table to show the probabilities of all the possible totals.
>
> | Total | Probability |
> |-------|-------------|
> | 2     |             |
> | 3     |             |
> | 12    |             |

Other rules can be invented for combining the scores when two dice are thrown. Make tables to find the probabilities of the various outcomes for each of these rules:

**D3**   The outcome is the *difference* between the scores on the two dice. For example: 5 on the blue, 2 on the red gives a difference of 3; also 2 on the blue, 5 on the red gives a difference of 3.

**D4**   The outcome is the *larger* of the scores on the two dice. When the scores are the same number, then that number is the outcome. For example $(4, 4) \mapsto 4$.

**D5**   The outcome is the *total* of the bottom numbers on two tetrahedral dice.

*A tetrahedron has four faces.*

**D6**   When three dice are thrown how many possible outcomes are there? Suggest a method for representing them. Find the probability of each possible outcome for
(a) the total of the scores on the three dice
(b) the largest of the scores on the three dice
(for example $(4, 1, 5) \mapsto 5$, $(4, 1, 4) \mapsto 4$).

### You could . . .

• Devise a game for a school fair which involves the rolling of dice with rules like those above.

# E : Another way to show outcomes

The outcomes when two dice are thrown can be shown on a **tree diagram** as on the right.

Each outcome is equally likely.

> **E1** Check that there are 11 ways of getting *at least one* six.
> What is the *probability* of getting
> **(a)** at least one six  **(b)** no sixes?

**(1)** The tree diagram has a large number of branches. If we are interested in *getting a six* and in *not getting a six* the tree diagram can be condensed like this:

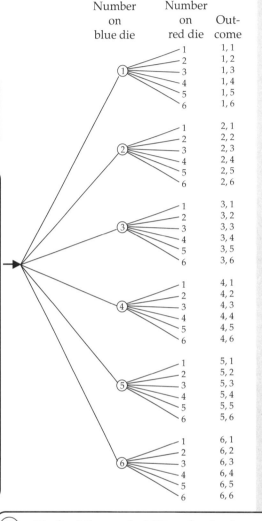

| | | Number on red die | Outcomes |
|---|---|---|---|
| | Not a 6 | Not a 6 | Not a 6, Not a 6 |
| Start | | 6 | Not a 6, 6 |
| | 6 | Not a 6 | 6, Not a 6 |
| | | 6 | 6, 6 |

Number on blue die

> Note that the outcomes here are not equally likely:
> the probability of a *six* is $\frac{1}{6}$
> the probability of *not a six* is $\frac{5}{6}$.

**(2)** Write the probabilities on the branches:

| Number on blue die | Number on red die | Outcomes |
|---|---|---|
| $\frac{5}{6}$ Not a 6 | $\frac{5}{6}$ Not a 6 | Not a 6, Not a 6 |
| | $\frac{1}{6}$ 6 | Not a 6, 6 |
| $\frac{1}{6}$ 6 | $\frac{5}{6}$ Not a 6 | 6, Not a 6 |
| | $\frac{1}{6}$ 6 | 6, 6 |

Start

**(3)** To find the probability of *not a 6* on the blue die and a 6 on the red die:
The probability of *not a 6* on the blue is $\frac{5}{6}$.
So you get *not a 6* on $\frac{5}{6}$ ths of your throws of the blue die.
Then the probability of a 6 on the red die is $\frac{1}{6}$.
So you get *not a 6* on the blue die and a 6 on the the red die on $\frac{1}{6}$ th of $\frac{5}{6}$ ths of your throws of the two dice.
This is $\frac{5}{36}$ ths of your throws.
So the probability of *not a 6* on the blue die and a 6 on the red die is $\frac{5}{36}$.

> **For discussion**
> • What simple operation on fractions does this correspond to?

> **E2** Work out the probabilities for the other outcomes in a similar way. Deduce the probability of getting at least one six.

Check with E1 above.

**E3**   (a)   Draw a full tree diagram to show the 16 possible outcomes
when two tetrahedral dice are thrown.
What are the probabilities of

The numbers on the bottom faces are used.

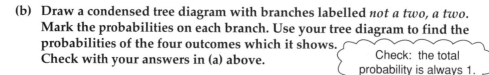

   (i)   2 twos
   (ii)   a two on the first throw and not a two on the second
   (iii)   not a two on the first throw and a two on the second
   (iv)   1 two only
   (v)   no twos at all?

   (b)   Draw a condensed tree diagram with branches labelled *not a two, a two*.
Mark the probabilities on each branch. Use your tree diagram to find the
probabilities of the four outcomes which it shows.
Check with your answers in (a) above.

Check: the total probability is always 1.

**E4**   Draw a tree diagram to show the outcomes when two coins are tossed.
Find the probabilities of the four outcomes using the tree diagram method and check
with your results in B1.

**E5**   A 'lucky dip' bag contains 3 red counters and 7 blue counters.
You dip into the bag and pull out a counter.
What is the probability it is (i) red (ii) blue?
The counter is put back and you dip in again.
Copy the tree diagram and mark the
probabilities on it.
Now find the probabilities of
   (i)   two reds
   (ii)   two blues
   (iii)   one of each
   (iv)   at least one red?

| First dip | Second dip | Outcome | Probability |
|---|---|---|---|
| red | red | red,red | |
| | blue | red, blue | |
| blue | red | blue, red | |
| | blue | blue, blue | |

In the previous example the 'red' branches in the tree diagram in E5 all had the same
probability. In the next example the probability at the second stage depends on what
happens at the first stage.

**E6**   The same 'lucky-dip' bag as in E5 is used but the first counter is not put back. Suppose
the first counter has been drawn and is red. How many reds are left in the bag? How
many counters are left in the bag?
So what is the probability that the counter on the second draw is red?
And what is the probability it is blue?
Copy the diagram in E5 and mark in the appropriate
probabilities.
Find the probabilities of
(i) two reds        (ii) two blues
(iii) one of each    (iv) at least one red.

**Note**
The probabilities for the second draw depend on the result of the first draw.
The result of the second draw is *dependent* on the result of the first draw.
In the previous examples the second event was *independent* of the first.

**E7**   Two red cards and two black cards are shuffled face-down.
A card is selected at random. It is not replaced.
Then another card is selected at random.
Draw a tree diagram to show the possible
outcomes and write the probabilities on it.
Find the probability of getting two cards of the same colour.

See the game on page 19

# F : Some probability problems

### A famous dice problem

A French gambler Chevalier de Méré found that when he made the bet that in 4 rolls of a die he would get at least one six he won in the long run.
He then reasoned that in 24 rolls of two dice he ought to get at least one double six. But he found that in the long run he lost.

In 1654 he asked the French mathematician Blaise Pascal (1623 – 1662) about these problems. Pascal analysed them and so began the study of probability.

*You* can analyse them in this way:

1. The tree diagram shows 2 rolls of a die.
What is the probability of NN?
So what is the probability of **at least one** six?

2. Draw (or imagine) a tree diagram for 3 rolls of a die.
What is the probability of NNN?
So what is the probability of **at least one** six?

3. Continue the argument to find the probability of at least one six in 4 rolls of a die. Is the probability greater or less than $\frac{1}{2}$?

4. What is the probability of not getting a double six when two dice are rolled?
So what is the probability of at least one double six in 24 rolls of two dice?
Is it greater than or less than $\frac{1}{2}$?

S stands for a six, N for not a six.

### Birth months and birthdays

What is the probability that Person B has a different birth month from Person A?
Assuming that Persons A and B have different birth months what is the probability that Person C has a different month from Persons A and B?
Deduce that the probability that the three of them have different birth months is $\frac{11}{12} \times \frac{10}{12}$ .

**Try this:**
How many people would you need in order that at least two have the same birth**day** (not necessarily the same year)?

What therefore is the probability that at least two of them have the same birth month?
Continue the argument for 4 people, and then for 5 people.
How many people would you need in order to make it worth betting that at least 2 of them have the same birth month?

# G : How many ways?

**Putting items in order**

You might have seen competitions like the one on the right which was taken from a cereal packet.

*How many entries would you need to make in order to cover all the possibilities?*

You have a choice of 8 letters to go in the first box. Having chosen one of them there are then 7 to choose from for the second box.

$$8 \times 7$$

So there are 56 ways of filling in the first two boxes.

Use your skill and judgement to put these domestic appliances in order of importance according to how you think they have made life easier.

A    Fridge/freezer
B    Automatic washing machine
C    Steam or dry iron
D    Vacuum cleaner
E    Dishwasher
F    Electric toaster
G    Tumble dryer
H    Shampoo polisher

*Win all these items. They are worth over £1000*

Enter the letters in the boxes

First there are 8 branches . . .

. . . and 6 branches on each of these.

. . .and 7 branches on each of these. . .

. . . then 6 branches on each of those!

**G1   Keep going to find the total number of different ways of filling in the coupon.**

**G2   The cereal packets cost 75p. Is it worth buying enough to cover all the possibilities?**

And then there is the tie-breaker!

*Why do most competitions include one of these?*

Think up a new brand name for the shampoo polisher:

_____

**G3   Suppose there were only 3 items to put in order of importance. How many possible arrangements would there be?**

**G4   Complete the table to show the number of arrangements for various numbers of items.**

| Number of items | Number of arrangements |
|---|---|
| 3 | |
| 4 | |
| 5 | |
| 6 | |
| 7 | |
| 8 | |

- There are 5 items in a competition. You have to pick out the 3 most important items and put them in order.

  For 1st position there is a choice of 5.
  For 2nd position there is a choice of 4.
  For 3rd position there is a choice of 3.
  $5 \times 4 \times 3$
  This gives 60 different arrangements. ○ ◯

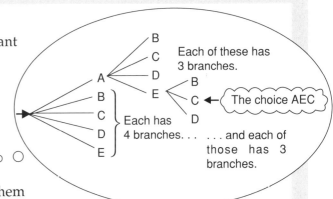

Each of these has 3 branches.

Each has 4 branches... ... and each of those has 3 branches.

The choice AEC

- Suppose now you did not have to put them in order but just *select* the 3 most important.

  Each selection of 3 items appears 6 times in the tree diagram.
  For example, A, B and C appear as

  |     |
  | --- |
  | ABC |
  | ACB |
  | BCA |
  | BAC |
  | CAB |
  | CBA |

  So the number of *selections* of 3 items is $60 \div 6$ which is 10.

*How we can be sure there are 6 ways to arrange 3 items*

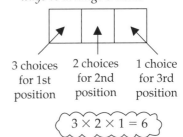

| 3 choices for 1st position | 2 choices for 2nd position | 1 choice for 3rd position |

$3 \times 2 \times 1 = 6$

**G5** (a) **How many *selections* of 3 items could be made from the 8 items in the breakfast cereal competition?**
(b) **How many selections of 4 items could be made from the 8?**

## Football pools

One competition in the football pools involves picking out matches which you think will be score draws. Suppose you were picking out 3 matches which you thought would be score draws from the 58 matches in the football league. First imagine putting them in order (as for the cereal packet competition).
You have a choice of 58 for the first, 57 for the second, 56 for the third.
So altogether there are $58 \times 57 \times 56$ different arrangements.
But each selection of 3 items will appear $3 \times 2 \times 1$ times in these different arrangements. So the number of possible *selections* of 3 matches is $\frac{58 \times 57 \times 56}{3 \times 2 \times 1}$.

In **score** draws teams score goals, for example 1-1, 2-2, etc. 0-0 is a **no-score** draw.

**G6** **Work out the number of selections.**

**G7** **The Treble Chance requires a choice of 8 matches. How many possible selections are there?**

Now you know why there isn't much chance of winning the pools!

## Coin tossing again

**G8** **When 5 coins are tossed how many ways are there to get 2 heads? Why is this the same as the number of ways of getting 3 heads?**

### For discussion
- How do the numbers arising in the pattern in Section C relate to the 'number of ways' method described above?

# H : Further activities

- Find out how to use a scientific calculator to generate random numbers.
  Use them to simulate throwing dice, tossing coins, etc.

- The program on the right simulates throwing dice.
  `RND(6)` gives a random number from 1 to 6.
  When you `RUN` the program line 10 will give a
  question mark.
  Enter the number of throws you want.

```
10  INPUT N
20  FOR I = 1 TO N
30  PRINT RND(6);
40  NEXT I
```

- This program simulates tossing a coin.
  `RND(2)` gives a random number from 1
  to 2 (in other words, 1 or 2).

```
10  INPUT N
20  FOR I = 1 TO N
30  R = RND(2)
40  R = 1 PRINT "T"; ELSE
    PRINT "H";
50  NEXT I
```

- Count up the numbers 1 to 6,
  or letters H and T, to find their
  frequencies.
  What happens
  to the relative
  frequencies as
  the number of
  'goes' increases?

  *You could use the computer to do the counting.*

- Use the printout to
  find how many
  throws are needed on
  average to get a 6.

- Modify the programs
  above for
  - throwing two dice
    and adding the
    scores
  - tossing two coins.

- Write a program to
  produce a table of
  random numbers
  from 0 to 9.

## Ernie

Ernie – Electronic Random Number Indicator Equipment – churns out no fewer than 185,000 Premium Bond winning numbers every month.

The odds against any particular number striking it lucky are 11,000 to 1, so given an average dose of good luck, the investor with £1,000 in Premium Bonds can look forward to getting a cheque once a year.

A saver with £5,000 in bonds could reasonably hope for five prizes, while the big gambler with £10,000 invested – and there are a startling 21,000 of them – could count himself unlucky not to get a cheque of some sort almost every month.

It is possible to put the maximum permitted £10,000 into Premium Bonds and still go a complete year without winning a single prize. But National Savings officials console big buyers with the impressive odds against this happening – 55,000 to 1.

- Five dice are rolled. Which would be the best bet: 2 pairs or 3 of a kind?

- *A* tosses one coin, *B* tosses two coins. If *B*'s coins show more heads than *A*'s coins, then *B* wins. If not, *A* wins. Who should win in the long run?

- One die has the numbers 1, 2, 2, 3, 3, 4 on its faces. Another die has the numbers 1, 3, 4, 5, 6, 8. The dice are rolled and the top numbers are added together. Find the probabilities of the possible totals.

  *Invent other sets of numbers which give the same results.*

- Four dice have these numbers on them:
  A: 0, 0, 4, 4, 4, 4
  B: 3, 3, 3, 3, 3, 3
  C: 2, 2, 2, 2, 6, 6
  D: 1, 1, 1, 5, 5, 5
  Show that in the long run A beats B, B beats C, C beats D, but A does not beat D.

  *Invent other examples.*

- How many cars would you need to observe in order that it is worth betting that at least two registration numbers end in the same pair of digits? Try it practically and then work it out theoretically.

- Find the probability of crossing a line in the roll-a-coin game on page 19 for various sizes of coins and squares.

  *Try triangles, hexagons, . . .*

- Alberto tosses a coin until he gets 2 heads, one after the other.
  Bettina tosses a coin until she gets a head followed by a tail.
  The person who achieves the result in the smallest number of tosses is the winner.
  Try it and then work it out theoretically.

  *A computer program?*

## A to Z

Sir,
Two friends and myself play Scrabble every week. Starting the game is done by drawing a tile out of a bag. The player drawing the tile nearest A begins.

Last evening the first player drew out an X and was certain she would not start the game. The second player drew Y and I drew Z. What are the odds against this happening I wonder?
Yours sincerely,

## Odds-on chance

Sir,
How is this for coincidence? I have been married twice. Both my wives were born on the same date: December 16.

My wife has been married twice. Both her husbands were born on September 9.

Yours truly,

**Some interesting books.**
How to take a chance *by D. Huff*
Lady luck *by W. Weaver*
The complete book of indoor games *by P. Arnold*

# Now try these . . .

1. Every day a factory making small electronic switches for computer keyboards tests 200 switches by taking groups of 10 switches at regular intervals throughout the day. Here is the record for one day:

| Total number of switches | 10 | 20 | 30 | 40 | 50 | 60 | 70 | 80 | 90 | 100 | 110 | 120 | 130 | 140 | 150 | 160 | 170 | 180 | 190 | 200 |
|---|---|---|---|---|---|---|---|---|---|---|---|---|---|---|---|---|---|---|---|---|
| Number which fail | 1 | 1 | 2 | 2 | 2 | 3 | 3 | 4 | 5 | 6 | 6 | 6 | 6 | 7 | 7 | 7 | 8 | 8 | 9 | 9 |

   Draw a graph to show the relative frequency of failure.
   Make an estimate of the probability of failure.
   Estimate how many switches might fail in a day's output of 30 000 switches.

2. (a) A bookmaker offers odds of 3-1. What is the probability of winning?
   (b) What are the odds that a six is scored when a die is rolled?

3. A pack of cards is shuffled and a card is selected. What is the probability of getting
   (a) a diamond      (b) a court card (that is a Jack or a Queen or a King)?

4. Using B for boy and G for girl make a list of all possible families with 4 children. Assuming that the probability that a child is a girl is $\frac{1}{2}$, find the probabilities of the various numbers of girls in families of 4 children.

5. Two symmetrical pentagonal spinners have the numbers 1 to 5 on them.
   The spinners are spun and the numbers are added together.
   Show all the possible outcomes either in a list or in a table.
   Find the probabilities of the various totals.
   Devise a game  (10p a go!) using the totals on the spinners.

   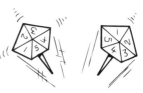

6. A card is chosen from a pack. It is replaced and a card is drawn again.
   By making a tree diagram find the probabilities of
   (a) 2 aces          (b) no aces          (c) one ace.

7. A bag contains 5 green counters and 7 yellow counters.  A counter is selected at random, replaced and another selection made.
   Draw a tree diagram to show the colours of each selection and mark on it the probabilities. Find the probabilities of
   (a) 2 greens        (b) 2 yellows        (c) one of each      (d) at least one green.

8. Find the probabilities in question 7 when the first counter is not replaced before the second is chosen.

9. On average the probability of any one particular day in June being fine (that is, not raining) is $\frac{2}{3}$. The probability that a fine day will be followed by a wet day is $\frac{1}{4}$. The probability that a wet day will be followed by another wet day is $\frac{1}{2}$.
   Find the probabilities for an average June month of having
   (a)   2 fine days in succession
   (b)   2 wet days in succession
   (c)   at least 1 fine day in any 2 successive days.

# Pattern and proof

On a calendar take a block of four numbers.
Multiply diagonally-opposite numbers and subtract.
For example, $4 \times 12 - 11 \times 5$.

| Sun | Mon | Tue | Wed | Thu | Fri | Sat |
|-----|-----|-----|-----|-----|-----|-----|
|     |     |     |     |     | 1   | 2   |
| 3   | 4   | 5   | 6   | 7   | 8   | 9   |
| 10  | 11  | 12  | 13  | 14  | 15  | 16  |
| 17  | 18  | 19  | 20  | 21  | 22  | 23  |
| 24  | 25  | 26  | 27  | 28  | 29  | 30  |

Try other blocks of four numbers.

Make a conjecture.

Explain why it happens.

---

Write down a three-digit number.

For example 742.

Repeat it to make a six-digit number.
Divide by 7.
Divide the result by 11.
Divide the result by 13.
Comment.

742742

Ignore any remainder at each stage.

Try some more.

Make a conjecture.

Explain why it happens.

---

Write down two numbers, for example 8 and 5.

| Square them | 64, 25 |
| Subtract | $64 - 25 = 39$ |
| Factorise | $39 = 3 \times 13$ |

How are the factors related to the original numbers?

Try some more:  8, 3
11, 6
etc.

Make a conjecture
$a^2 - b^2 = \ldots \times \ldots$

Can you prove it?

---

① Think of three digits.

② Arrange them to make the largest possible number.

③ Arrange them to make the smallest possible number.

④ Subtract the two numbers (put in a 0 in the hundreds position if necessary).

⑤ Repeat from ② using the three digits you finished up with in ④.

Try other starters.

Make a conjecture.

What happens with two-digit numbers? And four-digit numbers?

---

Conjecture : multiplying together the first $n$ prime numbers and adding 1 always makes a prime number.
For example:

| $n = 1$ | $2 + 1$ | $= 3$ |
| $n = 2$ | $2 \times 3 + 1$ | $= 7$ |
| $n = 3$ | $2 \times 3 \times 5 + 1$ | $= 31$ |
| $n = 4$ | $2 \times 3 \times 5 \times 7 + 1$ | $= 211$ |

True?        Undecided?        False?

Proof?

Counter-example

# A : For discussion

Three important steps in doing mathematics are

| 1. Observing | → | 2. Conjecturing | → | 3. Proving or disproving |

This is not always possible.

What is a **conjecture**?
A **conjecture** is an intelligent guess based on observing a pattern arising in some particular cases. It is usually a general statement about what is expected to happen in **all** cases.

The word *hypothesis* is sometimes used instead of *conjecture*.

*Look at these:*
$$3 + 9 = 12$$
$$1 + 7 = 8$$
$$9 + 11 = 20$$

*What do you notice?* . . . . . . . . . . . . . .   They are additions.

*What else?* . . . . . . . . . . . . . . . . . . . . .   Odd numbers are being added.

*And?* . . . . . . . . . . . . . . . . . . . . . . . . .   The results are even numbers.

*Can you link your observations to make a conjecture?* . . . . . . . . . . . . .   When two odd numbers are added the result is always an even number.

*Can you you find some more examples to support your conjecture?* . . . . . . . . . . . . . . . . . . . . .   $1 + 5 = 6$   and   $3 + 17 = 20$   and . . .

*Is that a proof?* . . . . . . . . . . . . . . . . . . .   No, but the conjecture looks more and and more as if it could be true.

*Can you prove it is true for any two odd numbers?*   Well, can *you*?

Try   even + odd
odd + even
What about subtraction?

*How many squares on a chessboard?* . . . . . . . . . . . . . . . . . .   64

*Are you sure?* . . . . . . . . . . . . . . . . . . . . .   Thinks! . . . 65. There's the big one as well.

*Go on* . . . . . . . . . . . . . . . . . . . . . . . . .   Ah! yes, there are lots. I can't count them all.

*Try smaller chessboards* . . . . . . . . . . . .

*Look for patterns.*
*Observe, make a general conjecture, prove.*

*How many squares on a chessboard?*

'2 by 2'

'3 by 3'

# B : Playing with numbers

### Think of a number

| | | | | |
|---|---|---|---|---|
| ① | Think of a number |
| ② | Add 7 |
| ③ | Multiply by 3 |
| ④ | Subtract 12 |
| ⑤ | Divide by 3 |
| ⑥ | Take away the number you thought of |

**1** Follow the sequence of instructions on the right.
Do it with several starters.

Make a conjecture.
Can you be sure that it always works?
(Have you tried *all* possible numbers?)

You cannot try *all* possible numbers but you *can* be sure by using a generalised method like this:
　　　Let the number thought of be $x$.
　　　Then at each stage you have

| | |
|---|---|
| ① | $x$ |
| ② | $x + 7$ |
| ③ | $(x + 7) \times 3$ which is $3x + 21$ |
| ④ | $3x + 21 - 12$ which is $3x + 9$ |
| ⑤ | $(3x + 9) \div 3$ which is $x + 3$ |
| ⑥ | $3$ |

Try these. Make conjectures. Then prove them.

**2**

| | |
|---|---|
| ① | Think of a number |
| ② | Multiply by 2 |
| ③ | Add 3 |
| ④ | Multiply by 6 |
| ⑤ | Add 6 |
| ⑥ | Divide by 12 |
| ⑦ | Take away the number you thought of |

**3**

| | |
|---|---|
| ① | Think of a number |
| ② | Add 9 |
| ③ | Multiply by 50 |
| ④ | Subtract 172 |
| ⑤ | Multiply by 20 |
| ⑥ | Subtract 560 |
| ⑦ | Divide by 1000 |
| ⑧ | Take away the number you thought of |

Invent some more yourself.

**4** Get someone to think of a number.
Then give them these instructions:
　　　Multiply by 5
　　　Add 7
　　　Multiply by 2
　　　Subtract 4
They tell you the result.
You can immediately tell them the number they thought of.

**How to do it**

Ignore the units digit (it is 0).
Subtract 1 from the rest of the number.
The result is the number they thought of.

Explain why it works.

Invent one yourself.

### Some calendar tricks

You need an old calendar.

| Sun | Mon | Tue | Wed | Thu | Fri | Sat |
|-----|-----|-----|-----|-----|-----|-----|
|     |     | 1   | 2   | 3   | 4   | 5   |
| 6   | 7   | 8   | 9   | 10  | 11  | 12  |
| 13  | 14  | 15  | 16  | 17  | 18  | 19  |
| 20  | 21  | 22  | 23  | 24  | 25  | 26  |
| 27  | 28  | 29  | 30  | 31  |     |     |

**1**  Ask someone to put a ring around a block of four numbers and to add them up.
They give you the total.
You can then immediately say what the numbers were.

**The secret**
Subtract 16.
Divide by 4 to get the first number.
Then use this pattern.

$+1$  $+6$  $+1$

**Why it works**
Let the top left number be $x$.
Then the number below it is $x + 7$ (one week, 7 days, later).
The top right number is $x + 1$.
The bottom right number is 7 days on, $x + 8$.
Check that the sum of the numbers is $4x + 16$.
Now explain the secret.

| $x$ | $x + 1$ |
|-----|---------|
| $x + 7$ | $x + 8$ |

---

**2**  Get someone to put a ring round a block of nine numbers.
Ask them for the lowest one. You immediately write a number on a piece of paper and ask them to add up the nine numbers in the block.
The number you wrote proves to be the correct total.
Explain the secret.

| Sun | Mon | Tue | Wed | Thu | Fri | Sat |
|-----|-----|-----|-----|-----|-----|-----|
|     |     |     |     | 1   | 2   | 3   |
| 4   | 5   | 6   | 7   | 8   | 9   | 10  |
| 11  | 12  | 13  | 14  | 15  | 16  | 17  |
| 18  | 19  | 20  | 21  | 22  | 23  | 24  |
| 25  | 26  | 27  | 28  | 29  | 30  | 31  |

**The secret**
Add 8 to the lowest number.
Multiply the result by 9.

---

**3**  In a block of 9 numbers, diagonally opposite numbers add up to the same number.
Explain why.
If someone gives you this number, can you determine all 9 numbers in the block?

```
14   15   16
21---22---23
28   29   30
```

---

**4**  Someone gives you the lowest number in the 'sock'.
How would you find the total?

---

**5**  Take a block of four numbers.
Multiply diagonally-opposite numbers and subtract.
$3 \times 9 - 2 \times 10 = 7$

| 2 | 3 |
|---|---|
| 9 | 10 |

Try some more. Make a conjecture. Prove it.

**You could . . .**
• Invent some more calendar tricks yourself.

# C : Patterns with numbers

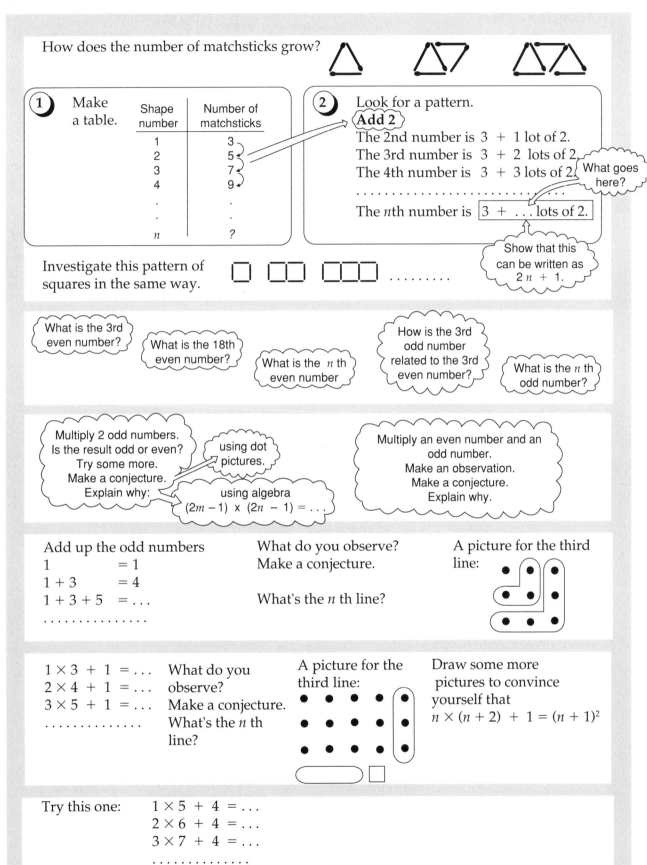

How does the number of matchsticks grow?

**1** Make a table.

| Shape number | Number of matchsticks |
|---|---|
| 1 | 3 |
| 2 | 5 |
| 3 | 7 |
| 4 | 9 |
| . | . |
| . | . |
| $n$ | ? |

**2** Look for a pattern.

Add 2

The 2nd number is $3 + 1$ lot of 2.
The 3rd number is $3 + 2$ lots of 2.
The 4th number is $3 + 3$ lots of 2.

What goes here?

. . . . . . . . . . . . . . . . . . . . . . . . . . . . . . . . .

The $n$th number is $\boxed{3 + \ldots \text{lots of 2.}}$

Show that this can be written as $2n + 1$.

Investigate this pattern of squares in the same way.

□  □□  □□□ . . . . . . . . .

What is the 3rd even number?

What is the 18th even number?

What is the $n$ th even number

How is the 3rd odd number related to the 3rd even number?

What is the $n$ th odd number?

Multiply 2 odd numbers. Is the result odd or even? Try some more. Make a conjecture. Explain why:

using dot pictures.

using algebra
$(2m - 1) \times (2n - 1) = \ldots$

Multiply an even number and an odd number. Make an observation. Make a conjecture. Explain why.

Add up the odd numbers
$1 = 1$
$1 + 3 = 4$
$1 + 3 + 5 = \ldots$
. . . . . . . . . . . . . .

What do you observe? Make a conjecture.

What's the $n$ th line?

A picture for the third line:

$1 \times 3 + 1 = \ldots$
$2 \times 4 + 1 = \ldots$
$3 \times 5 + 1 = \ldots$
. . . . . . . . . . . . .

What do you observe? Make a conjecture. What's the $n$ th line?

A picture for the third line:

Draw some more pictures to convince yourself that
$n \times (n + 2) + 1 = (n + 1)^2$

Try this one:
$1 \times 5 + 4 = \ldots$
$2 \times 6 + 4 = \ldots$
$3 \times 7 + 4 = \ldots$
. . . . . . . . . . . . .

## Triangle numbers

Make a list of the first 7 triangle numbers.

| | Triangle number |
|---|---|
| 1 | 1 |
| 2 | 3 |
| 3 | 6 |
| 4 | . |
| . | . |
| . | . |

Can you give
. . . the 10th triangle number?
. . . the 20th triangle number?
. . . the 100th triangle number?
*Is there a formula for the n th triangle number?*

### Did you know?
• Over 200 years ago Greek mathematicians such as Pythagoras used geometrical patterns to represent numbers. They called 1, 4, 9, . . . *square* numbers. We still refer to $3^2$ as "three squared".
1, 8, 27, . . . were called *cube* numbers.

## ① Putting it in pictures

Here is $T_4$ twice:

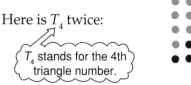

$T_4$ stands for the 4th triangle number.

There are . . . columns each with . . . dots.
So the number of dots is . . . × . . . = . . .
So the 4th triangle number $T_4$ is . . . ÷ 2

Draw a diagram for '$T_3$ twice' and then use this method.
Do another one.
Generalise for $T_n$ ← The $n$th triangle number

## ② Putting it without pictures

Here is the method above without the dot picture:

$$T_4 = 1 + 2 + 3 + 4$$
and $$T_4 = 4 + 3 + 2 + 1$$   Writing the sum in reverse order
Add up:
$$2T_4 = 5 + 5 + 5 + 5 = 4 \times 5$$
So $$T_4 = 4 \times 5 \div 2$$

• Do it for $T_5$
• Complete this for $T_n$:
$$T_n = 1 + 2 + \ldots + (n - 1) + n$$
$$T_n = n + (n - 1) + \ldots + 2 + 1$$
So $$2T_n = \ldots + \ldots + \ldots + \ldots + \ldots$$
$$= \ldots \times \ldots$$
and $$T_n = \ldots$$

---

1    3    6    10    . . .
Add two adjacent triangle numbers.
For example, 3 + 6. Try some more.
What sort of numbers do you get?
Make a conjecture. Draw dot patterns to explain why. Try to give the argument without dot patterns and then generalise it.

$1^3$                         = . . .      What sort of numbers are these? Do they have any connection with other numbers on this page?
$1^3 + 2^3$                 = . . .
$1^3 + 2^3 + 3^3$          = . . .
. . . . . . . . . . . . . . . . . .

Make a conjecture:
$$1^3 + 2^3 + \ldots + n^3 = \ldots$$

### Intersections

2 lines intersect in 1 point.

3 lines intersect in 3 points

4 lines intersect in 6 points
5 lines?
Keep going!
Make a conjecture about the number of intersections for $n$ lines.

*Rules*
No lines are parallel.
Only 2 lines cross at a point. All possible intersections must be shown.

Give formulae for
> the $2n$ th square number
> the $2n + 1$ th square number
> the $n + 1$ th triangle number
> the $n - 1$ th triangle number
> the $2n - 1$ th triangle number
> the $2n + 1$ th triangle number.

Multiply a triangle number by 8 and add 1.
Try some more. What sort of numbers do you get?
Make a conjecture. Can you prove it – by pictures?
　　　　　　　　　　　　　　　　　　 – by algebra?

**Some conjectures**

• Triangle numbers (other than 3) are never prime.
• For $n > 3$, $T_n - 1$ is never prime.
• Either $T_n + 1$ or $T_n + 2$ is prime.

True?　　　False?　　　Undecided?

Proof?　　Counter-example?

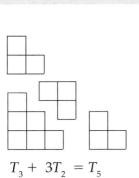

$$T_3 + 3T_2 = T_5$$

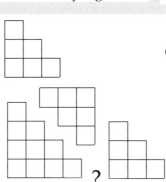

?

Growth?

Pattern?

Conjecture?

Proof?

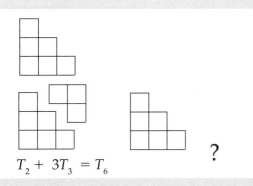

$$T_2 + 3T_3 = T_6$$

?

**An investigation**
What numbers can be written as sums of consecutive numbers?
For example
$$6 = 1 + 2 + 3$$
$$7 = 3 + 4$$
Can some numbers be written as sums of consecutive numbers in several ways?

$$
\begin{aligned}
1^2 &= \ldots \\
1^2 + 2^2 &= \ldots \\
1^2 + 2^2 + 3^2 &= \ldots \\
1^2 + 2^2 + 3^2 + 4^2 &= \ldots \\
1^2 + 2^2 + 3^2 + 4^2 + 5^2 &= \ldots \\
1^2 + 2^2 + 3^2 + 4^2 + 5^2 + 6^2 &= \ldots
\end{aligned}
$$

Find the sums and write out the first 8 lines.
Divide each sum by the corresponding triangle number.
Rewrite the results in a form which shows a pattern.
Make a conjecture

$$
\begin{aligned}
1 &= \ldots \\
3 + 5 &= \ldots \\
7 + 9 + 11 &= \ldots \\
13 + 15 + 17 + 19 &= \ldots
\end{aligned}
$$
. . . . . . . . . . . . . . . . . . . . . .

Find the sums and do some more.
What do you notice?
Make a conjecture and express it algebraically.
Can you prove it?

# D : Divisibility and prime numbers

Write down a three-digit number.
Repeat it to make a six-digit number.
Divide by 7.
Divide the result by 11.
Divide the result by 13.
Comment.
Try some more.
Make a conjecture.
Explain why it happens.

The problem on the left is from page 33.
One way to see what is happening is like this:
The three divisions are equivalent to a single division by 1001.
When a three-digit number abc is multiplied by 1001 the result is abcabc.
So, putting it in reverse,
abcabc ÷ 1001 = abc

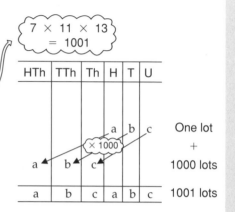

## Was the year 1972 a leap year?

Leap years are all divisible by 4.
So the question amounts to
*Is 1972 divisible by 4?*
You could find out by doing 1972 ÷ 4.
But since 100 is divisible by 4, so is 1900.
All you need to do therefore is check if 72 is divisible by 4.    Is it?

The same argument applies to any number and so to test that a number is divisible by 4 just check that the two-digit number made by the tens and units digits is divisible by 4.

### Did you know?
- Century years are only leap years when they are divisible by 400.   Why?

- Which of these years will be (or were) leap years?
  1996   2228   1922   1836

- Is 100 divisible by 8?
  Is 1000 divisible by 8?
  Devise a test for divisibility by 8.
  Write down some big numbers which are divisible by 8.

## More divisibility tests

To find if 2673 is divisible by 9 you could do the division or . . .

**1** Is 10 divisible by 9?
Is 100 divisible by 9?
Is 1000 divisible by 9?

**2** No, but   $10 = 9 + 1$
$100 = 99 + 1$
$1000 = 999 + 1$

All of these are divisible by 9.

**3** So think of $\dfrac{\text{Th} \mid \text{H} \mid \text{T} \mid \text{U}}{2 \mid 6 \mid 7 \mid 3}$ as $2000 + 600 + 70 + 3$
and rewrite it as
$(2 \times 999 + 2) + (6 \times 99 + 6) + (7 \times 9 + 7) + 3$
which is the same as
$2 \times 999 + 6 \times 99 + 7 \times 9 + (2 + 6 + 7 + 3)$

This is divisible by 9.

Is this divisible by 9?

- Try the method for some other numbers such as 8325, 64825, etc.
- Complete the statement : *To test for divisibility by 9 add up the digits. Then if . . . . . . . . . . . . .*
  Write down some big numbers which are divisible by 9 and some which are not.
- The same method also enables a test to be devised for divisibility by 3. Explain.
- Use the fact that $6 = 2 \times 3$ to devise a test for divisibility by 6.

### For discussion
$10 = 11 - 1$
$100 = 99 + 1$
$1000 = 1001 - 1$
  etc
So to test for divisibility by 11 . . .

## Prime numbers

Whole numbers which are not divisible by any other number, except 1 and themselves, are called **prime numbers**. For example, 7 is only divisible by 1 and 7. So 7 is a prime number.

Mathematicians have been interested in prime numbers for a long time. They have tried to answer questions like these:
- Are there any patterns in the prime numbers?
- Is there a formula which gives all the prime numbers?
- How are the prime numbers spread out? For example there are 25 between 1 and 100, 21 between 100 and 200. Do they 'thin out' the further you go?

| 1 | 2 | 3 | 4 | 5 | 6 | 7 | 8 | 9 | 10 |
|---|---|---|---|---|---|---|---|---|----|
| 11 | 12 | 13 | 14 | 15 | 16 | 17 | 18 | 19 | 20 |
| 21 | 22 | 23 | 24 | 25 | 26 | 27 | 28 | 29 | 30 |

| 131 | 132 | 133 | 134 | 135 | 136 | 137 | 138 | 139 | 140 |
|-----|-----|-----|-----|-----|-----|-----|-----|-----|-----|
| 141 | 142 | 143 | 144 | 145 | 146 | 147 | 148 | 149 | 150 |

Here is one way to find prime numbers.
On squared paper make a table of numbers as shown on the right.
The first square has been shaded out because 1 is not included as a prime number.

| 1 | 2 | 3 | 4̸ | 5 | 6̸ | 7 | 8̸ | 9 |
|---|---|---|---|---|---|---|---|---|

| 1 | 2 | 3 | 4̸ | 5 | 6̸ | 7 | 8̸ | 9̸ |
|---|---|---|---|---|---|---|---|---|

① Cross out all the numbers divisible by 2, but do not cross out 2.

② Cross out all the numbers divisible by 3, but do not cross out 3.

③ Do the same for 5, 7, and 11.

*Why don't you need to do 4, 6, 8, 9, 10?*

The numbers that are left are prime numbers.

*Check: there should be 35 prime numbers up to 150.*

## A conjecture about prime numbers

Make another table with 6 columns. Put a ring round the prime numbers.
Where do all the prime numbers occur?
About 500 years ago a conjecture was made like this:

> *Take any multiple of 6.*
> *Add 1 to it, and subtract 1 from it.*
> *Then either both or just one of the*
> *two numbers will be a prime number.*

Check to see if this conjecture is correct.

| 1 | ②  | ③  | 4 | ⑤  | 6 |
|---|---|---|---|---|---|
| ⑦  | 8 | 9 | 10 | ⑪  | 12 |
| ⑬  | 14 | 15 | 16 | ⑰  | 18 |

| 145 | 146 | 147 | 148 | ⑭⑨  | 150 |
|-----|-----|-----|-----|-----|-----|

## A formula for prime numbers?

The table shows $n^2 - n + 11$ for various values of $n$.
What sort of numbers are in the right hand column?

| $n$ | $n^2 - n + 11$ |
|---|---|
| 1 | 11 |
| 2 | 13 |
| 3 | 17 |
| 4 | 23 |

> **Did you know?**
> - The largest known prime number in 1992 was $2^{756839} - 1$ which has 227832 digits.

- Copy the table and extend it with $n$ as 5, 6, 7, 8.
  Are the numbers in the right-hand column prime numbers?
  Make a conjecture.
  Try some more values of $n$. Is your conjecture correct?
- Make a table for $4n^2 + 7$ with $n$ as 1, 2, 3, 4.
  Make a conjecture. Try some more values of $n$. Is your conjecture correct?

## Finding prime numbers by division

An obvious way to find out if a number $N$ is a prime number is to try dividing it by all the other numbers which might go into it. If none can be found, then $N$ must be a prime number.

For example,
    Is 65059 a prime number?
    First, using the divisibility tests,
    it is not divisible by 2, 3, 5 or 11.
    Try 7 (mentally!) − No
    Try 13 (very simple mentally!) − No
    Try 17. By calculator, $65059 \div 17 = 3827$
        So 65059 is *not* a prime number.

**For discussion**
- When testing a number $N$ for divisibility it is only necessary to use the prime numbers up to $\sqrt{N}$.

This computer program in BASIC tests to see if the number entered at line 10 is a prime. (Greater than 2)

```
10 INPUT N
20 FOR T = 2 TO SQR(N)
30 IF INT(N/T) = N/T
   THEN 60
40 NEXT T
50 PRINT "Prime":END
60 PRINT "Not prime"
```

> **D1** Test each of these numbers to see whether or not it is a prime number:
>    473    629    441    281    377
>    713    511    809    389    253
>    9269    2221    2173

A number which is not a prime number is called a **composite** number.
A composite number can be written as the product of prime numbers.
For example,

$$
\begin{aligned}
360 &= 2 \times 180 \\
    &= 2 \times 2 \times 90 \\
    &= 2 \times 2 \times 2 \times 45 \\
    &= 2 \times 2 \times 2 \times 3 \times 15 \\
    &= 2 \times 2 \times 2 \times 3 \times 3 \times 5 \\
    &= 2^3 \times 3^2 \times 5
\end{aligned}
$$

Study this example to see the strategy.

2, 3 and 5 are prime numbers.

> **D2** Write these numbers as products of prime numbers as in the example above.
>    (a) 84    (b) 2205    (c) 117 000    (d) 4807
>
> **D3** Which of these numbers are composite numbers? Write those which are composite as products of primes.
>    (a) 111    (b) 1111    (c) 11 111    (d) 111 111

**You could . . .**

- Find a set of 10 consecutive numbers which are composite. And a set of 20? And more?
  You could write a computer program to help find the 'gaps' in the prime numbers.

# E : Some famous conjectures

## The map colouring conjecture

The diagrams show some 'maps'. Make copies of them and colour them so that neighbouring regions have different colours. What is the smallest number of colours needed? Try it with some maps of your own design. Draw a complicated one and challenge a friend.

  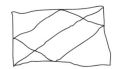

Instead of colouring you can use numbers 1, 2, 3 etc. for regions. Don't forget the outside (the 'sea'). Note that non-adjacent regions meeting at a point can be the same colour:

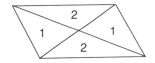

In 1853 a conjecture was made that *four* colours are sufficient to colour any map.
Although it was possible to **prove** that five colours were sufficient, mathematicians struggled for years to find a **proof** that any map could be coloured with at most four colours.

It was not until 1976 that a proof was found by two mathematicians at the University of Illinois.

## Goldbach's conjecture

In 1742 the German mathematician Christian Goldbach conjectured that every even number greater then 2 can be written as the sum of two primes.
For example:
    $4 = 2 + 2$
    $6 = 3 + 3$
    $8 = 3 + 5$
and so on . . .

*What is the smallest even number for which this can be done in two different ways?*

This conjecture has never been proved or disproved.

*Can you make a similar conjecture about odd numbers?*

## Fermat's conjecture

This is the most famous conjecture in mathematics. Pierre Fermat (1601 – 1665), a French mathematician, said that it was impossible to find numbers such that
    $a^n + b^n = c^n$
when $n$ was bigger than 2.

When $n$ is 2, it is Pythagoras' Theorem and there are an endless number of solutions. The most well known is
    $3^2 + 4^2 = 5^2$

There are lots of things like
    $3^3 + 4^3 + 5^3 = 6^3$
and    $2^2 + 11^2 = 5^3$
but none of them uses just three numbers *and* the same index throughout.

Fermat's conjecture has never been proved or disproved, though it is now generally accepted as being true.

*It may not be possible to find an exact solution but it is possible to get very close. For example $5^3 + 6^3$ is close to $7^3$. Can you find anything closer?*

# F : Disproving using counter-examples

The table shows $n^2 - n + 17$ when $n$ is $1, 2, 3, 4$.
What sort of numbers have been produced?
(Be more specific than 'odd numbers'.)

Try $n$ as $5, 6, 7, 8$.
Is the evidence mounting? Make a conjecture.
Continue testing with more numbers for $n$.
Is there a counter-example to your conjecture?

| $n$ | $n^2 - n + 17$ |
|---|---|
| 1 | 17 |
| 2 | 19 |
| 3 | 23 |
| 4 | 29 |

> A counter-example is a particular case for which a conjecture does not work. It proves that the conjecture is incorrect.

Find $2n^2 + 29$ when $n$ is $1, 2, 3, 4$.
Make a conjecture.
Test it by seeking a counter-example.
(You might spot one by looking carefully at the formula.)

A set of three *whole numbers* with no factors in common which could be the lengths of the sides of a right-angled triangle is called a *Pythagorean triple.*

Pythagoras' Theorem says that for a right-angled triangle
$c^2 = a^2 + b^2$

For example, $3, 4, 5$ is a Pythagorean triple because $3^2 + 4^2 = 5^2$,
  $5, 12, 13$ is another Pythagorean triple because $5^2 + 12^2 = 13^2$.

From these two examples a student made the conjecture that in a Pythagorean triple the largest number is one more than the middle number.

Another student refuted the conjecture with the counter-example $20, 21, 29$
($20^2 + 21^2 = 29^2$).

The first student modified the conjecture:
*one number in a Pythagorean triple exceeds another by 1.*

Test some more Pythagorean triples to see if you can find a counter-example.

Make some conjectures yourself about Pythagorean triples.

> Only one counter-example is needed to disprove a conjecture!

This program generates Pythagorean triples with the numbers not exceeding a number entered at the question mark when the program is run.

```
10    INPUT N
20    FOR A  =  1  TO N
30    FOR B  =  1  TO A
40    C  =  SQR (A*A  +  B*B)
50    IF C<> INT (C)  THEN 100
60    FOR I = 2 TO B/2
70    IF A MOD I  = 0 AND
      B MOD I  =  0 THEN 100
80    NEXT I
90    PRINT B, A, C
100   NEXT B
110   NEXT A
```

Investigate the conjecture
  *If $p$ is prime, then $2^p - 1$ is prime.*
True? False? Undecided?

# G : Proving by checking all possibilities

One way in which a conjecture or a result can be proved to be true is to check every possibility. Obviously this can only be done when there are not too many.
Here are some examples.

**How many squares can be made by joining the dots?**

Be systematic!

> There is 1 square with sides 2 units long.
> There are 4 squares with sides 1 unit long.
> There is 1 square at an angle (with sides √2 units long).

So there are 6 squares altogether.

> √2?
> Explain.

> You might find 'dotty' paper useful or a pinboard and rubber bands.

**G1** How many rectangles (including squares) can be made by joining the dots?

**G2** How many triangles can be made by joining the dots? (First find how many different types can be made. Be systematic!)

> What about a four-by-four board?

**How many nets are there for a tetrahedron?**

1. Start with a triangle for the base.

2. There have to be 3 more triangles.

3. One of them must join onto the first triangle like this, say.

> If it was joined on to one of the other sides, the 2 triangles could be rotated to this position.

**G3** Show that there is essentially only one position for the third triangle. How many essentially different positions are there for the fourth triangle?

**G4** Draw all the essentially different nets for a square-based pyramid.

**G5** Show that there are 11 different nets for a cube.

## Repeated subtractions

**G6** This is a simple version of one of the problems on page 33.

> This problem was first investigated by an Indian mathematician D.R. Kaprekar in about 1945.

  ① Write down a two-digit number.

  ② Reverse it.

> If you get a one-digit number put a zero in the tens place.

  ③ Subtract the smaller from the larger.

  ④ Using the result of ③ repeat steps ② and ③.

  ⑤ Continue repeating.

  Try it with various numbers. Make a conjecture.

**G7** When steps ① , ② and ③ are carried out the argument on the right shows that the result is a two-digit number which is a multiple of 9. Write down all the two-digit numbers whose digits add up to 9. By continuing steps ④ and ⑤ with them show that your conjecture is true (hopefully!).

> Let the number be $ab$ with $a > b$.
> $ab$ stands for $10a + b$.
> $ba$ stands for $10b + a$.
> So the result of the subtraction is
> $$(10a + b) - (10b + a)$$
> $$= 9a - 9b$$
> $$= 9(a - b)$$

**G8** When the first two stages of the procedure on page 33 are carried out with *three-digit* numbers the result is a multiple of 99. By considering all the possibilities determine what happens in the procedure.

> Try to prove this statement.

# H : Proving by deduction

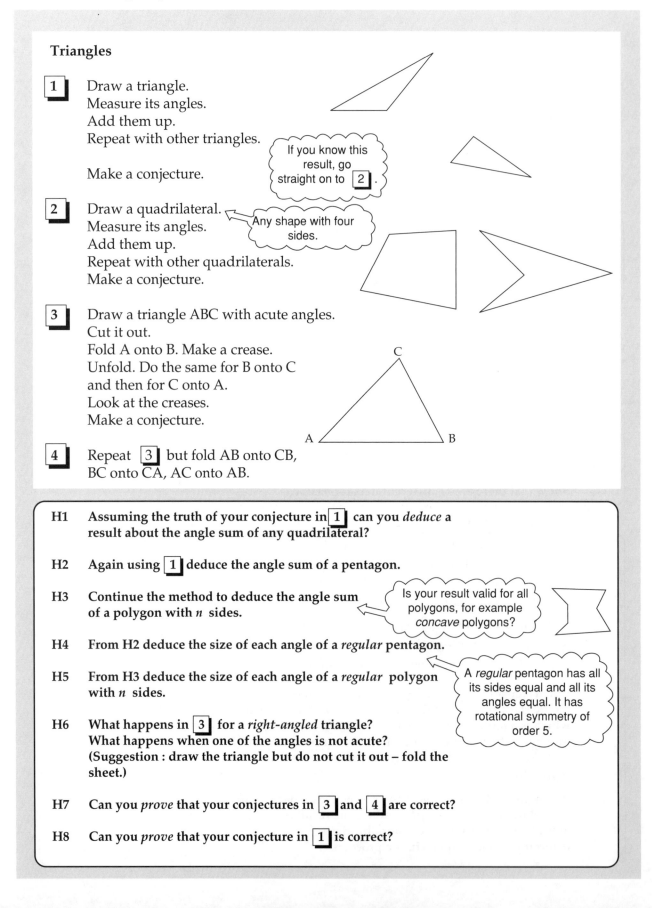

**Triangles**

**1**  Draw a triangle.
Measure its angles.
Add them up.
Repeat with other triangles.

Make a conjecture.

*If you know this result, go straight on to* **2** .

**2**  Draw a quadrilateral.
Measure its angles.
Add them up.
Repeat with other quadrilaterals.
Make a conjecture.

*Any shape with four sides.*

**3**  Draw a triangle ABC with acute angles.
Cut it out.
Fold A onto B. Make a crease.
Unfold. Do the same for B onto C
and then for C onto A.
Look at the creases.
Make a conjecture.

**4**  Repeat **3** but fold AB onto CB,
BC onto CA, AC onto AB.

**H1**  Assuming the truth of your conjecture in **1** can you *deduce* a result about the angle sum of any quadrilateral?

**H2**  Again using **1** deduce the angle sum of a pentagon.

**H3**  Continue the method to deduce the angle sum of a polygon with $n$ sides.

*Is your result valid for all polygons, for example concave polygons?*

**H4**  From H2 deduce the size of each angle of a *regular* pentagon.

**H5**  From H3 deduce the size of each angle of a *regular* polygon with $n$ sides.

*A regular pentagon has all its sides equal and all its angles equal. It has rotational symmetry of order 5.*

**H6**  What happens in **3** for a *right-angled* triangle?
What happens when one of the angles is not acute?
(**Suggestion : draw the triangle but do not cut it out – fold the sheet.**)

**H7**  Can you *prove* that your conjectures in **3** and **4** are correct?

**H8**  Can you *prove* that your conjecture in **1** is correct?

### Circles

**1** Using compasses draw a circle centre O.
Draw a diameter AB.
Choose any point P on the circumference.
Measure ∟APB.
Repeat for other positions of P.
Make a conjecture.

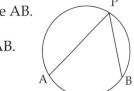

> **H9** Can you *prove* that your
> conjecture in **1** is true?

**2** Using compasses draw a circle.
Mark any two points A and B on the circumference.
Choose any point P on the circumference above AB.
Measure ∟APB.
Repeat for other positions of P above the line AB.
Make a conjecture.
What happens for positions of P below AB?

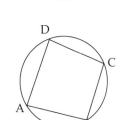

**3** Using compasses draw a circle centre O.
Mark two points A and B on the circumference.
Choose any point P on the circumference.
Join up as shown.
Measure ∟APB and ∟AOB.
Is there a relationship between them?
Repeat for another position of P.
Make a conjecture.
Try some more positions for P.

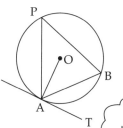

**4** Draw a circle and mark any four points on it.
Join them up to make a quadrilateral.
Measure ∟A and ∟C.
Is there a relationship between them?
Measure ∟B and ∟D.
Is there a relationship between them?
Repeat for other positions of the four points
on the circle.

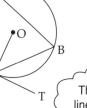

**5** Draw a circle and a chord AB.
Draw the tangent at A by first joining
the centre O to A and then drawing
the tangent AT at right angles to OA.
Mark any point P on the circle above AB.
Measure ∟APB and ∟BAT.
Make a conjecture.

> **Reminder**
> The tangent at A is a
> line which just touches
> the circle at A.

> **H10** If **3** was proved to be true explain how **1**, **2**, **4** and **5**
> could be deduced from it.
>
> **H11** Can you *prove* your conjecture in **3** ?

## Networks and polyhedra

**1** Draw a network. For example

This network has 5 regions
(counting the ' outside'),
4 junctions and 7 'streets'.

> A network is a set of lines ('streets')
> meeting at points ('junctions') and
> forming regions.
> When streets cross they form a
> junction. Fly-overs are not allowed!

Draw some networks yourself.
Enter the numbers for them in a table.

Is there a pattern?
(Suggestion: try adding 2 to
the number of streets.)
Make a conjecture.

|   | Number of regions $R$ | Number of junctions $J$ | Number of streets $S$ |
|---|---|---|---|
| ① | 5 | 4 | 7 |

**2** Make up a table showing the numbers
of faces, vertices and edges of
various polyhedra.
The polyhedra do not have to be **regular**
(symmetrical). Any three-dimensional
shapes such as off-cuts of wood would
do.
Is there a pattern? Make a conjecture.

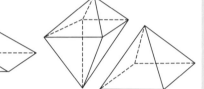

**For discussion**
- Is there a connection
  between **1** and **2**?
- Can you prove that **1**
  is true for any network?

## Prime numbers

As mentioned on page 41 mathematicians have for a long time been interested in
how prime numbers are spread out.
There are 25 prime numbers between 1 and 100 but only 16 between 1000 and 1100.
Do the primes get 'thinner on the ground' the further you go? Is there a largest
prime number?
These questions intrigued Greek mathematicians over 2000 years ago. Euclid
(about 300BC) made the conjecture that the primes go on for ever.
He developed a type of proof often used in mathematics.
In this case the proof goes like this:

> Assume that there is a largest prime number, $N$.
> Form the product of all the prime numbers up to $N$:
> $$2 \times 3 \times 5 \times \ldots \times N.$$
> This is certainly divisible by $2, 3, 5, \ldots N$.
> Add 1 to it.
> The resulting number is then not divisible by $2, 3, 5, \ldots N$.
> It is therefore *either* a prime number *or* it is divisible by
> a prime number greater than $N$.
> In both cases the assumption was incorrect and there
> is no largest prime.

**Proof by contradiction**
Assume the 'opposite' of
your conjecture. By logical
argument obtain a
contradiction. Hence the
assumption is false and
your conjecture is true.

# I : Pythagoras' Theorem

A *theorem* is a conjecture or result which has been proved. Most theorems start off as conjectures. Pythagoras' Theorem might have been conjectured from the pattern in the design below:

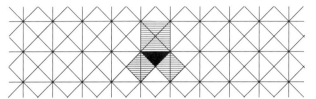

Look at the shaded squares on the three sides of the black triangle. The squares on the two shorter sides go together to make up the square on the longest side. Is this only because the triangle has two sides equal? Does the conjecture apply to *any* right-angled triangle?

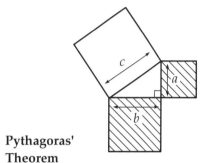

**Pythagoras' Theorem**
In a right-angled triangle the area of the square on the longest side is the sum of the areas of the squares on the other two sides.
So $c^2 = a^2 + b^2$.

Here are two geometrical methods which apply for *any* right-angled triangle.

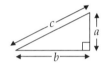

**1**

(1) In the diagram on the right four of the triangles have been put together to make a square. Prove that the shape in the middle is a square.

(2) Rotate the two lower triangles about their top corners to obtain the second diagram. Explain how this proves Pythagoras' Theorem.

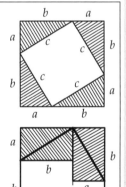

**Did you know?**
• In Egypt four thousand years ago right angles were marked out using a knotted rope with sides of lengths 3, 4 and 5 units.

$3^2 + 4^2 = 5^2$

In effect the Egyptians were using Pythagoras' Theorem as a relationship between *lengths*.
It is often used in that way today to calculate the length of one side of a right-angled triangle when the lengths of the other two sides are known.

**2**

(1) The diagram shows four of the triangles put together. Prove that the shape formed is a square and that the shape in the middle is a square of side $b - a$.

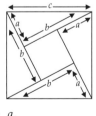

(2) Use the diagram to show that
$$c^2 = (b - a)^2 + 4 \times \tfrac{1}{2} ab$$

(3) Rewrite $(b - a)^2$ as $\ldots - \ldots + \ldots$

(4) Deduce from (2) and (3) that
$$c^2 = a^2 + b^2$$

**3**

Here is another method using trigonometry and algebra.

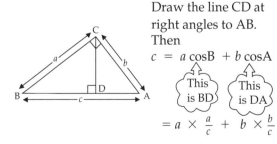

Draw the line CD at right angles to AB. Then
$$c = a\cos B + b\cos A$$

This is BD     This is DA

$$= a \times \frac{a}{c} + b \times \frac{b}{c}$$

Multiply by $c$:
$$c^2 = a^2 + b^2$$

# J : Rational and irrational numbers

From previous experience you will be aware that some fractions can be written as **terminating** decimals (for example, $\frac{1}{2} = 0.5$, $\frac{7}{40} = 0.175$) and others can be written as **recurring** decimals (for example, $\frac{1}{7}$ and $\frac{1}{17}$ ).
If you need to remind yourself try the questions below.

**J1**   Copy and complete the division to write $\frac{1}{7}$ as a decimal.
Convince yourself that it repeats with a cycle of 6 digits.
How could you have decided without doing the division
that there could not have been more than 6 digits?
By division find $\frac{2}{7}$ , $\frac{3}{7}$ , etc. and comment on the pattern in the repeating cycles of all
the sevenths.

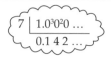

**J2**   On a calculator do $1 \div 17$. Write down the result from your calculator.
Repeat for  $\frac{2}{17}$ ,  $\frac{3}{17}$ ,  $\frac{4}{17}$ ,  $\frac{5}{17}$ .
Look at the numbers you have written down and deduce the complete cycle of repeating
digits for  $\frac{1}{17}$ .  How many digits are there in this cycle? How could you have decided
without doing the division that there could not have been more than 16 digits?

**J3**   In the same way find the repeating cycle of digits for $\frac{1}{19}$ .

**J4**   Investigate the thirteenths in the same way.

**J5**   What is the fraction (fully cancelled down) for the decimal 0.568?

**J6**   Decide whether the decimals for these fractions are terminating or recurring. Give the
decimals in each case:

$$\frac{1}{3} \ , \ \frac{1}{4} \ , \ \frac{1}{5} \ , \ \frac{1}{6} \ , \ \frac{1}{8} \ , \ \frac{1}{9} \ , \ \frac{1}{10} \ , \ \frac{1}{11} \ , \ \frac{1}{12} \ , \ \frac{1}{14} \ , \ \frac{1}{15} \ , \ \frac{1}{16} \ , \ \frac{1}{18} \ , \ \frac{1}{20}.$$

**J7**   Write down some numbers $n$ (greater than 20) such that $\frac{1}{n}$ gives a terminating decimal.
What can be said about $n$ when $\frac{1}{n}$ is a terminating decimal?

The fraction for a recurring decimal such
as $0.\dot{1}2\dot{3}$ can be found like this:

Let        $x = 0.123123123 \ldots$
Then multiplying by 1000 gives
     $1000x = 123.123123123 \ldots$
By subtraction
     $999x = 123$
and so
     $x = \frac{123}{999}$

Dividing both numbers by 3 gives the fraction  $\frac{41}{333}$ .

**Did you know?**
- A decimal such as 0.333 . . . which
  consists of 3 recurring is often written
  with a dot over the 3 : $0.\dot{3}$.
  0.142857142857 . . . which has a
  recurring cycle 142857 is written with
  a dot over the 1 and a dot over the 7:
  $0.\dot{1}4285\dot{7}$

**J8**   Find the fractions for these recurring decimals:
   (a) $0.\dot{3}2\dot{1}$       (b) $0.4\dot{5}$       (c) $0.4\dot{1}5\dot{8}$       (d) $0.67\ddot{1}$

Use a multiplier of
100 in this case.

**For discussion**
- Numbers such as 1, 2, 3, . . . are called **natural** numbers. They are the first numbers you met, arising in the context of counting.
- Sometimes it is useful to attach directions to numbers (3 below 0, 4 above 0, etc.). Numbers with directions are often written ⁻3, ⁺4, etc. Natural numbers with directions are often called **integers**. The upper height positive signs are usually omitted.

- Numbers such as $\frac{1}{7}$, $\frac{1}{2}$, $\frac{4}{3}$, $\frac{7}{4}$ are called **rational** numbers because they consist of *ratios* of two integers.
$\frac{1}{2}$, $\frac{2}{4}$, $\frac{3}{6}$, etc. are different ways of writing the same rational number. An integer such as 2 can be written as $\frac{2}{1}$, $\frac{4}{2}$, $\frac{6}{3}$, etc.

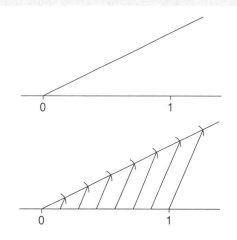

The number at A is $\frac{3}{10}$ or, as a decimal, 0.3.

The number at B is $\frac{3}{2}$ or $1\frac{1}{2}$ or, as a decimal, 1.5.

Rational numbers can be represented on a line (a ruler scale).

*For any rational number a point corresponding to it can be found on the number line.*
For example to find the positions for $\frac{1}{7}$, $\frac{2}{7}$, etc. draw a line through 0 at any angle as shown. With compasses set to any convenient radius step out 7 arcs along the line. Draw a line to join the last point of intersection to 1 on the number line. Then draw lines parallel to it. These lines then give positions for $\frac{1}{7}$, $\frac{2}{7}$, etc. Using this method any rational number can be 'placed' on the line.

*For any point on the number line is it possible to find a rational number corresponding to it?*
Most people's response is 'yes', but about two and a half thousand years ago Pythagoras showed that although there is a point on the line for √2, there is no **rational** number for it. (See the next page.)
Nor is there for √3, √5, √7 and many others!
Nor for $2^{\frac{1}{3}}$ (the cube root of 3), $10^{\frac{1}{4}}$, etc.
The rational numbers therefore are not sufficient to label every point on the number line.
The idea of a number (which until that time had meant *rational* number) had to be extended to include 'things' like √2. The new idea of number embraced the rational numbers and the **irrational** numbers such as √2, etc.
When an irrational number is written as a decimal it does not terminate or repeat.

**How to construct a point for √2**

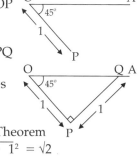

① Draw a line OP of length 1 at 45° to OA.
② Draw a line PQ of length 1 at right angles to OP.
③ Then by Pythagoras' Theorem OQ = $\sqrt{1^2 + 1^2}$ = √2

**Did you know?**
- An example of a non-terminating decimal which does not repeat is 0.123122312223 . . . This decimal therefore represents an irrational number.

The number of twos between the 1 and 3 is increased in each block of numbers.

- The number symbolised by π (circumference of a circle ÷ diameter of the circle) is also an irrational number.
In 1989 π was calculated to more than 2000 million decimal places. No pattern was apparent.

**For discussion**

Are these statements true or false? Prove those which are true.

- $\sqrt{2} + \sqrt{3} = \sqrt{2+3} = \sqrt{5}$   • $\sqrt{2} \times \sqrt{3} = \sqrt{2 \times 3} = \sqrt{6}$   • $\sqrt{8} = 2\sqrt{2}$

- $\dfrac{1}{\sqrt{2}} = \dfrac{\sqrt{2}}{2}$                • $\dfrac{\sqrt{27}}{\sqrt{3}} = 3$              • $\dfrac{1}{\sqrt{5}-1} = \dfrac{\sqrt{5}+1}{4}$

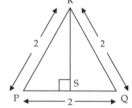

**J9**   In the diagram OB $= \sqrt{2}$ (by Pythagoras' Theorem).
Show that OC $= \sqrt{3}$.
Copy the diagram and continue the process
to obtain other square roots.

**J10**   Use triangle OAB to show that $\sin 45^0 = \dfrac{1}{\sqrt{2}}$.
Deduce also $\cos 45^0$.

**J11**   The triangle PQR is equilateral.
Use Pythagoras' Theorem to show that RS $= \sqrt{3}$.
Deduce $\sin 60^0$ and $\cos 60^0$.

**J12**   What is the sum of
(a) $\sqrt{2}$ and $-\sqrt{2}$   (b) $\sqrt{2}+1$ and $-\sqrt{2}+3$?
What is the product of
(a) $\sqrt{2}$ and $\sqrt{2}$   (b) $\sqrt{2}$ and $\sqrt{8}$   (c) $\sqrt{2}+1$ and $\sqrt{2}-1$?

**J13**   Give counter-examples to prove that these statements are false:
(a)   The sum of two irrational numbers is always irrational.
(b)   The product of two irrational numbers is always irrational.
(c)   The sum of two irrational numbers is always rational.
(d)   The product of two irrational numbers is always rational.

A proof by contradiction (see page 48) can be used to show that $\sqrt{2}$ is not a rational number.

Start by assuming it *is* a rational number in the form $\dfrac{p}{q}$, where $p$ and $q$ are integers with no factor in common.
Now $p$ and $q$ cannot both be even because then they have a factor of 2 in common.
So **either** ① $p$ is even and $q$ is odd   **or** ② ........   **or** ③ ........

In case ① $\sqrt{2} = \dfrac{\text{an even number}}{\text{an odd number}}$   and so, squaring, $2 = \dfrac{(\text{an even number})^2}{(\text{an odd number})^2}$.

Now an even number squared is a multiple of 4 (why?) and an odd number squared is odd.

So $2 = \dfrac{\text{a multiple of 4}}{\text{an odd number}}$   and therefore $2 \times$ an odd number $=$ a multiple of 4.

But this is impossible because $2 \times$ an odd number cannot have a factor of 4.

So case ① is not possible.

**J14**   What are the other two cases? Prove that they are impossible and so
establish the required contradiction.

# Now try these . . .

1. Think of a number. Add 5. Multiply by 4. Subtract 8. Divide by 4.
   By trying various starters make a conjecture.
   Prove your conjecture algebraically.

2. You are given the total of a 'parallellogram'
   of numbers from a calendar.
   How could you work out the four numbers?

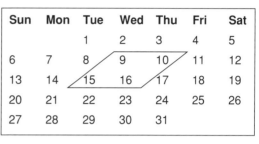

| Sun | Mon | Tue | Wed | Thu | Fri | Sat |
|---|---|---|---|---|---|---|
| | | 1 | 2 | 3 | 4 | 5 |
| 6 | 7 | 8 | 9 | 10 | 11 | 12 |
| 13 | 14 | 15 | 16 | 17 | 18 | 19 |
| 20 | 21 | 22 | 23 | 24 | 25 | 26 |
| 27 | 28 | 29 | 30 | 31 | | |

3. How many matchsticks are there in
   the $n$th shape ?

   (a)

   (b)

   (c)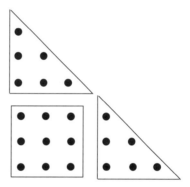

4. The pattern on the right suggests that
   $$T_6 = 3^2 + 2T_3.$$
   Investigate similar patterns for $T_4$ and $T_8$.
   Make a conjecture about $T_{2n}$.

5. These patterns show the first four hexagonal numbers $H_1$, $H_2$, $H_3$, $H_4$.

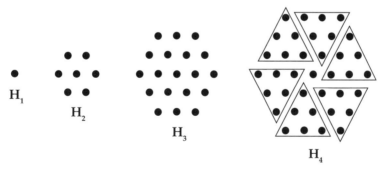

$H_1$   $H_2$   $H_3$   $H_4$

Use the triangles drawn on the fourth pattern to make a conjecture about the relationship
between the hexagonal numbers and the triangle numbers.
Check it with $H_3$, $H_2$ and $H_5$. What is $H_{20}$? Make a conjecture about a formula for $H_n$.

6. Write down any three digits. Make all possible two-digit numbers using them. Find the sum
   of these two-digit numbers. Find the sum of the original three digits. Make a conjecture
   about the relationship between these two sums. (You might need to try some more cases.)
   Prove your conjecture.

7. Find $n^2 - n + 41$ for $n = 1, 2, 3, 4$.
   Make a conjecture about the type of number produced.
   Test your conjecture for other values of $n$, seeking a counter-example.

8. Mark some points on a circle. Make all possible joins.
   Count the number of regions inside the circle.

2 points, 2 regions    3 points, 4 regions    4 points, 8 regions

Do the next one yourself. Take care to avoid multiple intersections. Tick off the regions as you count them.

   Make a conjecture. Test it with 6 points.

9. In 1556 the Italian mathematician Tartaglia made the
   conjecture that
   $1 + 2 + 4$
   $1 + 2 + 4 + 8$
   $1 + 2 + 4 + 8 + 16$
   . . . . . . . . . . . . . . . . .
   were alternately prime and composite. Test the conjecture.

10. A student claimed that the product of 3 consecutive numbers always had a factor of 12. For
    example, $2 \times 3 \times 4 = 24$, $3 \times 4 \times 5 = 60$. Test the conjecture.
    If you find a counter-example, modify the conjecture to state the largest factor.
    Test your conjecture and, if possible, prove it.

11. By considering as many possibilities as necessary prove that no square number can have 2
    as a units digit.

12. What are the units digits of (i) $23^5$ (ii) $17^5$ (iii) $12^5$?
    Make a conjecture about the units digit of any number raised to the fifth power. Prove it.

13. The angle DBC is called an *exterior* angle
    of the triangle ABC. Prove that an exterior
    angle of a triangle is equal to the sum of the
    opposite interior angles.

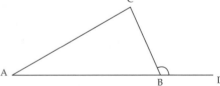

14. By considering the total angle turned through when
    'walking around' a pentagon find the sum of the
    exterior angles. Deduce the exterior angles for a *regular* pentagon,
    and hence find the internal angle of a regular
    pentagon. Generalise for an $n$–sided polygon.

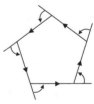

15. Find the fractions for these recurring decimals:
    (a) $0.8\dot{2}\dot{7}$    (b) $0.7\dot{5}$    (c) $0.3\dot{4}\dot{2}$

16. Prove these statements:
    (a) $\sqrt{5} \times \sqrt{20} = 10$    (b) $\dfrac{1}{\sqrt{3}} = \dfrac{\sqrt{3}}{3}$    (c) $(\sqrt{3} + 1)(\sqrt{3} - 1) = 2$

# The mathematics of music

How is sound made?

What is *pitch*?

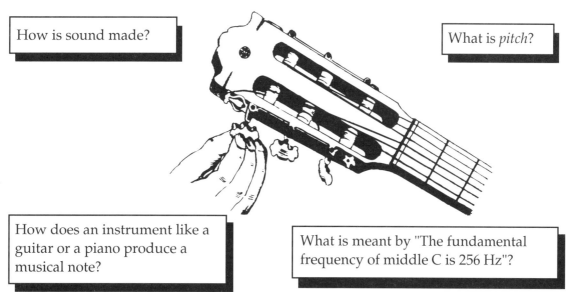

How does an instrument like a guitar or a piano produce a musical note?

What is meant by "The fundamental frequency of middle C is 256 Hz"?

"Pythagoras made a . . . . highly practical contribution which figures in every performance by a jazz pianist or string quartet. This was his discovery of the underlying mathematics of the musical scale. Pythagoras found that a marvellous connection existed between musical harmony and the whole numbers we count by – 1, 2, 3, 4, 5 and so on. Pluck a string and sound a note, then pluck an equally taut string twice as long and you hear a new note just one harmonic octave below the first. Starting with any string and the note it sounds, you can go down the scale by increasing the length of the string according to simple fractions expressible as the ratios of whole numbers.

For instance: 16/15 of a C-string gives the next lower note B, 6/5 of it gives A, 4/3 of it gives G, 3/2 of it gives F, 8/5 of it gives E, 16/9 of it gives D, and exactly 2 of it gives C again, an octave lower.

Pythagoras discovered the whole-number relationships between C, F, G and low C and between their equivalents in any scale. From this find he progressed to the firm conviction that all harmony, all beauty, all nature can be expressed by whole-number relationships."

*Life Science Library, Mathematics (Time-Life Books)*

Name the notes.
What is an octave?
Why are the white and black notes arranged in this way?

# A : Distances on a guitar

You will need a guitar.

Measure the distances of the frets from the bridge.  Record them in a table:

| Number of fret | Distance from bridge (in cm) |
|----------------|------------------------------|
| 1 | |
| 2 | |

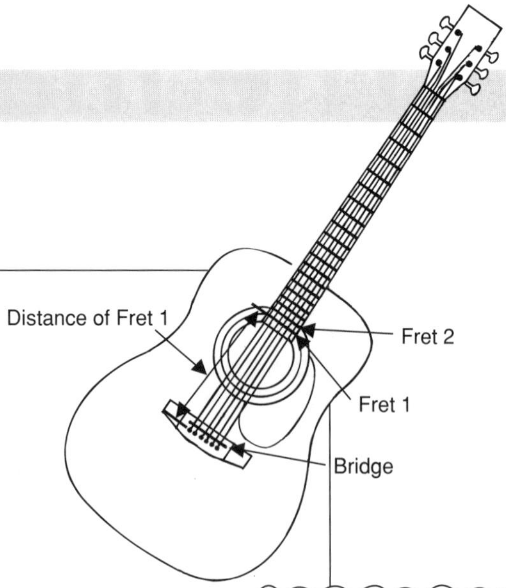

Distance of Fret 1

Fret 2

Fret 1

Bridge

Plot a graph:

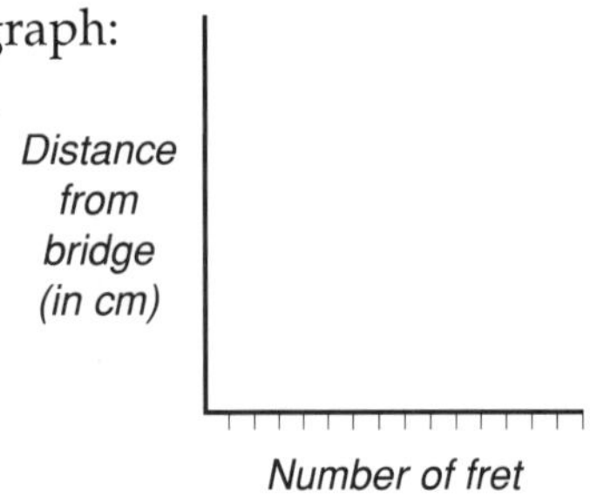

*Distance from bridge (in cm)*

*Number of fret*

How do the distances increase?

Do they go up by equal amounts?

Do they go up by equal multiplying factors?

How does a guitar player get different notes from a guitar?

And a violin player?

What are 'stopped' and 'open' strings?

How are stringed instruments tuned?

**For discussion**

Which fret is double the distance from the bridge of fret number 1?

Which fret is double the distance from the bridge of fret number 2?

Try some more.

Comment.

How would you find the distance for fret number 10 from the distance for fret number 9?

How would you find the distance $d_n$ for fret number $n$ from the distance $d_{n-1}$ for fret number $n-1$?

Obtain a formula connecting $d_n$ and $d_{n-1}$.

Obtain a formula for $d_n$ in terms of $n$.

# B : Frequency and length

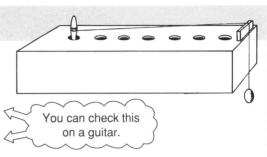

When a string is kept under a constant tension, the pitch of the note emitted (the *frequency*) depends on the length of the string: as the length increases the frequency decreases.

You can check this on a guitar.

It can be shown that
when the length is *multiplied by 2*, the frequency is *divided by 2*
when the length is *multiplied by 3*, the frequency is *divided by 3*. And so on.
**When the length is multiplied by k, the frequency is divided by k.**

A guitar string of length 60 cm gave a note with a frequency of 200 Hz.

Copy and complete the table to show the corresponding length and frequency for the same type of string under the same tension:

| Length $l$ (in cm) | Frequency $f$ (in Hz) |
|---|---|
| 60 | 200 |
| 30 | |
| | 100 |
| 15 | |
| | 300 |
| 75 | |

Put in some numbers yourself.

Check that $l \times f$ is always the same.

How can $f$ be found from $l$?
Write a formula: $f = \ldots$

How can $l$ be found from $f$?
Write a formula: $l = \ldots$

Plot a graph to show the relationship between $l$ and $f$.

- $f$ is said to be *inversely proportional* to $l$: when $l$ increases, $f$ decreases, and vice versa.

- Give some other situations in which this type of relationship occurs.

**B1** A string of length 40 cm emits a note of frequency 260 Hz.
   **(a)** What frequency would be emitted by a length of 20 cm of the same string under the same tension?
   **(b)** What is the relationship between the length $l$ cm of a string of that type under the same tension and the frequency $f$ Hz of the note emitted?
   **(c)** Find $f$ when $l$ is 50.
   **(d)** Find $l$ when $f$ is 200.
   **(e)** Plot a graph to show the relationship.

# C : Natural scales

Over 2000 years ago Pythagoras found that strings whose lengths were related by some simple fractions produced notes which harmonised well.

Call the length of a particular string $L$.
Then a string of length $\frac{4}{5}L$ produces a note which goes well with the note from the string of length $L$.

Similarly strings of length $L$ and $\frac{3}{4}L$, $L$ and $\frac{2}{3}L$, $L$ and $\frac{3}{5}L$, $L$ and $\frac{1}{2}L$ produce pleasant notes.

Two other notes, *ray* and *te*, were added using strings of lengths $\frac{8}{9}L$ and $\frac{8}{15}L$.
Neither of these two notes harmonised well with *doh* but they made a pleasant sequence when all the notes were played together.

The eight notes form a scale which spans an *octave*.

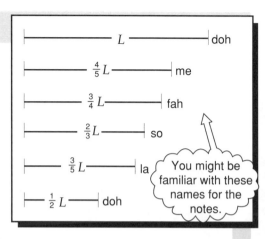

You might be familiar with these names for the notes.

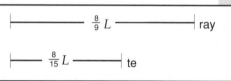

> **C1**  Taking $L$ as 180 find the lengths of the strings for the other notes of the octave.

It is now possible to find the relationships between the *frequencies* of the notes produced.

The length for *ray* is the length for *doh* **multiplied by** $\frac{8}{9}$.

So the frequency for *ray* is the frequency for *doh* **divided by** $\frac{8}{9}$.

**Reminder**
When the length is multiplied by $k$ the frequency is divided by $k$.

But **dividing by** $\frac{8}{9}$ is the same as **multiplying by** $\frac{9}{8}$.

**Reminder**
Dividing by $\frac{a}{b}$ is the same as multiplying by $\frac{b}{a}$.

So when the frequency for *doh* is $F$, the frequency for *ray* is $\frac{9}{8}F$.

> **C2**  Copy and complete the table to show the frequencies of the notes.

| | Length | Frequency | |
|---|---|---|---|
| doh | $L$ | $F$ | |
| ray | $\frac{8}{9}L$ | $\frac{9}{8}F$ | |
| me | $\frac{4}{5}L$ | | |
| fah | $\frac{3}{4}L$ | | Leave room for another column needed later. |
| so | $\frac{2}{3}L$ | | |
| la | $\frac{3}{5}L$ | | |
| te | $\frac{8}{15}L$ | | |
| doh | $\frac{1}{2}L$ | | |

Taking one of the C notes as *doh* gives a *scale of C* – the 8 white notes on a piano starting from C.

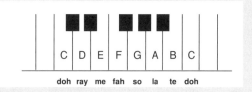

C3   The frequency of middle C is 256 Hz.  Use the frequency column in your answer to C2 to find the frequencies of the other notes of the octave which starts on middle C and finishes on the C above middle C.

C4   What is the  frequency of the C two octaves above middle C?

C5   What is the frequency of the C one octave lower than middle C?

Look back at the table in C2.

Each frequency can be calculated from the one above it.  For example

- the frequency of *ray* is $\frac{9}{8}\times$ the frequency of *doh*.
  So the *multiplier* is $\frac{9}{8}$ which is 1.125 as a decimal.

  $$\frac{9}{8}\times\boxed{?}=\frac{5}{4}$$

- the frequency of *me* is $\frac{8}{9}\times\frac{5}{4}\times$ the frequency of *ray*.
  So the *multiplier* is $\frac{8}{9}\times\frac{5}{4}$ which is 1.111 (to 3 decimal places).

  $$\frac{9}{8}\times\boxed{\frac{8}{9}\times\frac{5}{4}}=\frac{5}{4}$$

  To 'cancel' the effect of $\frac{9}{8}$.

C6   Find the other multipliers and fill them in on a copy of the table:

|       | Length          | Frequency        | Multiplier                                     |
|-------|-----------------|------------------|------------------------------------------------|
| doh   | $L$             | $F$              |                                                |
| ray   | $\frac{8}{9}L$  | $\frac{9}{8}F$   | $\frac{9}{8}=1.125$                            |
| me    | $\frac{4}{5}L$  | $\frac{5}{4}F$   | $\frac{8}{9}\times\frac{5}{4}=1.111$           |
| fah   | $\frac{3}{4}L$  | $\frac{4}{3}F$   |                                                |

*A calculator challenge*

The notes produced by strings of length $L$ and $\frac{2}{3}L$ are said to form a *perfect fifth*.  The frequency of the second note is $\frac{3}{2}\times$ the frequency of the first note.

The ancient Greeks and the Chinese found that 12 'fifths' approximates to 7 octaves.  Check by calculating $(\frac{3}{2})^{12}$ and $2^7$.

About 40 BC a Chinese scholar sought a better approximation.  He found that 41 'fifths' corresponded to 24 octaves.  Check!

Encouraged by this he went further and found that 53 'fifths' corresponded to . . . octaves.

Find it!

Look at your table in C6.

*Check that 1.067 occurs twice and that the other five numbers are approximately equal and are close to $(1.067)^2$.*

Writing $m$ for 1.067 gives approximate relationships between the frequencies of the notes as shown on the right.

Note that the multiplier between *me* and *fah* and between *te* and *doh* is $m$ to the power of 1. The other notes are connected by the multiplier $m$ to the power of 2.

> The notes are separated by a *semi-tone*.

> The notes are separated by a *tone*.

| doh | |
|---|---|
| | $m$ |
| te | |
| | $m^2$ |
| la | |
| | $m^2$ |
| so | |
| | $m^2$ |
| fah | |
| | $m$ |
| me | |
| | $m^2$ |
| ray | |
| | $m^2$ |
| doh | |

Taking C as *doh* gives a **scale of** C:

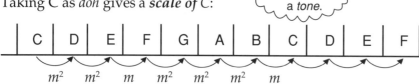

| C | D | E | F | G | A | B | C | D | E | F |
|---|---|---|---|---|---|---|---|---|---|---|

$m^2$　$m^2$　$m$　$m^2$　$m^2$　$m^2$　$m$

Suppose now we take D as *doh* to obtain a **scale of** D.

The multiplier from D to E is $m^2$ and so E is *ray*.

The multiplier from E to F is $m$ but to obtain the note *me* a multiplier $m^2$ is needed. So an extra note is required between F and G. It is called F sharp ($F^\#$) or G flat ($G^b$). On a piano it is a black note.

**C7**　Continue the multiplier argument to show that for a scale of D another note will be needed between C and D.

**C8**　By considering scales of E, F, etc. show that a further three notes will be required (making 5 in all). Name these notes as sharps.

**Find out**
- Why are the extra notes sometimes called *sharps* and sometimes *flats*?

When these extra notes are put in for all possible octaves, the piano keyboard looks like this:

> You should now be able to name all the notes on the piano and know why the black notes are there and why they are arranged in that way.

Middle C

# D : The equal-tempered scale

In the previous section the frequencies obtained from the fractional lengths were related *approximately* by the multipliers

$$m^2 \quad m^2 \quad m \quad m^2 \quad m^2 \quad m^2 \quad m$$

An *exact* relationship could be obtained if $m$ was chosen so that $m^2 \times m^2 \times m \times m^2 \times m^2 \times m^2 \times m$ was 2.

*The frequency is doubled from doh to doh.*

This gives $m^{12} = 2$

and so $m$ is the twelfth root of 2:

$$m = 2^{\frac{1}{12}}$$

*To find $2^{\frac{1}{12}}$ on a calculator, first do 1 ÷ 12 and put the result in memory. Then enter 2, press $x^y$, press memory read, press =.*

**D1**   **Check that $m$ is 1.0595 (to 4 decimal places).**

*On some calculators there is a quicker way.*

With this value of $m$ the 12 notes from C to C are then all related by the same multiplying factor. The frequencies on this **equal-tempered scale** are close to the frequencies on the natural scale obtained from fractional lengths (as described in the previous section). The differences are not large and can be accommodated by most people.

*From D1 the multiplying factor for a semitone is about 1.06*

**D2**   **Calculate the frequencies of the 12 notes from middle C to the next C up on an equal-tempered scale (that is to say with a multiplier of $2^{\frac{1}{12}}$ ).**

**Compare the frequencies of D, E, F, G, A, B, C with those on the natural scale (see your answer to C3).**

| Note | Frequency (in Hz) |
|------|-------------------|
| C    | 256               |
| C#   |                   |
| D    |                   |
| D#   |                   |
| E    |                   |
| F    |                   |
| F#   |                   |
| B    |                   |
| C    |                   |

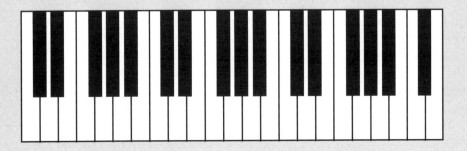

# E : Music by computer

Type in the program on the right in BBC BASIC.

Run the program and enter 53.

Then try 101.

Try some other inputs.

```
10    INPUT N
20    SOUND 1,-15,N,10
30    SOUND 1,-15,N + 8,10
40    SOUND 1,-15,N + 16,10
50    SOUND 1,-15,N + 20,10
60    SOUND 1,-15,N + 28,10
70    SOUND 1,-15,N + 36,10
80    SOUND 1,-15,N + 44,10
90    SOUND 1,-15,N + 48,10
```

## Understanding the SOUND statement

The SOUND statement is of the form

```
SOUND C, A, P, D
```

C is the *channel*.

Musical notes are obtained using channels 1, 2 and 3. The program above just uses channel 1. The three channels can be used for chords. There is also a channel 0 which gives a noise.

A is the *amplitude*.

This determines the loudness: 0 for silence, −15 for maximum loudness.

P is the *pitch* (frequency).

0 gives the lowest note, 255 the highest note. 53 gives middle C. Adding 4 increases the pitch by a semi-tone.

D is the *duration*.

This is in twentieths of a second. So 20 gives 1 second, 10 gives $\frac{1}{2}$ second, etc. Any number from 1 to 255 can be used.

## How the program works

When N is 53, line 20 gives middle C. In line 30 the pitch number is increased by 8, giving the note two semi-tones above middle C, which is D.
And so on.
In this way the program gives an equal-tempered scale:

|  | C | D | E | F | G | A | B | C |
|---|---|---|---|---|---|---|---|---|
| Number of semi-tones |  | 2 | 2 | 1 | 2 | 2 | 2 | 1 |
| Pitch number | 53 | 61 | 69 | 73 | 81 | 89 | 97 | 101 |

Try the program on the right to obtain all the twelve notes from middle C to the next C. Line 30 gives a pause (amplitude 0). Experiment with the program: vary the amplitudes, durations and pauses. Modify the program to give the twelve notes starting with any note.

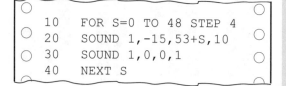

```
10    FOR S=0 TO 48 STEP 4
20    SOUND 1,-15,53+S,10
30    SOUND 1,0,0,1
40    NEXT S
```

# F : Bell ringing

Bell ringers often try to ring a set of bells in all possible orders.

For 2 bells there are only
2 possible orders:

1  2
2  1

> Not very interesting, and indistinguishable when the bells are rung continuously.

---

**F1**   **Write out all the possible orders for 3 bells:**

    1   2   3
    1   3   2
        etc.

**How many are there? How many possible orders are there for 4 bells? And for 5 bells?**

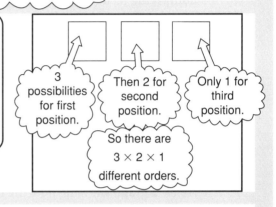

> 3 possibilities for first position.

> Then 2 for second position.

> Only 1 for third position.

> So there are
> $3 \times 2 \times 1$
> different orders.

---

Two rules are followed in *change ringing*:
- a bell may not move more than one place up or down
- usually a bell may not stay in the same place more than twice.

---

Here is a way to ring the changes on 3 bells using the rules.
The lines help to show how the position in which each bell is rung moves.

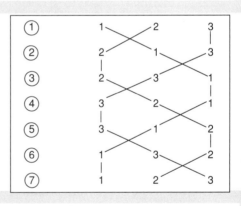

**F2**   **Find a different way to ring the changes with 3 bells. Trace the path of each bell. Compare the pattern of the lines with the one shown on the right.**

---

With 4 bells it's harder!
Here is one way:
*Interchange the 'outside' pairs.*
*Interchange the 'inside' pair.*
Repeating these interchanges three more times will bring

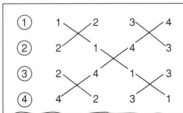

> This method is called Plain Bob Minimus.

you back to 1 2 3 4 on row ⑨ but not all possible changes will have been rung. So on row ⑧ just before you get back to 1 2 3 4 *interchange the right hand pair only* to give 1 3 4 2 for row ⑨. Repeat the whole process starting with 1 3 4 2 and you should get 1 4 3 2 for row ⑯. Then interchange the right-hand pair and repeat the process.

**F3**   **Write out all the changes. (There are 24 of them.)**

### You could . . .

- Investigate changes on 5 bells!
- Find out more about the mathematics of bell ringing.

# Now try these . . .

1.  The table shows the distances from the bridge of the first five frets of a guitar.
    Show that the distances increase by a constant multiplying factor (approximately).
    Calculate the approximate distances from the bridge of fret 13 and of fret 20.

    | Number of fret | Distance in cm |
    |----------------|----------------|
    | 1              | 21.8           |
    | 2              | 23.0           |
    | 3              | 24.4           |
    | 4              | 25.8           |
    | 5              | 27.4           |

2.  A violin string of length 40 cm is tuned to 440 Hz.
    What frequency of note would be obtained from a string of the same type with length 20 cm under the same tension?
    Write down an algebraic relation between the frequency and the length for strings of that type under the same tension.
    *Sketch* a graph showing how the frequency depends on the length.

3.  (a) String 2 is five sixths of the length of String 1.
    What is the relationship between the frequencies ($f_2$ and $f_1$ respectively) of the notes they produce? (Assume throughout this question that the strings are of the same thickness and under the same tension.)

    (b) String 3 is four ninths of the length of String 1.
    What is the relationship between their frequencies ($f_3$ and $f_1$)?

    (c) What is the relationship between the frequencies of String 3 and String 2?

4.  On a piano the note A above middle C is tuned to 440 Hz. Find the frequencies of the white notes from middle C to the next C up on an equal-tempered scale.

5.  The frequency $f$ (in hertz) of a vibrating string is given by

    $$f = \frac{\sqrt{T/m}}{2l}$$

    where   $l$ is the length of the string in cm
    $T$ is its tension in newtons
    $m$ is its mass per unit length in kg per metre.

    (a) (i) Find $f$ when $l$ is 0.3, $T$ is 9 and $m$ is 0.0004.
        (ii) Find $l$ when $f$ is 220, $T$ is 21.7 and $m$ is 0.0007.

    (b) What is the effect on $f$ of
        (i) multiplying $l$ by 3
        (ii) multiplying $T$ by 9?

# Curves

**Did you know?**
- The longest single span of a suspension bridge is 1410 metres long, across the Humber estuary.

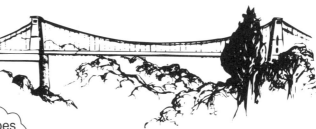

Find out about shapes of bridges.

**Controlled grazing**

A goat is fastened to one corner of a hut by a long chain.

What shape is the goat able to graze over? If the hut measures 2 metres by 4 metres, what area of ground can the goat reach? Try it for different lengths of chain. Suppose there is a tree placed somewhere in the field. What difference will that make?

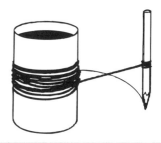

**Around and out**

Wrap a length of string around a cylinder. Stand the cylinder upright on a piece of paper. Put a pencil through a loop in the end of the string and then unwind the string from the cylinder.

Keep the string pulled out taut as you do this, and the pencil in contact with the paper so that it draws as it unwinds.

**Follow, follow, follow, . . .**

A woman, child, man and dog are standing in a park at the corners of a square.
Suddenly they all start walking:
- the woman towards the child
- the child towards the man
- the man towards the dog
- the dog towards the woman

What shape are the curves each one follows?
What happens if they move at different speeds?

W →    C ↓

D ↑    M ←

**Equations of curves**

What do the graphs with these equations look like?

$y = x^2$

$y = ax^2$

$y = a(x + b)^2$

$y = ax^2 + c$

And this one?

$y = \dfrac{a}{x}$

**Design**

# A : Some history

A penny is circular:

But when you look at a penny the shape you see is not normally a circle:

A cone of light rays.

**For discussion**
- Look at some circular objects. What actually do you see? How does the shape depend on the position of your eye?

It was possibly such an idea which led Greek mathematicians in about 350 BC to consider the geometry of the cone. They asked the question *What shapes arise from taking slices of a cone?*

 A slice parallel to the base is a **circle**.

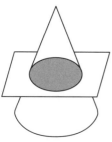

This corresponds to looking at a coin from directly above.

 Now imagine the plane of the slice being tilted. A slice at an angle like this is an **ellipse**.

This corresponds to looking at a coin from the side.

 As the plane continues to tilt it reaches a position where it is parallel to the side of the cone.

The curve formed is now no longer closed like the ellipse. It is called a **parabola**.

Let the plane continue to tilt. The curve is now more open than the parabola. It is called a **hyperbola**.

 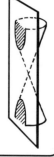

Strictly it is half of a hyperbola. The other half comes from using a double cone.

The Greeks studied the properties of these shapes obtained from cross-*sections* of a *cone*. They called the shapes *conic sections*.

**You could ...**
- Make models to show the conic sections. Some suggestions: card, acetate, Plasticine.

Have a look at some conic sections:

Tilt a tumbler of water or a funnel.

Put a funnel in a bowl of water.

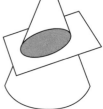

Cut slices through the upper part of a plastic squash bottle.

 Try slicing some circular objects:
a cucumber
a carrot
a sausage
a wooden dowel
a plastic drain-pipe

 What shadows can be made from a circle?

Some time later another method to obtain an ellipse was found.

You need two drawing pins, a loop of string, a piece of paper, and a board. Arrange them as shown. Put a pencil in the loop and move it round keeping the string taut.

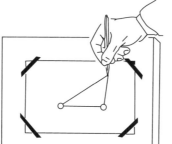

Experiment by
– changing the length of the string
– changing the distance between the pins (or holes).

Alternatively, make two holes in a piece of card. Put the string through the holes and tie the ends underneath.

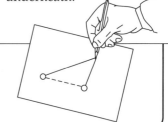

Each drawing pin is at a *focus* of the ellipse.

Plural: *foci*

A circle could be thought of as an ellipse in which the two foci are coincident.

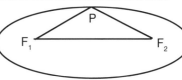

$PF_1 + PF_2$ is constant.

## Some more curves to draw

Draw a straight line.
Mark a dot, not on the line.
Put in a point which is the same distance from the dot as it is from the line.
Put in lots of points which meet that condition.
Draw a curve through all the points.

• Point

• Dot

Line

Try moving the point closer to the line . . . and further away.

Try other rules, such as: the points must be half as far from the dot as from the line.

Try other fractions.

What curves do you get?

. . . . . or twice as far from the dot as from the line.

Try three times as far, one and a half times as far . . . . .

*How was it known that the curve obtained by the 'pins and string' method was actually an ellipse as defined by the sections of a cone method?*

A proof was found in 1822 by fitting two spheres in a cone to touch an elliptical section. It can be shown that for any point on the ellipse the sum of its distances from the points of contact of the spheres with the section is constant. These points of contact are the foci.

The Greeks were mainly interested in the *properties* of the conics. It was not until 1609 that Kepler discovered that the planets moved in ellipses with the sun at a focus. The orbits are actually very close to circles. Isaac Newton (1680) went further. He showed that the force of gravity due to an object such as the sun or the earth was inversely proportional to the square of the distance from that object. It was a consequence of that relationship that an orbiting object would move in an ellipse.

*Why was this a revolutionary idea? (Excuse the pun.)*

**You could . . .**

- A simple model to show the foci can be made from two table tennis balls in a cylinder of acetate sheet. Some thought is needed to cut the ellipse. Can you prove that the spheres touch the ellipse at its foci?

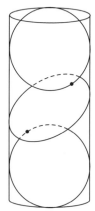

As you might have realised the *dot-line* methods on page 67 give rise to the parabola, ellipse and hyperbola. These methods show that the three types of curve can all be defined in the same way:

A point moves so that its distance from a fixed point is *k* × its distance from a fixed line.

When *k* is 1 a parabola
    is obtained.
When *k* is less than 1, an
    ellipse is obtained.
When *k* is greater than 1,
    a hyperbola is obtained.

*F is the focus.*

$$PF = k \times PQ$$

This is usually taken as the definition of the 'conics'. The *pins and string* property and the *sections of a cone* property can be deduced from it.

# B : Parabolas

The Greeks obtained parabolas as sections of a cone when the plane was parallel to the edge of the cone.

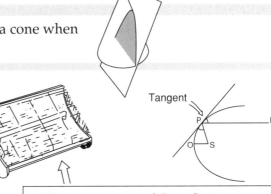

One of the properties of a parabola which they found was that if the focus S was joined to any point P on the parabola and a line PR drawn so that the two marked angles were equal (angle of reflection = angle of incidence), then PR was parallel to OS. This property is the basis of an electric fire (or car headlamp or radar aerial).

Tangent

The cross-section of the reflecting surface is a parabola. The element is at the focus of the parabola. The rays are reflected and emerge parallel.

The parabola is also important because it is the curve formed by an object such as a ball when thrown or a cannon ball or a shell from a gun (ignoring the effect of air resistance).

## Making parabolas

### Parabolas from straight lines

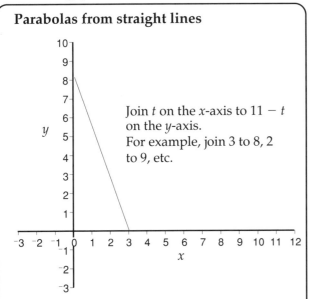

Join $t$ on the $x$-axis to $11 - t$ on the $y$-axis.
For example, join 3 to 8, 2 to 9, etc.

To make the curve look more like a parabola extend the axes and continue to join $t$ to $11 - t$.
For example, $\quad ^-1 \to 11 - {}^-1 \quad = 12$
$\qquad\qquad\quad 13 \to 11 - 13 \quad = {}^-2$

Try it when the lines are not at right angles.

The curve formed looks effective when the lines are *stitched* using thread.

### Paper folding

Use thin paper or tracing paper.

Mark a dot about 2 cm from the edge, and about half way down.

Fold the paper over so that the edge near the dot falls exactly on the dot.

Unfold and draw a line along the crease.

Do this folding and drawing several times.
As you draw more and more lines, you should see a curve forming.

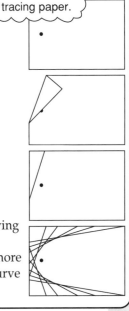

Try this computer program:

```
10   MODE 1
20   FOR X = 0 TO 1000 STEP 40
30   MOVE X,0
40   Y = 900 - X
50   DRAW 0,Y
60   FOR I = 0 TO 200:NEXT I
70   NEXT X
```

# Graphing parabolas

In the sixteenth century a great advance in mathematics was made when points were defined by *coordinates*. Then curves were defined by *equations* connecting the coordinates. Geometrical properties could then be expressed in algebra.

A parabola, for example, is defined by the equation $y = x^2$.

**Did you know?**
- René Descartes (French) defined the position of a point by giving two numbers – its distances from two fixed lines.

In honour of Descartes, these numbers are called *cartesian* coordinates.

What other ways are there of giving a position?

---

**B1**   On fine grid graph paper plot points whose coordinates satisfy the equation

$$y = x^2$$

| $x$ | $x^2$ |
|-----|-------|
| $^-3$ | |
| $^-2$ | |
| $^-1$ | 1 |
| 0 | 0 |
| 1 | |
| 2 | 4 |
| 3 | |

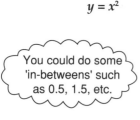
You could do some 'in-betweens' such as 0.5, 1.5, etc.

**Reminder**
$^-1^2$ is $^-1 \times ^-1$ which is $^+1$ or just 1
$^-2^2$ is $^-2 \times ^-2 = 4$ etc

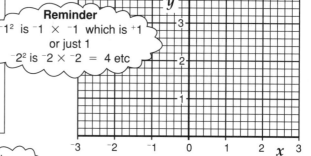

**Join the points carefully with a smooth curve.**   Use a sharp pencil.

---

**B2**   On the same sheet of graph paper draw the graph with equation
$$y = x^2 + 1$$
Check that you agree that for a given $x$ number the $y$ number for **B2** is 1 more than for **B1**. Do you agree that this means that the graph for **B2** is the graph for **B1** moved up by 1?

Translated by 1 up.

| $x$ | $x^2 + 1$ |
|-----|-----------|
| $^-3$ | |
| $^-2$ | |
| $^-1$ | |
| 0 | |
| 1 | |

To avoid confusion label the graphs with their equations.

---

**B3**   Now draw the graphs with equations

  (a)  $y = x^2 + 3$

  (b)  $y = x^2 - 2$

Use the same sheet as for B1 and B2.

**For discussion**
- Describe the family of graphs with equation
$$y = x^2 + c$$
How can they be obtained from the graph with equation $y = x^2$?

**B4** On another sheet of graph paper draw again the graph with equation $y = x^2$.

(a) On the same sheet draw the graph with equation
$$y = (x - 1)^2$$
What is the relationship between the two graphs?

(b) On the same sheet draw the graph with equation
$$y = (x + 2)^2$$
How does it relate to the graph with equation $y = x^2$?

| $x$ | $(x - 1)^2$ |
|-----|-------------|
| -3  |             |
| -2  |             |
| -1  |             |
| 0   |             |
| 1   |             |

**For discussion**
- Describe the family of graphs with equation $y = (x + c)^2$.

**B5** Use your graph with equation $y = (x - 1)^2$ in **B4** to draw on the same sheet the graph with equation
$$y = (x - 1)^2 + 2 \quad \Leftarrow$$

Do not make a table for this equation.

In the same way use your graph in **B4(b)** to obtain the graph with equation
$$y = (x + 2)^2 - 3$$

**For discussion**
- How can the family of graphs with equation
$$y = (x + c)^2 + d$$
be obtained from the graph with equation $y = x^2$?

**B6** On another sheet of graph paper draw again the graph with equation $y = x^2$.

(a) On the same sheet draw the graph with equation
$$y = 2x^2$$
What is the relationship between the two graphs?

(b) On the same sheet draw the graph with equation
$$y = \tfrac{1}{2} x^2$$
How does it relate to the graph with equation
$$y = x^2?$$

**Reminder**

$2x^2$ means $\boxed{2} \times \boxed{x^2}$

**For discussion**
- Describe the family of graphs with equation $y = k x^2$.
  What happens when $k$ is negative?
  How can they be obtained from the graph with equation $y = x^2$?

**You could ...**
- Investigate the families of graphs using a computer graph plotter.

A ball is thrown.  Ignoring air resistance its path can
be taken as a parabola with equation

$$y = 2x - 0.2x^2$$

To plot its path find the
height for various
horizontal distances.

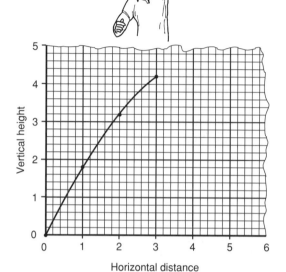

| $x$ | $2x - 0.2x^2$ |
|---|---|
| 0 | 0.0 |
| 1 | 1.8 |
| 2 | 3.2 |
| 3 | 4.2 |
| 9 | |
| 10 | |

The first four points have
been plotted.

**B7** Copy and complete the table. (Hint: the path is symmetrical!) Then draw the graph on
your own sheet of graph paper.

**B8** The equation  of the path of a ball is

$$y = 1.6x - 0.08x^2$$

where $y$ is the height above ground level and $x$ is the distance horizontally.
Draw up a table with $x$ from 0 to 20 in steps of 2.
Plot the graph.

**B9** The equation of the cable of a suspension bridge is

$$y = 0.01x^2 + 3$$

No need to do ⁻50 to 0
because of symmetry.

with $x$ going from ⁻50 to 50.
Draw up a table with $x$ from 0 to 50 in steps of 10.
Plot the graph with $x$ from ⁻50 to 50.

**B10** Bends in roads are often designed as parabolas.
The equation of one edge of a road is

$$y = 20 - 0.002\,x^2$$

Plot its graph taking $x$ from ⁻100 to 100 in steps of 20.

**B11** The equation of a concrete bridge is

$$y = -\frac{1}{20}x^2 - 1$$

where $y$ is the depth below the road surface.
Plot its graph taking $x$ from ⁻10 to 10.

# C : Circles

A slice through a cone parallel to the base gives a circle.

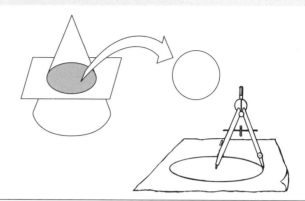

Circles are familiar shapes. The usual way of drawing them is with compasses.

---

Here is another way to obtain a circular arc.

Mark two dots on a sheet of paper about 5 cm apart or put two drawing pins through a sheet on a board.
Cut a piece of card to make an angle roughly as shown.
Put the card on the paper so that the edges pass through the dots (or are in contact with the pins). Make a mark at the point of the angle. Move the card slightly and make another mark. Continue the process.

Try it again with a right-angled piece of card.

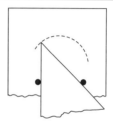

**For discussion**
• How can you be sure that the curve produced is part of a circle and that when the angle is 90⁰ a semi-circle is produced? See page 47.

---

### The equation of a circle

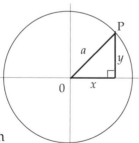

A circle of radius $a$ is formed when the point P moves so that its distance from 0 is always $a$.

Let P have coordinates $(x,y)$. Then by Pythagoras' Theorem
$$x^2 + y^2 = a^2$$
This relationship is true for all positions of P.
It is the *equation of the circle*.

The equation can be rearranged in the form $y = \ldots$ like this:
Start with $x^2 + y^2 = a^2$
Subtract $x^2$ from both sides:
$$y^2 = a^2 - x^2$$
Take the square root:
$$y = \pm \sqrt{a^2 - x^2}$$
Note that for a given $x$, $y$ can have two values, one positive and one negative.

---

**C1** Plot a circle of radius 4 using the equation
$$y = + \sqrt{16 - x^2}$$
by first making a table. Draw axes with $x$ and $y$ both going from ⁻5 to 5.

| $x$ | $\sqrt{16 - x^2}$ |
|-----|-------------------|
| 0   |                   |
| 0.5 |                   |
| 1   |                   |
| 3.5 |                   |
| 4   |                   |

Because of symmetry no further calculation is needed to plot the points when $y$ is ⁻$\sqrt{16 - x^2}$, nor when $x$ is negative.
Plot appropriately to obtain the complete circle.

# D : Ellipses

We see ellipses all the time although we do not register them as ellipses.

Two thousand years ago the Greeks studied ellipses as sections of a cone.

In the seventeenth century ellipses became of interest when it was discovered that the planets moved around the sun in elliptical orbits.

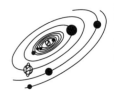

## Making ellipses

### Sliding ladder

A ladder slides down a wall. What is the path of a point such as P?

You will need a ruler.

Draw the two lines at right angles. Make the ladder 10 cm long. Choose a point 7 cm from the top say. Move the ruler so that *0* is on one line and *10* is on the other. Mark in the position of the point as you move the ruler.

What shape do you get?

Vary the position of the point.

Try it with 'ladders' in the other quadrants.

### Paper folding

Draw and cut out a circle 10 cm in diameter.

Mark a point in the circle anywhere between the centre and the edge.

Crease the paper circle by folding it over, so as to make the edge just touch the marked point:

Repeat with other creases.

The more times you make a crease the better the curve which results.

> Try marking the point in different positions in the circle.

Try it on a computer:

```
10   MODE 1
15   MOVE 1200,0:DRAW 0,0:MOVE 0,1000
20   FOR X = 0 TO 1000 STEP 40
30   PLOT 69,0.7*X,0.3*SQR(1000000-X↑2)
60   FOR I = 0 TO 200:NEXT I
70   NEXT X
```

> An amended version of the program in Section B.

> Can you see what line 30 is doing? Hint: Pythagoras.

# An ellipse from its equation

**D1** Plot the graph with equation

$$y = \pm 2 \times \sqrt{1 - \frac{x^2}{16}}$$

For example:

when $x$ is 1, $y$ is $\pm 2 \times \sqrt{1 - \frac{1}{16}} \approx \pm 1.94$

So plot (1, 1.94) and (1, ⁻1.94).

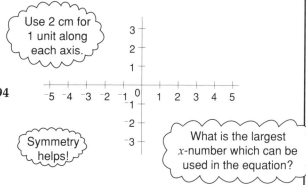

Use 2 cm for 1 unit along each axis.

Symmetry helps!

What is the largest $x$-number which can be used in the equation?

**D2** Repeat for $y = \pm 3 \times \sqrt{1 - \frac{x^2}{25}}$

using the same sheet as for D1.

Any equation of the form

$$y = \pm b \times \sqrt{1 - \frac{x^2}{a^2}}$$

gives an ellipse.

The equation in D1 can be rewritten like this:

Start with

$$y = \pm 2 \sqrt{1 - \frac{x^2}{16}}$$

Divide both sides by 2:

$$\frac{y}{2} = \pm \sqrt{1 - \frac{x^2}{16}}$$

Square both sides:

$$\left(\frac{y}{2}\right)^2 = 1 - \frac{x^2}{16}$$

Add $\frac{x^2}{16}$ to both sides:

$$\frac{x^2}{16} + \left(\frac{y}{2}\right)^2 = 1$$

Rewrite $\left(\frac{y}{2}\right)^2$ as $\frac{y^2}{4}$:

$$\boxed{\frac{x^2}{16} + \frac{y^2}{4} = 1}$$

How does the symmetry of the graph show up in the equation?

**D3** In the same way rearrange

$$y = \pm b \sqrt{1 - \frac{x^2}{a^2}}$$

## You could ...

- Try plotting graphs of ellipses with various values for $a$ and $b$.
  What do $a$ and $b$ tell you about the graph?
  What happens when $a = b$?
- You could try it using a computer graph plotter.

## For discussion

- An ellipse is a stretched circle.

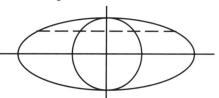

- The equation of a circle of radius 4 is

$$x^2 + y^2 = 16$$

which can be written as

$$\frac{x^2}{16} + \frac{y^2}{16} = 1$$

# E : Hyperbolas

The Greeks studied the hyperbola as a section of a double cone.

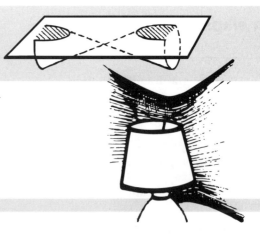

The hyperbola does not occur as frequently as the parabola and the ellipse although it can be seen sometimes as the shadow from a lamp shade.  It arises more often as the graph of relationships in physics.

## Making hyperbolas

### Hyperbolas from straight lines

On graph paper draw lines from $a$ on the $x$-axis to $\frac{36}{a}$ on the $y$-axis.

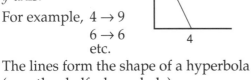

For example, $4 \to 9$
$\qquad\quad 6 \to 6$
$\qquad\quad$ etc.

The lines form the shape of a hyperbola (or rather half a hyperbola).

Try it with this computer program:

*Almost the same as the program in Section B.*

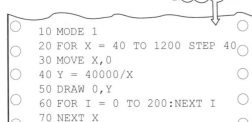

```
10 MODE 1
20 FOR X = 40 TO 1200 STEP 40
30 MOVE X,0
40 Y = 40000/X
50 DRAW 0,Y
60 FOR I = 0 TO 200:NEXT I
70 NEXT X
```

### Paper folding

You will need a sheet of thin paper or tracing paper.

Draw a circle. Mark a dot just outside it.

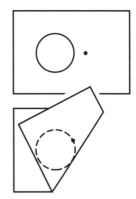

Fold the paper so that the dot is on the circle. Unfold and draw a line along the crease.

Repeat a number of times.

The lines should form a hyperbola.

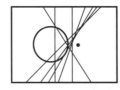

*Try changing the position of the dot.*

## Graphing hyperbolas

The equation of a hyperbola can be written in the form

$$y = \pm\, b \sqrt{\frac{x^2}{a^2} - 1}$$

Take $a$ as 2, say, and $b$ as 1 and plot the graph.

Try other values for $a$ and $b$.

*Don't forget $x$ can be negative.*

### You could . . .

- Show that the equation can be rearranged as
$$\frac{x^2}{a^2} - \frac{y^2}{b^2} = 1$$

- Draw some hyperbolas using a computer graph plotter.

# Another form for the equation of a hyperbola

Equations of hyperbolas can be put in the simple form

$$xy = \text{constant}$$

For example, taking the constant as 24 gives the equation

$$xy = 24$$

This can be rewritten as

$$y = \frac{24}{x}$$

When $x$ is 1, $y$ is 24.
When $x$ is 0.5, $y$ is 48.
When $x$ is $^-2$, $y$ is $^-12$.
And so on.

**An important feature**
When $x$ increases, $y$ decreases towards 0.
When $x$ decreases towards 0, $y$ increases.

Is there a point on the graph when $x$ is 0?

**E1**  **Draw the hyperbola with equation  $xy = 24$.**
**Then on the same sheet plot hyperbolas with equations**
$$xy = 60$$
$$xy = 120$$
**Label the graphs with their equations, and compare them.**

Suggestion: take 2 cm for 10 cm on both axes.

Graphs in the shape of hyperbolas often arise from *relationships*.

A rectangle has an area of 24 cm². The relationship between its sides of lengths $x$ cm and $y$ cm is
$$xy = 24.$$
From the graph you drew above the width could be found for any length. (Ignore the negative part!)

The pressure $p$ atmospheres  and volume $v$ cm³ of a gas at constant temperature are related by
$$pv = \text{constant}.$$
For example, when the constant is 24, the relationship would be shown by one of the graphs in E1.

**E2**  **The average speed $v$ mph and the time $t$ hours  to travel 80 miles are related by**
$$vt = 80$$
**Plot a graph to show the relationship.**

The relationship can be rearranged as $t = \frac{80}{v}$ .

Another common relationship in physics is of the form
$$y = \frac{\text{constant}}{x^2}$$
It is called an *inverse square law*.
For example, the force of gravity is *inversely* proportional to the square of the distance from the earth.

**E3**  **Take the constant as 60 and plot the graph with equation**
$$y = \frac{60}{x^2}$$
This is not a hyperbola.
**Compare it with the graph whose equation is $y = \frac{60}{x}$ .**

# Now try these . . .

1.  Draw two parallel lines as shown.
    Join points on the lines using the mapping

    $$x \mapsto \frac{12}{x}$$

    For example, $3 \mapsto \dfrac{12}{3} = 4$. So join 3 to 4.

    What shape is obtained?

    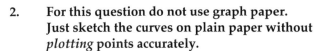
    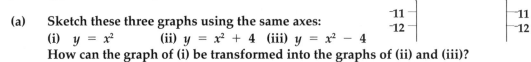

2.  For this question do not use graph paper.
    Just sketch the curves on plain paper without
    *plotting* points accurately.

    (a)  Sketch these three graphs using the same axes:
         (i)  $y = x^2$      (ii) $y = x^2 + 4$   (iii) $y = x^2 - 4$
         How can the graph of (i) be transformed into the graphs of (ii) and (iii)?

    (b)  Sketch these two graphs on another set of axes:
         (i)  $y = (x - 3)^2$   (ii)  $y = (x + 3)^2$

    (c)  Sketch these three graphs on another set of axes:
         (i)  $y = 4x^2$      (ii)  $y = \frac{1}{4} x^2$   (iii)  $y = {}^-2x^2$
         How can the graph with equation $y = x^2$ be transformed into the graphs of (i),
         (ii) and (iii)?

3.  In appropriate units the equation of the suspension cable of the Humber bridge is
    approximately

    $$y = \frac{2.45}{10000} \, x^2 + 40$$

    On graph paper label the $x$-axis from $^-700$ to 700 and the $y$–axis from 0 to 160. (The
    height of the bridge is small compared with its length! Use the same scale on both
    axes.)
    The road is represented by a horizontal straight line at $y = 40$.
    The supporting columns are vertical at $x = {}^-700$ and $x = 700$.
    Plot the graph taking $x$ at intervals of 100.

4.  Write down a formula to find the time $t$ hours to travel a distance of 100 miles at an
    average speed of $v$ mph.
    On graph paper plot a graph to show the relationship between $v$ and $t$.

5.  *Sketch,* on plain paper using the same axes, the graphs with equations

    $$y = \frac{12}{x} \quad \text{and} \quad y = \frac{12}{x^2}$$

    Label each graph with its equation.

# Three-dimensional structures

**How good are you at drawing
three-dimensional objects?**

Draw  a  die
       a  brick
       a  table (with a rectangular
          top and four legs)
       a  television set.

Get someone
to criticize your
drawings.

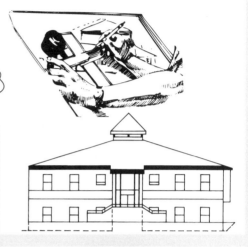

The diagram shows
a regular tetrahedron
whose edges are
diagonals of a cube.

What shapes are
left when the tetrahedron
is taken out?

What is the
volume of the
tetrahedron?

Can any other such
tetrahedra be formed
in the cube?

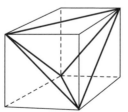

Play three-dimensional
Noughts and Crosses.

How can you
keep a record of
the moves?

**Design**

# A : Making three-dimensional structures

*In order to understand the geometry of three dimensions you will find it helpful to make some simple structures. You can then use them for the other pages of this chapter.*

Here are some ways of making three-dimensional structures.

### Using "girders"
This is a simple and cheap method.
You will need strips of card about 2 cm wide.
They can be cut on a slide-type guillotine from sheets of A4 card.
Score each strip along the centre and fold to make a girder. Fix the girders together using either a quick-setting glue or a contact adhesive.

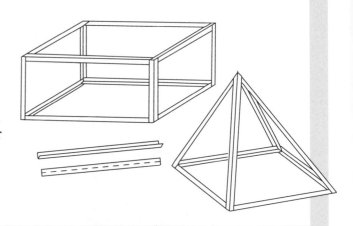

### Using straws
Plastic straws can be fixed together using pipe cleaners. To make the corners of a cuboid bend the pipe cleaners at three points to make three prongs at right angles.
Alternatively, straws can be joined using thread.

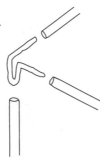

### Using sticks
Small structures can be made by fixing cocktail sticks together using contact adhesive.

A large square-based pyramid can be made using garden canes or thin dowel, held together at the corners with lumps of Plasticine. This is suitable for use as a demonstration model.

*You will find it helpful for pages 81 to 91 to have a cuboid, a cube and a square-based pyramid. The dimensions are not critical.*

### Some further ideas

Add some strips or straws to a cube to show one of the tetrahedra "inside" it.

Make a tetrahedron from cocktail sticks. Compare its rigidity with that of a cube.

# B : How to draw cubes and cuboids

**Oblique drawings**

① Draw a square.

② Draw a second square, the same size as the first one, "behind" it and to one side. The edges of the two squares must be parallel to each other.

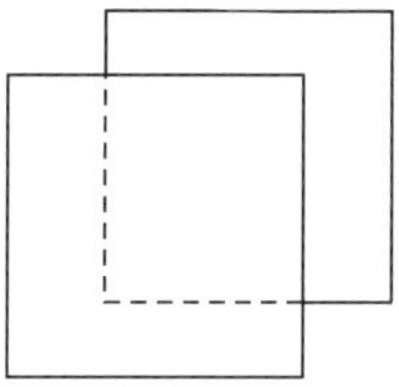

③ Join the corresponding corners of the two squares.

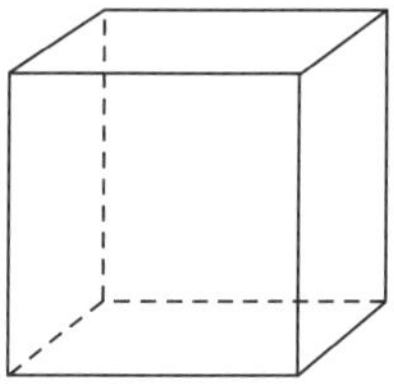

**Experiment** with this idea.

Make a collection of drawings to show various effects. Try moving the second square into different positions

- across
- up
- down
- across and up

Try making the second square a different size.

Get some actual cubes and cuboids and find viewing positions in which they match up with your drawings.

**For discussion**

- The edges of a cube are all the same length.
    *Are the edges in your drawings all the same length?*
- The faces of a cube are all squares.
    *Are the faces in your drawings all squares?*
- The angles of a cube or cuboid are all right angles.
    *Are the angles in your drawings all right angles?*

**B1** Draw some things using the oblique method – for example: a chair, a microwave cooker, . . .

**B2** If you did not use the oblique drawing method above when drawing a brick, a table and a television (see page 79), use it now to draw them.

## Isometric drawings

The oblique drawing of a cube started with the front face drawn as a square and looking flat on the paper. The top and side faces went away from it at an angle. Diagrams are often drawn with none of the faces of the object appearing to be flat on the paper. One such method is called **isometric** drawing.

You will need some isometric paper. Draw the lines shown on the right. You can make the shape look more like a cube by making some lines heavy and others lighter or dotted. Try it.

### For discussion
- Are the edges of your drawing all the same length?
- Are the faces all squares?
- Are the angles all right angles?

What does *isometric* mean?
What angles do the sloping lines make with the horizontal?

**B3** Make isometric drawings of some common objects. You could try some of the things suggested on the previous pages.

## Perspective drawings

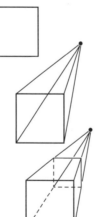

1. Start with a square.

2. Mark a point anywhere above it and off to one side. Draw lines joining the corners of the square to that point.

3. Draw lines parallel to the edges of the square to make the back face.

**B4** Try it yourself. Experiment with different positions for the point.

**B5** Make perspective drawings of some common objects such as those suggested on the previous pages.

### Did you know?
- Perspective began to be used in the fifteenth and sixteenth centuries by artists such as Uccello, Francesca and Dürer.
- The point to which the lines are drawn is called the *vanishing point*.
- Artists and architects normally do perspective drawings with a *vanishing line*. The other horizontal edges of the cube would then meet on the vanishing line.

### Find out
- Obtain more information about the development of perspective. You will find details in some books on art.

# C : Calculating lengths and angles

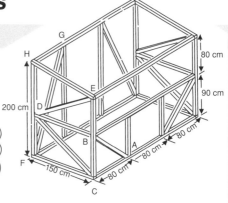

The diagram shows the framework for a garden shed.

From the measurements given the lengths of the diagonal struts can be found.
For example, the length of AB can be found like this:

> Note that in the calculations in this chapter the need for joints and overlaps has been ignored.

**either** make a scale drawing

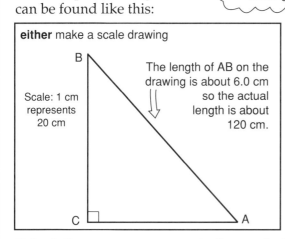

Scale: 1 cm represents 20 cm

The length of AB on the drawing is about 6.0 cm so the actual length is about 120 cm.

**or** use Pythagoras' Theorem

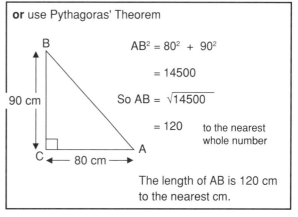

90 cm

$AB^2 = 80^2 + 90^2$

$= 14500$

So $AB = \sqrt{14500}$

$= 120$ to the nearest whole number

The length of AB is 120 cm to the nearest cm.

Calculations are more accurate than scale drawings, but scale drawings are usually accurate enough for practical work and they can serve as a check that the calculation has been done correctly.

> **C1** Find the lengths of the struts CD, DE and FG.
>
> **C2** Find the length of the sloping part of the roof (EH).

*In order for water to drain off the roof, the slope must be greater than $10^0$.*
*Does this roof satisfy that condition?*

The angle of slope can be found

**either** by making a scale drawing

The angle is about $10^0$.

Scale: 1 cm represents 20 cm.

**or** by using trigonometrical tangents

$\tan e^0 = \dfrac{30}{150} = 0.2$

So $e^0 = 11.3^0$ to the nearest tenth

30 cm

150 cm

> Is the roof steep enough?

> **C3** The diagram shows a garden frame.
> What length of glass is needed for it?
> What is the angle of slope of the glass?

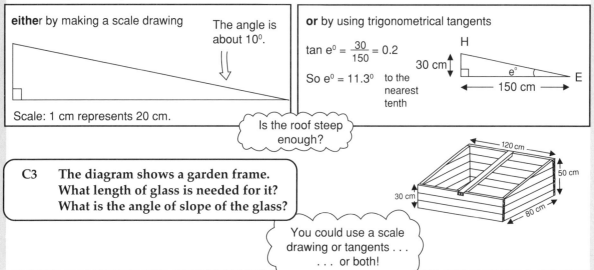

> You could use a scale drawing or tangents . . .
> . . . or both!

*An artist's drawing table is being designed.*
*The pivot for the table is to be at a height of 1 metre above*
*the floor.  The legs are to be 90 cm apart at the floor.*

The length of metal needed for the legs can be
calculated by putting in the line of symmetry of the
triangle formed by the legs.
Then by Pythagoras' Theorem

$$AC^2 = 45^2 + 100^2$$
$$= 12025$$

*to 2 decimal places*

So  $AC = \sqrt{12025} = 109.66$
*The length of the legs is therefore*
*110 cm to the nearest centimetre.*

The horizontal strut DE is 25 cm up from the floor.
Since the height of C is 100 cm, the strut is $\frac{1}{4}$ of the way
*up*.  This means that it is $\frac{3}{4}$ of the way *down* from C.
So its length will be $\frac{3}{4}$ of the length of AB.
The length of the strut is therefore 67.5 cm.

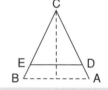

**C4**   The back of the frame is to be made
rigid by using two struts as shown.
How long is each strut?
(Suggestion: put in the line of symmetry.)

**C5**   The diagram shows a trestle.
Its height is 60 cm and the distance between
the outside edges at the bottom is 50 cm.
(a)  What is the length of AB?
(b)  At what angle should the timber be cut
at A?
(c)  The bottom edge of the horizontal piece
DE is 15 cm down from B.  How long is
it?
(d)  The bottom edge of the horizontal piece
FG is 20 cm up from the ground.
How long is FG?
(e)  Find the approximate length of the
diagonal struts. (The struts are attached
at the mid-point of the top of the
trestle.)

**C6**   The diagram shows a roof structure.
The sloping timbers are at an angle of
50⁰ to the horizontal.
(a)  What is the height of the roof
structure?
(b)  How long are the sloping timbers?
(c)  The horizontal timbers are one-third
of the way up.  How long are they?

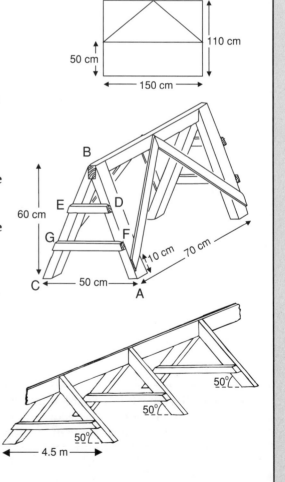

# D : Cuboid structures

*To follow the explanation on this page you need a cuboid. A "skeleton" model made from card "girders" is best, or it could be made from straws or sticks. Alternatively a cardboard box with two faces cut out can be used. A piece of card can be cut to make the section shown below. Also, if the room in which you are working is a cuboid it can be a useful visual aid.*

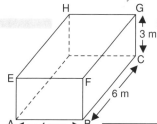

The diagram shows a room.

*How far is it diagonally across the floor?*

(1) Draw a diagram of the floor as seen from above.

(2) By Pythagoras' Theorem
$$AC^2 = 4^2 + 6^2 = 52$$

So $AC = \sqrt{52} = 7.21$ (to 2 decimal places)

*The length of the diagonal is therefore 7.21 m to 2 d.p. (that is, 7 m 21 cm to the nearest cm).*

**You could . . .**

- Measure the length, width and height of some cuboid-shaped rooms.
  Calculate the diagonal distances across the floor and the walls.

---

**D1** How far is it diagonally across (a) the front wall (AF) (b) the side wall (BG)?

---

**How long is the main diagonal AG of the room?**

(1) Look at the shaded triangle.

(2) Re-draw it as as shown below. AG can now be found by Pythagoras' Theorem because AC is known (see above).
$$AG^2 = AC^2 + 3^2 = 52 + 3^2 = 61$$

So $AG = \sqrt{61} = 7.81$ to 2 d.p.

*The length of the main diagonal is therefore 7.81 m to the nearest cm.*

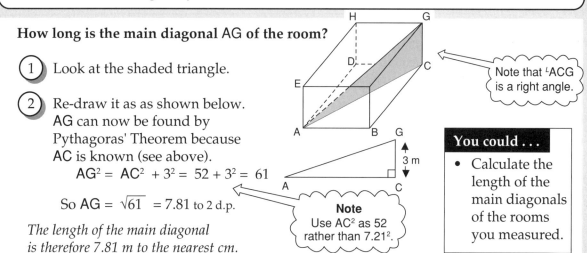

Note that ∠ACG is a right angle.

**Note**
Use $AC^2$ as 52 rather than $7.21^2$.

(Why?)

**You could . . .**

- Calculate the length of the main diagonals of the rooms you measured.

---

**D2** Find the length of the main diagonal of a room with a floor measuring 5 m by 7 m and a height of 3 m. (Find (floor diagonal)² first.)

**D3** What is the length of the longest stick which will fit in a box measuring 70 cm by 80 cm by 25 cm?

**D4** Find the length of the main diagonal of a cube of edge length 1 m. What would it be for a cube of edge length (a) 2 m (b) $x$ m?

**For discussion**
- How can the length of the main diagonal be found from the three measurements of a room? (Hint: where did 52 come from in the calculation above?)

# E : Pyramid structures

*To follow the explanation in this section you need a square-based pyramid made from card "girders" or straws or sticks. It need not be to scale. Use card to make the triangular sections shown below.*

The diagram shows a roof structure like the one in the photograph on page 79.
The top point T is vertically above the centre of the square base. The edges of the square are 3 m long. The architect decided that a height of 2 m would give a pleasing appearance.
In order to estimate the cost of the building, and later to build it, the lengths of the sloping edges are needed.

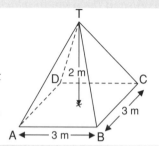

*Here are two ways to find the lengths of the sloping edges.*
*Work through them with the help of a model pyramid.*

## Method 1

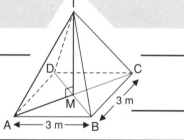

①   Look at triangle ATM. Pythagoras' Theorem could be used to find AT if we knew AM.

> Can AM be found?

②   Yes. Look at triangle AMN, where N is the mid point of AB.
AN is 1.5 metres (half of AB) and so is NM (half of BC).
So by Pythagoras' Theorem
$$AM^2 = AN^2 + NM^2$$
$$= 1.5^2 + 1.5^2$$
$$= 4.5$$
So $AM = \sqrt{4.5}$

> **Note: AM does not have to be found for use in ③ below. All that is needed is AM².**

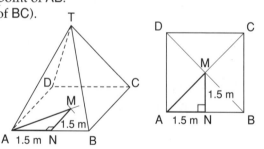

③   Now go back to triangle ATM.
Again using Pythagoras' Theorem
$$AT^2 = AM^2 + \ldots .$$
$$= 4.5 + \ldots .$$
$$= \ldots .$$
So $AT = \ldots . = \ldots .$ to 2 decimal places

The length of a sloping edge of the pyramid is therefore . . . . to 2 decimal places.

The diagram on the left also enables us to find the angle which the sloping edge AT makes with the horizontal.

$$\tan \angle TAM = \frac{2}{\sqrt{4.5}} = 0.943 \text{ to 3 d.p.}$$

So      $\angle TAM = 43^0$   to the nearest degree.

> This point about angles is taken up at the end of Method 2.

   **E1    Copy and complete ③ above.**

## Method 2

 Look at triangle ATN.
Since $\angle$ANT is a right angle,
Pythagoras' Theorem could be
used to find AT if we knew NT.

 *Can NT be found?*

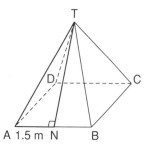

---

 Yes. Look at triangle TNM.
NM is 1.5 m (half of BC).
So by Pythagoras' Theorem

$$NT^2 = NM^2 + MT^2$$
$$= 1.5^2 + 2^2$$
$$= 6.25$$

So NT $= \sqrt{6.25}$

*No need to work it out here.*

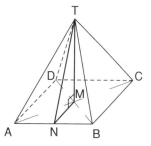

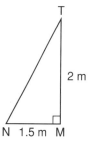

---

③ Now go back to triangle ATN.
Again using Pythagoras' Theorem

$$AT^2 = \ldots + NT^2$$
$$= \ldots + 6.25$$
$$= \ldots$$

So NT $= \sqrt{\ldots} = \ldots$ to 2 decimal places.

*This is why you did not need to work out NT.*

The length of a sloping edge is therefore . . . . m to 2 decimal places.

---

**E2** Copy and complete ③ above.

*Check with E1.*

---

### Another angle on it

*What angle does the face TAB make with the horizontal base?*

Look at the diagrams in the second panel above.
The angle which the face **TAB** makes with the horizontal base is angle TNM.
From the triangle on the right of the second panel

$$\tan \angle TNM = \frac{2}{1.5} = \ldots \text{ to 3 d.p.}$$

So $\angle$TNM $= \ldots$ to the nearest degree

The angle which the sloping face **TAB** makes with the base is . . . . to the nearest degree.

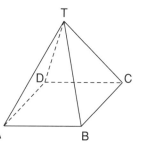

**For discussion**

• The angle which the *edge* TA makes with the horizontal is not the same as the angle which the *face* TAB makes with the horizontal. Why not? How can the angle between two planes be found?

**A useful model** Folded card, like a Christmas card with two corners cut off.

---

**E3** Copy and complete the last four lines above.

**E4**   In the pyramid structure on the right
ABCD is a square of edge length 4 m.
T is 3 m above the centre of the square.
Find AT   (a)   by first finding AM² where
          M is the centre of the square,
          (b)   by first finding NT where N is
          the mid-point of the edge AB.
What angle does the edge AT make with the base?
What angle does the face TAB make with the base?

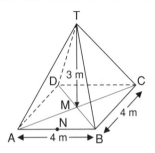

**E5**   A roof structure in the form of a pyramid has a
rectangular base measuring 3 m by 2 m.
The top of the pyramid is 1.5 m above the centre of the
base.
Find the length of a slanting edge.
What angle does the face TAB make with the base?
What angle does the face TBC make with the base?

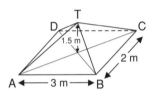

**E6**   The diagram shows the roof structure above the entrance
hall to a building.
The rectangular ceiling measures 5 m by 7 m.
The top T is 3 m above the mid-point E of the edge AD.
A card model is to be made of the pyramid based on
ABCD.
Find     (a)   the length of AT,
         (b)   the length of BT.
Draw to scale a net of the pyramid.
Check that it folds up correctly.
Calculate the angle which TA makes with the horizontal.
Explain why this is also the angle which the face TAB
makes with the horizontal.
Calculate the angle which BT makes with the horizontal.
Is this also the angle which the face TBC makes with the
horizontal base? If not, calculate that angle.

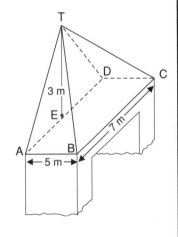

**E7**   The diagram shows a roof structure with a regular
hexagon as base.  The apex of the roof is vertically
above the centre of the base.
The edges of the hexagon are of length 2 m and
the height is 4 m.
Find the length of a sloping edge.
Find the angle which a sloping edge makes with
the horizontal base.
Find the angle which one of the faces makes with
the horizontal base.

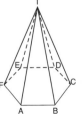

**Note:**
A regular hexagon is
made up from 6
equilateral triangles.

How can this diagram
be drawn without using
a protractor?

# F : Coordinates in three dimensions

In *two dimensions* positions of points can be determined by giving *two* distances, the coordinates of the point. For example, the x-coordinate of P is 3, and the y-coordinate is 2. P is determined by the number pair (3, 2).

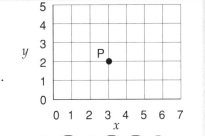

The distance of P from the origin can be found by using Pythagoras' Theorem:

$$OP^2 = 3^2 + 2^2 = 13$$
$$\text{So } OP = \sqrt{13} = 3.61 \text{ to 2 d.p.}$$

What other ways are there to fix the position of a point in two dimensions?

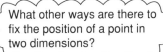

In the same way the distance between any two points can be found by using Pythagoras' Theorem.
For example, with P and Q as shown on the right,

$$PQ^2 = 4^2 + 5^2 = 41$$
$$\text{So } PQ = \sqrt{41} = 6.40 \text{ to 2 d.p.}$$

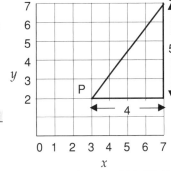

**F1** Find the distance of each of these points from the origin:
  (a) (5, 7)   (b) ($^-$3, $^-$4)   (c) (1, 1)   (d) (a, a)

**F2** Find the distances between the pairs of points:
  (a) (1, 2) and (4, 6)   (b) (3, 5) and (7, 10)   (c) ($^-$2, 0) and (3, 12)

In *three dimensions* the position of a point can be determined by *three* coordinates. Usually called x, y and z.
For example, the x-coordinate of P is 5, the y-coordinate is 4 and the z-coordinate is 2.
P is determined by the number triple (5, 4, 2).
To find the distance OP, first find $ON^2$, using Pythagoras' Theorem:

$$ON^2 = 5^2 + 4^2$$

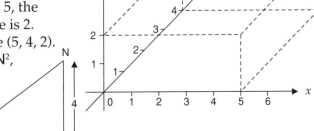

Then find $OP^2$:

$$OP^2 = ON^2 + 2^2$$
$$= 5^2 + 4^2 + 2^2$$
$$= 45$$

Notice the pattern here.

$$\text{So } OP = \sqrt{45} = 6.71 \text{ to 2 d.p.}$$

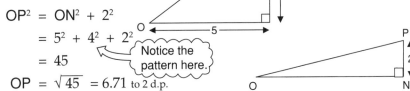

**F3** What is the distance of each of these points from the origin?
  (a) (4, 2, 1)   (b) (1, 2, 2)   (c) (1, 1, 1)   (d) (k, k, k).

**F4** Draw a diagram to show how to find the distance between the points (3, 2, 1) and (7, 5, 7).
  Find the distances between the pairs of points:
  (a) (1, 5, 4) and (3, 8, 10)   (b) (1, 3, 2) and (5, 7, 9)   (c) (1, 2, 3) and (4, 5, 6).

# G : Further activities

### Shortest route

An electric cable is being taken from P to
Q along the walls, floor or ceiling.
Find the shortest length of cable needed
and show its path.

Invent some other problems about
shortest routes when P and Q are not at
corners.

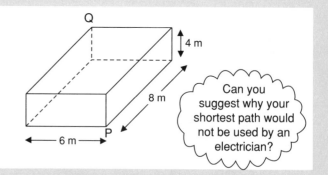

Can you
suggest why your
shortest path would
not be used by an
electrician?

### Whole number lengths

Check that the length of the main
diagonal of this box is 3 m.

A whole
number.

Find other whole number
measurements for boxes so that the
main diagonal is also a whole
number.

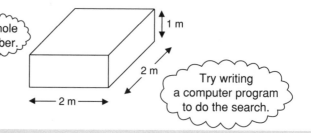

Try writing
a computer program
to do the search.

### Three-dimensional Noughts and Crosses

|     | Player | Move      |
|-----|--------|-----------|
| 1.  | B      | (1, 1, 3) |
| 2.  | W      | (1, 0, 3) |
| 3.  | B      | (0, 0, 2) |
| 4.  | W      | (1, 3, 2) |
| 5.  | B      | (3, 2, 3) |
| 6.  | W      | (2, 3, 0) |
| 7.  | B      | (0, 2, 0) |
| 8.  | W      | (0, 3, 0) |
| 9.  | B      | (2, 0, 2) |
| 10. | W      | (0, 1, 2) |
| 11. | B      | (1, 2, 0) |
| 12. | W      | (1, 2, 1) |
| 13. | B      | (1, 2, 3) |
| 14. | W      | (3, 1, 2) |
| 15. | B      | (2, 2, 1) |
| 16. | W      | (3, 1, 1) |
| 17. | B      | (1, 0, 2) |
| 18. | W      | (1, 3, 0) |
| 19. | B      | (0, 1, 0) |
| 20. | W      | (2, 1, 2) |
| 21. | B      | (3, 2, 0) |
| 22. | W      | (1, 1, 2) |

Here is a record of a game
between two players Black (B)
and White (W).
On move 22 with the counter
placed on (1, 1, 2) the game was
won. Actually, two winning
lines were formed on that move.
What were the coordinates of the
points on the two winning lines?

How many lines are possible in
the game of Three-dimensional
Noughts and Crosses?

When given a set of four points
in coordinate form how can you
tell if they form a winning line?

### A three-dimensional puzzle

How can a block of
wood be cut so that it
would just fit into each
of these three holes in
a sheet of metal?

### Designing three-dimensional structures

Study some three-dimensional structures (roofs, skylights,
etc.).
Do some calculations and make models.

# Now try these . . .

1. Three cubes are put together to make an L-shape. Draw diagrams to show
   (a) an oblique view        (b) an isometric view        (c) a perspective view.

2. The diagram shows the structure
   of a building.
   What is the height of the top of
   the building?
   What is the angle of slope of
   the roof?

3. The drawing shows the framework of a
   garden shed.
   (a) Make a scale drawing to show the back
        view. The vertical support is half-way
        along at the back. (Represent each
        piece of timber by a line.)
   (b) Using your drawing find the length of
        the diagonal struts.
   (c) Check your accuracy in (b) by
        *calculating* the length of the diagonal
        struts.
   (d) Calculate
        (i)    AB (the bottom of the window is
             half-way up the front)
        (ii)   CD
        (iii) AD
        (iv) the angle of slope of the roof.

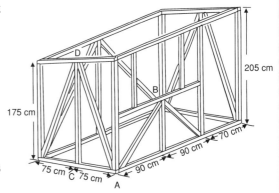

4. A box measures 80 cm by 40 cm by 50 cm.
   What is the length of the longest rod which could be fitted into it?

5. The drawing (not to scale) shows a television mast OT which
   has four stay-wires fastened to its top (at T) and to the
   ground at A, B, C, and D. The points ABCD form a square
   with sides of length 32 metres. O is the centre of the square.
   The angle of elevation of T from A is $57^0$.
   Calculate :
   (a)    the distance AO
   (b)    the height of the mast
   (c)    the length of one stay-wire
   (d)    the angle of elevation of the top of the
          mast from a point E which is midway between C and D
   (e)    the new angle of elevation of the top of the mast
          from A if the height of the mast were doubled.

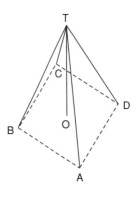

6. The drawing (not to scale) shows a wedge ABCDEF.
   Faces ABCD and BEFC are both rectangles and are at right angles to each other.
   AB = 20 cm   AD = 10 cm   $\llcorner$FDC = $18^0$

   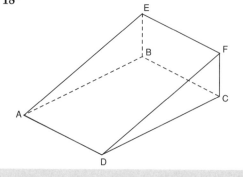

   Calculate:
   (a)   the height CF
   (b)   the length of the edge DF
   (c)   $\llcorner$CAD
   (d)   the length of the diagonal AF
   (e)   $\llcorner$FAC

7. The drawing shows the top of a building in the shape
   of a pyramid with a rectangular base. The apex is
   above the centre of the base.
   (a)   Find the length of a sloping edge.
   (b)   Find the angle which a sloping edge makes
         with the base.
   (c)   Find the angle which the face on the right
         of the pyramid makes with the base.

   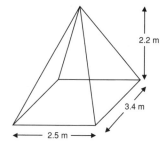

8. A roof structure is made from square-based pyramids
   as shown.
   (a)   How long are the sloping pieces?
         (Treat the connector as a point – that is
         to say, ignore the lengths which will
         need to be cut off the sloping pieces in
         order that they fit the connector.)
   (b)   At what angle would the top end of the
         sloping pieces need to be cut?

   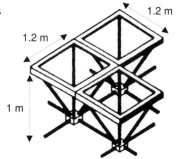

9. The net on the right folds up to make a pyramid with
   the vertex above the centre of the base. When the
   pyramid is made up what will be the vertical height?

   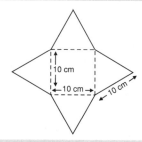

10. Show that the points with coordinates (2, 4, 7) and (1, 2, 8) are equi-distant
    from the origin.
    Find the distance between the two points.

# The best design

### Maximising area

Queen Dido of Syria fled to Africa when her husband was murdered. She asked King Jarbos for some land. "How much do you want?" he said. "As much as can be spanned by the hide of an ox" she replied. The King did not think that was much and her request was granted. However, the Queen was crafty. She cut up the hide into strips and knotted them together to make a loop. How did she arrange the loop to maximise the area?

### Designing a tank

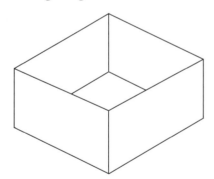

An open tank with a square base is needed to contain 50 litres of liquid. Sheet metal costs £10 per square metre. What dimensions would you recommend for the cheapest tank?

### Designing a tennis-ball package

Tennis balls are sometimes packed in boxes of six, and sometimes in tubes of four. Compare the 'efficiency' of the two methods by finding the percentage of waste space in each case.

# A : Maximising area

**A farmer has 40 metres of wire fencing. The farmer wishes to make a rectangular enclosure to contain as large an area as possible.**

The problem can be analysed mathematically like this :

Suppose the length is $x$ metres and the width is $y$ metres.
Then, since the farmer has 40 metres of fencing

$$2x + 2y = 40$$

and so, dividing by 2,

$$x + y = 20 \qquad \dots \dots \text{(i)}$$

The area is $xy$ square metres.

Now from equation (i)

$$y = 20 - x$$

The area can therefore be written as
$x(20 - x)$ square metres.

Thus if $x$ is 15 the area is $15 \times 5 = 75$ square metres.

To find the greatest area, various numbers can be tried for $x$.

| $x$ | $x(20 - x)$ |
|-----|-------------|
| 0 | $0 \times 20 = 0$ |
| 1 | $1 \times 19 = 19$ |
| 2 | $2 \times 18 = 36$ |
| 3 | $3 \times 17 = 51$ |
| . | . |
| . | . |
| . | . |
| . | . |

**A1**   **By trying other numbers find the greatest area.**

The way in which the area depends on $x$ can also be shown graphically :

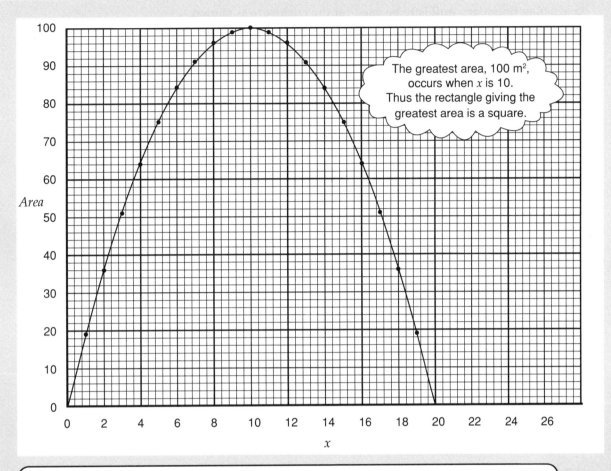

The greatest area, 100 m², occurs when $x$ is 10. Thus the rectangle giving the greatest area is a square.

**A2** Use the graph to find the dimensions of a rectangular enclosure of area 80 m². Is there more than one solution?

**A3** Use the graph to solve the equation
$$x(20 - x) = 40$$

$x(20 - x)$ can be written as
$$x \times 20 - x \times x$$
or as
$$20x - x^2$$

**For example**
$$6 \times (20 - 6) = 6 \times 20 - 6 \times 6$$

**A4** Use the graph to solve the equations

(a) $x(20 - x) = 50$

(b) $20x - x^2 = 30$

(c) $x^2 - 20x + 60 = 0$

**A5** The farmer wishes to make a rectangular enclosure with 60 metres of fencing.
What dimensions would you recommend to obtain the greatest area?
Generalise the problem for any length of fencing.

**An existing boundary wall is to be used for the enclosure as shown. Again 40 metres of fencing are available.**

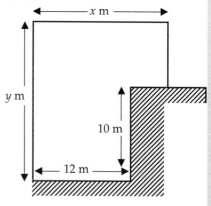

So      $x + y + (y - 10) = 40$

> Which length is this on the diagram?

Thus      $x + 2y - 10 = 40$

and so      $x + 2y = 50$      . . . . . (1)

The area of the enclosure (in m²) is

$$xy - 10x + 120 \qquad \text{. . . . . (2)}$$

Area of ABCD    Area of AEGD    Area of AEFH

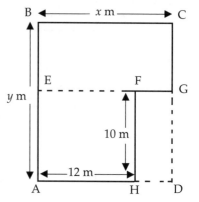

This expression for the area involves both $x$ and $y$. From equation (1), $y$ can be found in terms of $x$ :

$$2y = 50 - x$$

and so      $y = \dfrac{50 - x}{2}$

The area can now be found in terms of $x$ by substituting for $y$ in (2). The area (in m²) is

$$x\left(\frac{50 - x}{2}\right) - 10x + 120$$

This formula can be rewritten as

$$\frac{50x - x^2}{2} - 10x + 120$$

and then as

$$25x - \frac{1}{2}x^2 - 10x + 120$$

> Check these steps.

and finally as

$$15x - \frac{1}{2}x^2 + 120$$

Here is a computer printout showing the area with $x$ going from 12 to 30 in steps of 2.

| x | f(x) |
|---|------|
| 12 | 228.0 |
| 14 | 232.0 |
| 16 | 232.0 |
| 18 | 228.0 |
| 20 | 220.0 |
| 22 | 208.0 |
| 24 | 192.0 |
| 26 | 172.0 |
| 28 | 148.0 |
| 30 | 120.0 |

The printout was obtained with this program. It can be used to evaluate any function.

```
10  INPUT "f(x)= "F$
20  INPUT "Least x= "A
30  INPUT "Greatest x= "B
40  INPUT "Step= "H
50  PRINT "   x     f(x)":PRINT
60  FOR X= A TO B STEP H
70  PRINT X"      "EVAL(F$)
80  NEXT X
```

**A6** Can you determine from the printout the value of $x$ which gives the maximum area? If necessary, re-run the program with a different step length, or use a calculator.

**A7** In the printout $x$ went up to 30. Is it possible for $x$ to be greater than 30 or less than 12?

**A8** Draw a graph to show the area. Suggested scales : 1 cm for 2 metres across the page, and 1 cm for 20 m² up the page. You could include $x$ values from 0 to 12 although they are not actually possible in this problem.

**A9** A rectangular enclosure is to be built with 40 m of fencing using an existing wall as shown on the right. Show that the area is

$$\frac{x(40-x)}{2} \ \ m^2$$

Draw up a table giving the area for various values of $x$. Use the computer program if you wish.
Plot a graph of the area.
What dimensions would you recommend for the maximum area?

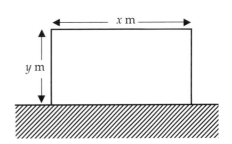

**A10** Repeat A9 for 60 m of fencing.

**A11** Make a conjecture about the dimensions which give the maximum area for a length of L metres of fencing.

Can you prove your conjecture?

**A12** (a) Use the diagram on the right to show that the area (in m²) of the enclosure on the opposite page is $xy - 10(x - 12)$.
By 'removing the brackets' check that this is the same as (2) on the opposite page.

Reminder
$a - (b - c) = a - b + c$

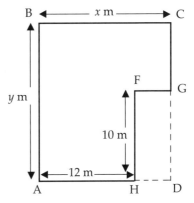

(b) Use the diagram on the right to show that the area (in m²) is also
$12y + (x - 12)(y - 10)$
Check that this is the same as (2) on the opposite page.

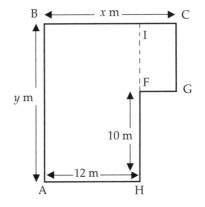

# B : Quadratic functions

## Using a computer graph plotter

The problems in Section A gave rise to functions of the form

$$x \mapsto ax^2 + bx + c$$

Functions of this form, where the highest power of $x$ is 2, are called *quadratic* functions. Their graphs are parabolas. You drew some parabolic graphs on pages 70 to 72.

A computer graph plotter can be used to investigate the graph with equation

$$y = ax^2 + bx + c$$

for various values of $a$, $b$ and $c$.

Here are two examples :

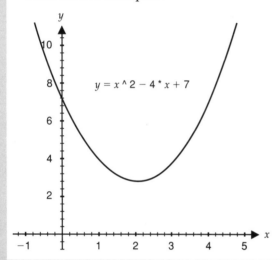

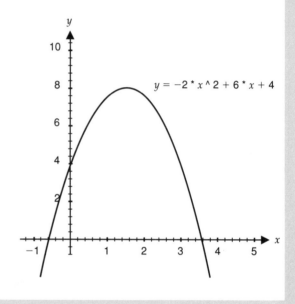

To investigate the graphs it is worth developing a strategy such as

- take $b$ and $c$ as 0.
  Try various numbers for $a$, positive and negative.

- take $b$ as 0.

- take $c$ as 0.

    etc.

Try to predict the value of $x$ at the bottom point (or top point) of the graph with equation
$$y = ax^2 + bx + c$$
Take $a$ as 1 to begin with.

Use the graphs to solve equations such as

$$x^2 + 6x + 5 = 0$$
$$x^2 - 2x - 6 = 0$$
$$x^2 + 2x + 1 = 0$$

**You could . . .**

- Write an account of your investigation and illustrate it with graphs drawn yourself.

## Graph sketching

It is often useful to be able to do a rough sketch of the graph with equation $y = ax^2 + bx + c$ without having to evaluate $ax^2 + bx + c$ or use a computer graph plotter. This page and the next one show how to do such a sketch rapidly.

On page 71 you drew the graph with equation $y = (x + 2)^2$ and you saw that it was a translation of the graph with equation $y = x^2$ by 2 to the left. You also saw that the graph with equation $y = (x - 1)^2$ was a translation of the graph with equation $y = x^2$ by 1 to the right.

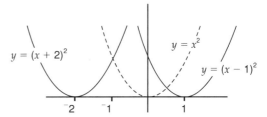

Now $(x + 2)^2$ can be written in the form $ax^2 + bx + c$ by using an area diagram or table as on the right:

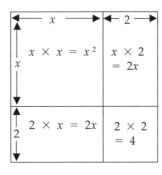

$$(x + 2)^2 = x^2 + 4x + 4$$

This is then in the form $ax^2 + bx + c$ where $a$ is 1, $b$ is 4 and $c$ is 4.

So the graph with equation $y = x^2 + 4x + 4$ could be sketched rapidly by realising that $y = x^2 + 4x + 4$ is the same as $y = (x + 2)^2$.

---

**B1**   Write in the form $ax^2 + bx + c$ by using 'area diagrams' or tables:
  (a) $(x + 1)^2$     (b) $(x + 5)^2$     (c) $(x + 1\frac{1}{2})^2$

**B2**   Write in the form $(x + \dots)^2$
  (a) $x^2 + 6x + 9$       (b) $x^2 + 10x + 25$        (c) $x^2 + 5x + \frac{25}{4}$

**B3**   Use B2 to sketch the graphs with equations
  (a) $y = x^2 + 6x + 9$     (b) $y = x^2 + 10x + 25$     (c) $y = x^2 + 5x + \frac{25}{4}$

---

In the same way $(x - 1)^2$ can be written in the form $ax^2 + bx + c$ by thinking of it as $(x + {}^-1)^2$ and using a table as on the right.
  $(x - 1)^2 = (x + {}^-1)^2 = x^2 + {}^-2x + 1 = x^2 - 2x + 1$

| | $x$ | $^-1$ |
|---|---|---|
| $x$ | $x^2$ | $x \times {}^-1$ |
| $^-1$ | $^-1 \times x$ | $^-1 \times {}^-1$ |

---

**B4**   Using tables (if necessary) write in the form $ax^2 + bx + c$:
  (a) $(x - 2)^2$              (b) $(x - 3)^2$              (c) $(x - \frac{1}{2})^2$

**B5**   Write in the form $(x - \dots)^2$
  (a) $x^2 - 6x + 9$       (b) $x^2 - 10x + 25$        (c) $x^2 - 5x + \frac{25}{4}$

**B6**   Use B5 to sketch the graphs with equations
  (a) $y = x^2 - 6x + 9$     (b) $y = x^2 - 10x + 25$     (c) $y = x^2 - 5x + \frac{25}{4}$

**B7**   Write in the form $y = ax^2 + bx + c$:
  (a) $y = (x + 2)^2 + 3$     (b) $y = (x + 1)^2 + 2$
  (c) $y = (x + 5)^2 - 25$     (d) $y = (x - 1)^2 + 4$
  (e) $y = (x - 3)^2 - 9$     (f) $y = (x - \frac{1}{2})^2 + 1$

**For discussion**
- How can graphs be sketched rapidly for the equations in B7?

The process in B7 can also be done the other way round.

For example, $x^2 + 6x + 11$ can be written in the form $(x + \ldots)^2 + \ldots$ like this:

**1** Find the missing number in the brackets:
The number of $x$s in $x^2 + 6x + 11$ is 6.
The missing number is therefore 3.
So $x^2 + 6x + 11 = (x + 3)^2 + \ldots$

This is called **completing the square.**

**2** Find the missing number at the end :
$(x + 3)^2$ is $x^2 + 6x + 9$
To make 9 up to 11, 2 needs to be added.
So $x^2 + 6x + 11 = (x + 3)^2 + 2$

This now enables the graph to be sketched rapidly using the method on pages 70 and 71.

Start with the graph with equation $y = x^2$

Translate it by 3 to the left to give the graph with equation $y = (x + 3)^2$

Translate it by 2 up to give the graph with equation $y = (x + 3)^2 + 2$

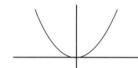
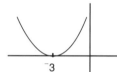
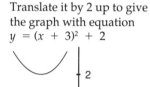

As a second example consider $x^2 + 8x + 15$.
It can be written in the form $(x + \ldots)^2 + \ldots$ like this:

**1** Find the missing number in the brackets:
The number of $x$s in $x^2 + 8x + 15$ is 8.
The missing number is therefore 4. $\Leftarrow 8 \div 2$
So $x^2 + 8x + 15 = (x + 4)^2 + \ldots$

**2** Find the missing number at the end:
$(x + 4)^2$ is $x^2 + 8x + 16$
We want 15 not 16 so we have to add $^-1$, or equivalently subtract 1:
$x^2 + 8x + 15 = (x + 4)^2 - 1$

To sketch the graph use the method on pages 70 and 71:

Start with the graph with equation $y = x^2$

Translate it by 4 to the left to give the graph with equation $y = (x + 4)^2$

Translate it by 1 down to give the graph with equation $y = (x + 4)^2 - 1$

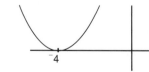
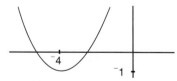

**B8** Write in the form $y = (x + \ldots)^2 + \ldots$
(a) $y = x^2 + 4x + 5$     (b) $y = x^2 + 2x + 3$
(c) $y = x^2 + 3x + 4$     (d) $y = x^2 + 2x - 3$
(e) $y = x^2 - 2x - 8$     (f) $y = x^2 - 5x - 0.75$

**B9** Make sketches of the graphs in B8.

**For discussion**
• How can $ax^2 + bx + c$ be rewritten when $a$ is not 1?
For example,
$2x^2 + 12x - 31 = \ldots (x + \ldots)^2 - \ldots$
$^-x^2 + 4x + 5 = \ldots\ldots\ldots\ldots$

In the second example on the opposite page the graph with equation $y = x^2 + 8x + 15$ crossed the $x$-axis twice. To find the $x$-coordinates at these points we need to solve the equation

$$x^2 + 8x + 15 = 0$$

It can be rewritten (see opposite) as

$$(x + 4)^2 - 1 = 0$$

Add 1 to both sides:

$$(x + 4)^2 = 1$$

Take the square root of both sides:

$$x + 4 = 1 \text{ or } {}^-1$$

**Reminder**
$1 \times 1 = 1$
${}^-1 \times {}^-1 = 1$

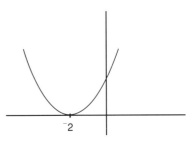

When $x + 4 = 1$ then $x = {}^-3$.
When $x + 4 = {}^-1$ then $x = {}^-5$.

So the equation has two solutions : $x = {}^-3$ and ${}^-5$.
The graph crosses the $x$-axis when $x = {}^-3$ and when $x = {}^-5$.

The first example on the opposite page shows that the graph with equation $y = x^2 + 6x + 11$ does not cross the $x$-axis.
So the equation $x^2 + 6x + 11 = 0$ does not have any solutions.

This can be seen from the algebra also:

$x^2 + 6x + 11$ can be written as $(x + 3)^2 + 2$
So $x^2 + 6x + 11 = 0$ when $(x + 3)^2 + 2 = 0$
This gives $(x + 3)^2 = {}^-2$
and so $x + 3 = \pm\sqrt{{}^-2}$
But $\sqrt{{}^-2}$ cannot be found (at least not in the number system in which we usually work).
There are therefore no solutions of the equation $x^2 + 6x + 11 = 0$.

It can also be seen directly from $(x + 3)^2 + 2 = 0$.
$(x + 3)^2$ cannot be negative. Its least value is 0.
So $(x + 3)^2 + 2$ is greater than or equal to 2 and certainly cannot be 0.

On page 99 $(x + 2)^2$ was written as $x^2 + 4x + 4$.
Solving the equation $x^2 + 4x + 4 = 0$ therefore amounts to finding where the graph with equation $y = (x + 2)^2$ crosses the $x$-axis.
The graph is shown on the right. It does not cross the $x$-axis – it touches it (the $x$-axis is a *tangent* to the graph).
There is only one solution $x = {}^-2$.

This can also be obtained algebraically:

$$(x + 2)^2 = 0 \implies x + 2 = 0 \implies x = {}^-2$$

**For discussion**
- How can equations such as
  $$2x^2 + 12x - 31 = 0$$
  and
  $${}^-x^2 + 4x + 5 = 0$$
  be solved?
- Apply the method to the equations on page 95.

**B10** Use the method above to find the points at which the graphs in B9 **(d) – (f)** cross the $x$-axis.

**B11** Solve these equations (if possible):
(a) $x^2 - 2x - 15 = 0$
(b) $x^2 - 2x - 9 = 0$
(c) $x^2 - 2x + 3 = 0$
(d) $x^2 + 5x + 5.25 = 0$
(e) $x^2 + 6x + 9 = 0$
(f) $x^2 + 6x = 0$

# C : Maximising volume

An open box is to be made from a sheet of card measuring 50 cm by 80 cm by cutting out the shaded pieces, and then folding along the dotted lines.

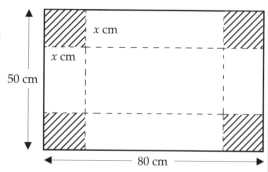

The volume (cm³) of the box is

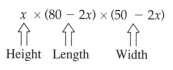

$$x \times (80 - 2x) \times (50 - 2x)$$

Height  Length  Width

*x* has to be less than 25. Why?

Thus when *x* is 5, the volume is $5 \times 70 \times 40$ cm³ which is 14000 cm³.

Here is a computer printout showing the volume for various values of *x* :

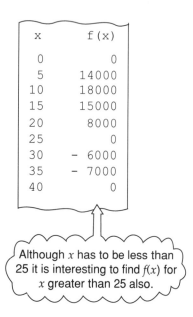

| x | f(x) |
|---|---|
| 0 | 0 |
| 5 | 14000 |
| 10 | 18000 |
| 15 | 15000 |
| 20 | 8000 |
| 25 | 0 |
| 30 | − 6000 |
| 35 | − 7000 |
| 40 | 0 |

Although *x* has to be less than 25 it is interesting to find *f*(*x*) for *x* greater than 25 also.

### For discussion

• The formula for the volume can be re-written like this :

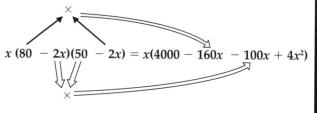

$$x (80 - 2x)(50 - 2x) = x(4000 - 160x - 100x + 4x^2)$$

$$= 4000x - 260x^2 + 4x^3$$

The highest power of *x* is 3.

$4000x - 260x^2 + 4x^3$ is a *cubic* polynomial.

### You could . . .

• Use a computer graph plotter to investigate the graphs of *cubic* polynomials.

---

**C1**　Use the table to draw the graph with equation

$$y = x \times (80 - 2x) \times (50 - 2x)$$

(You might need to calculate the volumes for some other values of *x*.)
What is the maximum volume which can be obtained?

**C2**　Another piece of card measures 50 cm by 50 cm.
A box is to be made as shown above.
Find the volume when corners measuring *x* cm by *x* cm are removed and write it as a cubic polynomial.
What is the maximum volume?

A computer graph plotter could be used to solve this.

**C3**　Repeat for a card measuring 40 cm by 90 cm.

A tin is to be made to contain 250 ml of soup.
It is required to find the dimensions for the
least amount of metal.

Let the height be $h$ cm and the radius $r$ cm.
Then

$$\pi r^2 h = 250 \quad \ldots \ldots (1)$$

> **Reminder**
> Volume of a cylinder = $\pi r^2 h$
> Circumference of a cylinder = $2\pi r$

Imagine the tin unrolled.
The length of the rectangular "side" is equal to
the circumference of the circular top (or bottom)
which is $2\pi r$ cm.

The surface area (in cm²) is

$$\pi r^2 + \pi r^2 + 2\pi rh \quad \ldots \ldots (2)$$

The surface area depends on $r$ and $h$.

From (1)
$$h = \frac{250}{\pi r^2}$$

> Use equation (1) to
> eliminate $h$ so that the
> surface area is a
> function of $r$ only.

Now substitute for $h$ in (2) :
the surface area is
$$\pi r^2 + \pi r^2 + 2\pi r \times \frac{250}{\pi r^2}$$

> Check the algebra
> here.

$$= 2\pi r^2 + \frac{500}{r}$$

Thus when $r$ is 3 the surface area is $2\pi \times 3^2 + \frac{500}{3}$ cm²

which is 223.22 cm² (to 2 d.p.).

The computer printout on the right shows the surface area for
various values of $r$.

| | |
|---|---|
| 1 | 506.28 |
| 2 | 275.13 |
| 3 | 223.22 |
| 4 | 225.53 |
| 5 | 257.08 |
| 6 | 309.53 |
| 7 | 379.30 |
| 8 | 464.62 |
| 9 | 564.49 |
| 10 | 678.32 |

**C4** It looks as if the radius to give the least surface area is between 2 cm and 5 cm.
Do another RUN of the program or use a calculator to find the radius to 1 decimal place.
Find the height corresponding to this radius.

**C5** Draw a graph to show the surface
area as a function of $r$.

**C6** Make a conjecture about the
relationship between the height
and the radius to give the least
surface area. Try another example
with a different volume.

**C7** A cylindrical water butt (no top) is to
be made with a volume of 1000 litres.
Find the dimensions for the least amount
of metal.

**You could . . .**

- In the method above the 'seam' at the
side has been ignored. Make a
reasonable estimate of the width of the
seam. Modify the surface area formula
(2) to include the seam and find the
dimensions to minimise the surface
area.

Improve the model further by allowing
for the rims at the top and bottom of the
tin.

# Now try these . . .

1. Mirrors measuring 40 cm by 30 cm are being wrapped in clear plastic film which is then heat-sealed. 1 cm is needed on the edges shown for heat sealing.
   Which method uses the least amount of film?

   Method 1                          Method 2

   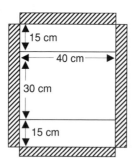   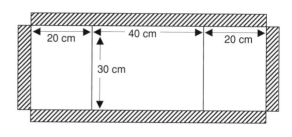

   Suppose now that the mirrors measure $a$ cm by $b$ cm (where $a > b$).
   Show that the area for the first method is
   $$2ab + 2a + 4b + 4 \text{ cm}^2$$
   Find the area for the second method.
   What is the difference in area between the two methods?
   What advice would you give to the machine operator so that the most economical method was used?

2. A water channel is being made by bending a sheet of metal of width 1 metre along the dotted lines to give a rectangular cross-section.

   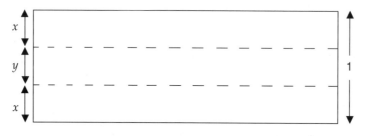

   Dimensions in metres

   Show that the area of the cross-section is $x(1 - 2x)$ m$^2$.
   Find the value of $x$ which gives the maximum flow along the channel.

3. By writing the following equations in the form $y = (x + \ldots)^2 + \ldots$ sketch the graphs:

   (a) $y = x^2 - 6x + 4$     (b) $y = x^2 + 4x - 1$     (c) $y = x^2 + 3x + 1.25$

   (d) $y = x^2 - 8x + 17$     (e) $y = x^2 + 4x$     (f) $y = x^2 + x + 1$

4. Solve (if possible) the equations:

   (a) $x^2 + 10x + 9 = 0$     (b) $x^2 - 4x - 7 = 0$     (c) $x^2 - 8x + 16 = 0$

   (d) $x^2 + x - 4 = 0$     (e) $x^2 + 2x + 4 = 0$     (f) $x^2 - 3x + 3 = 0$

# Further trigonometry

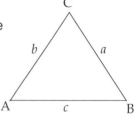

A surveyor has to measure up a triangular plot of
land so that a drawing can be made of it.

He could measure the three sides
*or* he could measure one side and
the two angles at each end of it
*or* he could measure . . . .

Thinking about the measurements in
this way can lead to the question:

*What information (sides and angles) is
needed to specify a triangle exactly?*

You might find the panel on the right
helpful in exploring the question.

• Draw triangles with these specifications:

  ① $c = 5$ cm $\quad b = 4$ cm $\quad a = 2.5$ cm

  ② $c = 5$ cm $\quad A = 40^0$ $\quad b = 6$ cm

  ③ $c = 5$ cm $\quad A = 50^0$ $\quad B = 60^0$

• Show that there are *two* possible triangles
with
  $\quad c = 5$ cm $\quad b = 4$ cm $\quad B = 45^0$

Use a calculator to find

$\sin 42^0 \qquad \sin (180^0 - 42^0)$

$\cos 42^0 \qquad \cos (180^0 - 42^0)$

Try some other similar examples.
Devise a method to find the sine and
cosine of angles between $90^0$ and $180^0$.

What is the area
of this triangle?

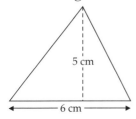

What is the area
of this triangle?

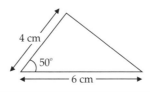

Generalise to obtain a
formula for the area of a
triangle when the
lengths of two sides and
the angle between them
are given.

**Design**

# A : The sine rule

The triangle on the right has been drawn given the length of side *c* and the sizes of the angles A and B.

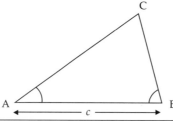

From this information it is possible to *calculate* the lengths of the other two sides.

---

**①** Draw a line from C at right angles to AB as shown. The triangle is now split into two *right-angled* triangles.

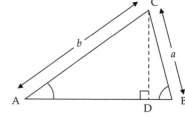

From the left-hand triangle
  CD = *b* sin A

From the right-hand triangle
  CD = *a* sin B

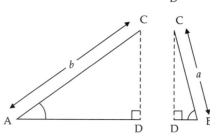

So   *a* sin B = *b* sin A

Dividing both sides of this equation by sin B gives

$$a = \frac{b \sin A}{\sin B}$$

Then dividing both sides by sin A gives

$$\frac{a}{\sin A} = \frac{b}{\sin B}$$

---

**②** Draw a line from B at right angles to AC as shown.

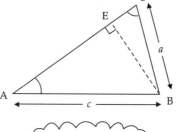

From triangle ABE
BE = *c* sin A

From triangle BCE
BE = *a* sin C

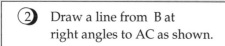

You might find it helpful to rotate the page so that AE is horizontal.

So   *a* sin C = *c* sin A

Dividing both sides of this equation first by sin C then by sin A gives

$$\frac{a}{\sin A} = \frac{c}{\sin C}$$

---

**③** Putting the two results from ① and ② together gives

$$\frac{a}{\sin A} = \frac{b}{\sin B} = \frac{c}{\sin C}$$

This is called the **sine rule.**

Given the length of one side of a triangle and the angles at each end of it, the sine rule can be used to calculate the lengths of the other two sides.

For example, in the triangle on the right $c = 5$ cm, $A = 56^0$ and $B = 42^0$. The lengths of $a$ and $b$ have to be calculated.

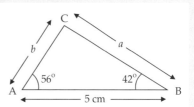

First, find the third angle:
$$C = 180^0 - 56^0 - 42^0$$
$$= 82^0$$

**Reminder**
The three angles of a triangle add up to $180^0$.

Then from the sine rule,
$$\frac{a}{\sin 56^0} = \frac{b}{\sin 42^0} = \frac{5}{\sin 82^0}$$

| | |
|---|---|
| Omitting the central part of the equation gives $$\frac{a}{\sin 56^0} = \frac{5}{\sin 82^0}$$ Multiplying both sides by $\sin 56^0$ gives $$a = \frac{5}{\sin 82^0} \times \sin 56^0$$ $$= 4.19 \text{ (to 2 dp)}$$ | Omitting the first part of the equation gives $$\frac{b}{\sin 42^0} = \frac{5}{\sin 82^0}$$ Multiplying both sides by $\sin 42^0$ gives $$b = \frac{5}{\sin 82^0} \times \sin 42^0$$ $$= 3.38 \text{ (to 2 dp)}$$ |

So the other two sides are of lengths 4.19 cm and 3.38 cm (to 2 dp).

**A1** Calculate the lengths of the sides $a$ and $b$ of the triangle in which
$c = 8$ cm, $A = 62^0$, $B = 53^0$

**A2** Calculate the lengths of the other two sides of the triangles:
(a) $a = 10$ cm, $B = 34^0$, $C = 87^0$
(b) $b = 9.2$ cm, $A = 43^0$, $C = 35^0$

**A3** A surveyor is unable to gain access to one corner of a triangular field. The surveyor measures the length of the side opposite the inaccessible corner, 56 metres, and the angles at each end of it, $47^0$ and $65^0$. Calculate the lengths of the other two sides.

**A4** Calculate the areas of the triangles in A1, A2 and A3.

**A5** The diagram shows the results of a survey of a field. Calculate the area of the field.

**For discussion**
• What happens in the argument on the opposite page when angle B is greater than $90^0$?

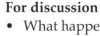

**A6** In a triangle $c = 8$ cm, $A = 35^0$ and $a = 5$ cm.
Draw a line 8 cm long for side AB.
Draw a line through A at $35^0$ to AB, making it about 10 cm long.
With compasses set to a radius of 5 cm draw an arc of a circle centred at B.
Hence show that there are two possible triangles with the given measurements.
Use the sine rule to show that $\sin C = 0.918$ (to 3 dp).
Use the inverse sine on your calculator to find one solution for C.
Deduce a second solution for C. (Hint : $\sin (180^0 - x^0) = \sin x^0$)
Use the sine rule to find the length of $b$ in both cases.

# B : The cosine rule

The triangle on the right has been drawn given the lengths of sides $b$ and $c$ and the size of angle A.

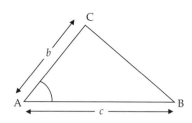

> **For discussion**
> - Show that it is not possible to find the length of the other side using the sine rule.

Another method is needed to find the length of side $a$.

Draw a line CD at right angles to AB as shown.
Let the length of CD be $h$.
Let the length of AD be $d$. Then the length of DB is $c - d$.

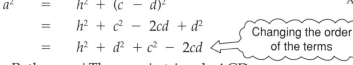

By Pythagoras' Theorem in triangle BCD

$$
\begin{aligned}
a^2 &= h^2 + (c - d)^2 \\
&= h^2 + c^2 - 2cd + d^2 \\
&= h^2 + d^2 + c^2 - 2cd
\end{aligned}
$$

> Changing the order of the terms

But by Pythagoras' Theorem in triangle ACD
$$h^2 + d^2 = b^2$$

So $\quad a^2 = b^2 + c^2 - 2cd$

But from triangle ACD, $d = b \cos A$

So $\quad a^2 = b^2 + c^2 - 2\,c \times b \cos A$

$\qquad = b^2 + c^2 - 2\,bc \cos A$

> This is called the **cosine rule.**

The cosine rule can be used to find $a$ when $b$, $c$ and A are given.
For example, in the triangle on the right
$$b = 6 \text{ cm} \quad c = 7 \text{ cm} \quad A = 50^0$$
So from the cosine rule
$$a^2 = 6^2 + 7^2 - 2 \times 6 \times 7 \times \cos 50^0$$

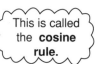

> **For discussion**
> - What happens to the cosine rule when A is $90^0$?

> **B1** Complete the calculation to find $a$.

The cosine rule can also be used to find angle A when the lengths of the three sides of the triangle are known.
For the triangle on the right
$$5^2 = 6^2 + 8^2 - 2 \times 6 \times 8 \times \cos A$$

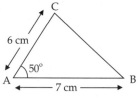

> **B2** Show that cos A $= \frac{75}{96}$ and hence find A.

**B3** $b = 4$ cm     $c = 6$ cm     $A = 68^0$    Calculate $a$.

**B4** $a = 3$ cm     $b = 4$ cm     $c = 6$ cm   Calculate A.

**B5** $b = 7$ cm     $c = 6$ cm     $A = 115^0$   Calculate $a$.

**B6** $a = 9$ cm     $b = 6$ cm     $c = 5$ cm   Calculate A.

**B7** Two people start walking from the same place at the same time on level ground.
One person walks at 4 km per hour going North and the other walks at 3 km per hour going North-East. After 3 hours, how far apart will they be?

There are two other versions of the cosine rule which follow from the one on the opposite page by noting the pattern:

$$b^2 = a^2 + c^2 - 2ac \cos B$$

$$c^2 = a^2 + b^2 - 2ab \cos C$$

**For discussion**
• What happens in the argument on the opposite page when A is greater than $90^0$?

**B8**   $a = 11$ cm     $c = 12$ cm     $B = 49^0$    Calculate $b$.

**B9**   $a = 10$ cm     $b = 13$ cm     $c = 15$ cm   Calculate B.

**B10**   $a = 5$ cm     $b = 8$ cm     $C = 32^0$    Calculate $c$.

**B11**   $a = 21$ cm     $b = 20$ cm     $c = 15$ cm   Calculate C.

When the three sides of a triangle are known, the cosine rule can be used to find one of the angles. It is then normally easier to use the sine rule to find a second angle rather than use another version of the cosine rule.

**B12** In B4 use the sine rule to calculate angle B.

**B13** $a = 8$ cm     $b = 9$ cm     $c = 10$ cm
Calculate the three angles of the triangle.

**B14** Use the cosine rule when $a = 5$ cm, $b = 7$ cm, $c = 12$ cm to find A.
Make a sketch to explain your result.

**B15** Use the cosine rule to try to find A when
$a = 12$ cm     $b = 5$ cm     $c = 6$ cm
Make a sketch to explain your result.

**You could ...**
• Given any three measurements of a triangle (except three angles), describe a systematic method to find the other three measurements (where possible).
You could express your method as a computer program.

# Now try these . . .

1.  Calculate the lengths of sides $a$ and $b$ of the triangle ABC in which
    $c = 7$ cm,  A $= 49^0$,  B $= 73^0$.
    Calculate the area of the triangle.

2.  Calculate the lengths of the other two sides of the triangles:
    (a)  $a = 9.2$ cm  B $= 35^0$  C $= 68^0$
    (b)  $b = 12$ cm  A $= 117^0$  B $= 24^0$

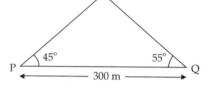

3.  Two boats at P and Q are racing to reach
    the buoy at R.
    How far does each boat have to go?

4.  Show that there are two possible triangles such that
    $a = 8$ cm  B $= 42^0$  $b = 6$ cm
    Calculate the other angles and side in each case.

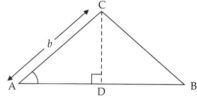

5.  How can CD be found from $b$ and A?
    Deduce a formula for the area of the
    triangle in terms of $b$, $c$ and A.

6.  (a)  A regular hexagon is inscribed in a circle
        of radius 10 cm.
        What is the angle between the 'spokes'?
        What is the area of the triangle OAB?
        Deduce the area of the hexagon.
    (b)  Repeat for a regular octagon inscribed
        in a circle of radius 10 cm.

7.  $b = 2$ cm  $c = 3$ cm  A $= 60^0$  Calculate $a$.

8.  $a = 6$ cm  $b = 7$ cm  $c = 9$ cm  Calculate A.

9.  $a = 4$ cm  $b = 2$ cm  C $= 41^0$  Calculate $c$.

10. $a = 4.8$ cm  $b = 7.1$ cm  $c = 5.5$ cm  Calculate the largest angle.

11. Two planes leave simultaneously from the same airport. One flies East at a speed
    of 150 mph, the other on a course of $250^0$ at 170 mph. Calculate how far apart the
    two planes are 2 hours after leaving the airport.

12. By applying Pythagoras' Theorem to the triangles ABE and ACE obtain the
    cosine formula in the form

    $$c^2 = a^2 + b^2 - 2ab \cos C$$

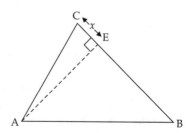

# Transforming by numbers

Apply the mapping
$(x, y) \mapsto (y, x)$
to the shaded flag.
What geometrical
transformation
has taken place?

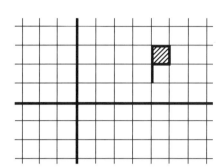

Write the mappings for each
of these transformations in
the form $(x,y) \mapsto (\ldots, \ldots)$

Reflection in the $y$-axis

Reflection in the $x$-axis

Rotation about (0,0) through $180^0$

Rotation about (0,0) through
$90^0$ anti-clockwise

Rotation about (0,0) through
$90^0$ clockwise

Reflection in the line $y = {}^-x$

Enlargement centre the origin
with a scale factor of 3

What are the **inverses** of these
transformations?

Find the area of the
parallelogram.

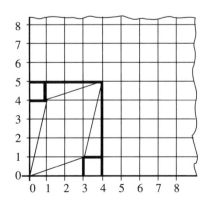

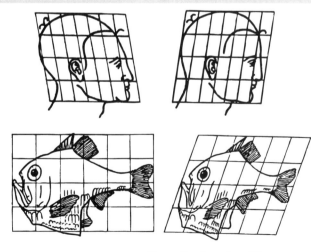

From *On Growth and Form*
by D'Arcy Thompson

# A : Mappings and matrices

The mappings on the previous page were all of the form

$$(x, y) \mapsto (ax + by, cx + dy)$$

where *either* $a$ or $b$ *or* $c$ or $d$ was 0.

For example,

$(x, y) \mapsto (y, x)$ can be written as $(x, y) \mapsto (0x + 1y, 1x + 0y)$
$(x, y) \mapsto (^-x, y)$ can be written as $(x, y) \mapsto (^-1x + 0y, 0x + 1y)$

---

**A1**    Write these mappings in the form $(x, y) \mapsto (ax + by, cx + dy)$:
(a)   $(x, y) \mapsto (x, ^-y)$
(b)   $(x, y) \mapsto (y, ^-x)$
(c)   $(x, y) \mapsto (^-y, ^-x)$

---

It is more interesting to choose some numbers for $a$, $b$, $c$ and $d$ which are not 0s or 1s.
Consider for example, $(x, y) \mapsto (4x + 3y, 2x + 6y)$.
Apply it to the vertices of the shaded square on the right:
$(1, 0) \mapsto (4, 2)$   and   $(0, 1) \mapsto (3, 6)$.

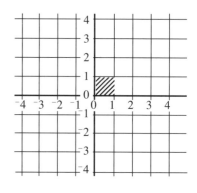

---

**A2**    What points do (0, 0) and (1,1) map to?

**A3**    On half-centimetre squared paper draw $x$- and $y$-axes from $^-8$ to 16, and mark the points which the four corners of the shaded square map to. Join them up. It is important to take care to draw the lines accurately through the points. Check that you get a parallelogram.

**A4**    Apply the same mapping to the vertices of each of the squares labelled A, B and C on the lower diagram. On your diagram for A3 draw the resulting parallelograms (take care to be accurate) labelling them A', B', and C'. Then do it for squares D, E, F, G and H.
You should find that the grid of squares is transformed into a grid of parallelograms.

---

The shaded square with vertices at (0, 0), (1, 0), (0, 1), (1, 1) is called the **unit square**.

---

**A5**    Apply these mappings to the grid of nine squares as above. Start with the unit square. Label the parallelograms A', B', etc. (For (a) you will need an $x$-axis from $^-8$ to 14 and a $y$-axis from $^-6$ to 12.)
(a)   $(x, y) \mapsto (5x + 2y, x + 4y)$
(b)   $(x, y) \mapsto (2x + y, ^-x + 3y)$
(c)   $(x, y) \mapsto (3x - 2y, x + 4y)$

**A6**    Show that the mapping $(x, y) \mapsto (2x + y, 6x + 3y)$ 'squashes' the unit square onto a straight line. What does it do to the other squares?

**A7**    Write the mapping $(x, y) \mapsto (x, y)$ in the form $(x, y) \mapsto (ax + by, cx + dy)$.
What does this mapping do to the grid of squares?

**For discussion**
• Can you be sure that all the points on the line from (0, 0) to (1, 0) map to points on the line from (0, 0) to (4, 2)?

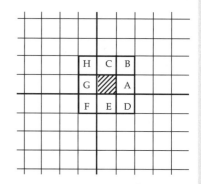

**For discussion**
• When the *image* of the unit square is known the *image* of the whole grid of squares can be drawn rapidly.

It is usual to write a mapping such as $(x, y) \mapsto (4x + 3y, 2x + 6y)$
in a slightly different form:

$$\begin{bmatrix} x \\ y \end{bmatrix} \mapsto \begin{bmatrix} 4 & 3 \\ 2 & 6 \end{bmatrix} \begin{bmatrix} x \\ y \end{bmatrix}$$

This encourages the idea that the numbers 4, 3, 2 and 6 are the important things in the mapping.

$\begin{bmatrix} 4 & 3 \\ 2 & 6 \end{bmatrix}$ is called a **matrix**. 4, 3, 2 and 6 are the **elements** of the matrix.

Notice that the new $x$-coordinate $4x + 3y$ is obtained by
'running along' the first row of the matrix and 'diving down' $\begin{bmatrix} x \\ y \end{bmatrix}$,
multiplying corresponding numbers and adding as you go.
Similarly the new $y$-coordinate $2x + 6y$ is obtained by running
along the second row of the matrix and diving down.

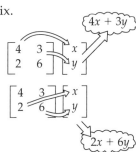

For example, $\begin{bmatrix} 4 & 3 \\ 2 & 6 \end{bmatrix} \begin{bmatrix} 5 \\ 1 \end{bmatrix}$ is $\begin{bmatrix} 23 \\ 16 \end{bmatrix}$ $\leftarrow 4 \times 5 + 3 \times 1$ $\leftarrow 2 \times 5 + 6 \times 1$

---

**A8** Work out

(a) $\begin{bmatrix} 4 & 3 \\ 2 & 6 \end{bmatrix} \begin{bmatrix} 1 \\ 5 \end{bmatrix}$ (b) $\begin{bmatrix} 4 & 3 \\ 2 & 6 \end{bmatrix} \begin{bmatrix} 5 \\ -1 \end{bmatrix}$ (c) $\begin{bmatrix} 4 & 3 \\ 2 & 6 \end{bmatrix} \begin{bmatrix} 1 \\ -5 \end{bmatrix}$

(d) $\begin{bmatrix} 4 & 3 \\ 2 & 6 \end{bmatrix} \begin{bmatrix} -5 \\ 1 \end{bmatrix}$ (e) $\begin{bmatrix} 4 & 3 \\ 2 & 6 \end{bmatrix} \begin{bmatrix} -7 \\ -1 \end{bmatrix}$

**A9** Write the mappings in A5 in matrix form: $\begin{bmatrix} x \\ y \end{bmatrix} \mapsto \begin{bmatrix} \bullet & \bullet \\ \bullet & \bullet \end{bmatrix} \begin{bmatrix} x \\ y \end{bmatrix}$

---

To find the matrix for $(x, y) \mapsto (y, x)$, first write the mapping as $(x, y) \mapsto (0x + 1y, 1x + 0y)$.

Then the matrix is $\begin{bmatrix} 0 & 1 \\ 1 & 0 \end{bmatrix}$

---

**A10** Write the mappings in A1 in matrix form.
**A11** What is the matrix for the 'stay-put' mapping in A7?

---

**For discussion**

$\begin{bmatrix} 4 & 3 \\ 2 & 6 \end{bmatrix} \begin{bmatrix} 1 \\ 0 \end{bmatrix} = \begin{bmatrix} 4 \\ 2 \end{bmatrix}$ ← Where do the numbers 4 and 2 occur in the matrix?

$\begin{bmatrix} 4 & 3 \\ 2 & 6 \end{bmatrix} \begin{bmatrix} 0 \\ 1 \end{bmatrix} = \begin{bmatrix} 3 \\ 6 \end{bmatrix}$ ← Where do the numbers 3 and 6 occur in the matrix?

For any given matrix how can you tell immediately where $\begin{bmatrix} 1 \\ 0 \end{bmatrix}$ and $\begin{bmatrix} 0 \\ 1 \end{bmatrix}$ map to?

How can you find rapidly where $\begin{bmatrix} 1 \\ 1 \end{bmatrix}$ maps to?

What matrix maps $\begin{bmatrix} 1 \\ 0 \end{bmatrix}$ to $\begin{bmatrix} 2 \\ 3 \end{bmatrix}$ and $\begin{bmatrix} 0 \\ 1 \end{bmatrix}$ to $\begin{bmatrix} 1 \\ 4 \end{bmatrix}$?

Invent some more.

# B : Combining mappings

*How can the result of combining two mappings be found using matrices?*

The plural of **matrix** is **matrices**.

Suppose we start with the mapping $(x, y) \mapsto (4x + 3y, 2x + 6y)$.
Think of it as changing the coordinates $(x, y)$ to new coordinates
$(X, Y)$ where $X = 4x + 3y$ and $Y = 2x + 6y$.
So the first mapping is $(x, y) \mapsto (X, Y)$.

Secondly, do the mapping $(X, Y) \mapsto (7X + 5Y, 8X + 10Y)$
Since $X = 4x + 3y$ and $Y = 2x + 6y$, the final coordinates can be written in terms of
$x$ and $y$:

$$7X + 5Y \quad = \quad 7 \times (4x + 3y) \quad + \quad 5 \times (2x + 6y)$$
$$= \quad (7 \times 4 + 5 \times 2)x \quad + \quad (7 \times 3 + 5 \times 6)y$$

$$8X + 10Y \quad = \quad 8 \times (4x + 3y) \quad + \quad 10 \times (2x + 6y)$$
$$= \quad (8 \times 4 + 10 \times 2)x \quad + \quad (8 \times 3 + 10 \times 6)y$$

So the single mapping equivalent to the two is

$$(x, y) \mapsto ((7 \times 4 + 5 \times 2)x + (7 \times 3 + 5 \times 6)y \,, (8 \times 4 + 10 \times 2)x + (8 \times 3 + 10 \times 6)y) \quad \ldots\ldots *$$

This is $(x, y) \mapsto (38x + 51y, 52x + 84y)$, although in order to see the pattern it is better to leave it as in .

Now consider the process in matrix form:

The first mapping is $\quad \begin{bmatrix} x \\ y \end{bmatrix} \mapsto \begin{bmatrix} X \\ Y \end{bmatrix} \quad$ where $\begin{bmatrix} X \\ Y \end{bmatrix} = \begin{bmatrix} 4 & 3 \\ 2 & 6 \end{bmatrix} \begin{bmatrix} x \\ y \end{bmatrix}$

The second mapping is $\quad \begin{bmatrix} X \\ Y \end{bmatrix} \mapsto \begin{bmatrix} 7 & 5 \\ 8 & 10 \end{bmatrix} \begin{bmatrix} X \\ Y \end{bmatrix}$

Call this matrix **A**

So the combined mapping is

Call this matrix **B**

$$\begin{bmatrix} x \\ y \end{bmatrix} \mapsto \begin{bmatrix} X \\ Y \end{bmatrix} \mapsto \begin{bmatrix} 7 & 5 \\ 8 & 10 \end{bmatrix} \begin{bmatrix} X \\ Y \end{bmatrix}$$

Substituting for $\begin{bmatrix} X \\ Y \end{bmatrix}$ gives

$$\begin{bmatrix} x \\ y \end{bmatrix} \mapsto \begin{bmatrix} 7 & 5 \\ 8 & 10 \end{bmatrix} \begin{bmatrix} 4 & 3 \\ 2 & 6 \end{bmatrix} \begin{bmatrix} x \\ y \end{bmatrix}$$

This is BA $\begin{bmatrix} x \\ y \end{bmatrix}$.

Note that A is the matrix for the mapping which is done first and B for the one which is done second. Notice the order in which they are written.

But from * the single mapping equivalent to the two can be written as

$$\begin{bmatrix} x \\ y \end{bmatrix} \mapsto \begin{bmatrix} 7 \times 4 + 5 \times 2 & 7 \times 3 + 5 \times 6 \\ 8 \times 4 + 10 \times 2 & 8 \times 3 + 10 \times 6 \end{bmatrix} \begin{bmatrix} x \\ y \end{bmatrix}$$

The question is :

> *How can these numbers be obtained from the elements*
> *of the two matrices A and B?*

- Look at the top left element : $7 \times 4 + 5 \times 2$
  Note where the numbers come from:
  7 and 5 are in matrix B
  4 and 2 are in matrix A

$$\overset{B}{\begin{bmatrix} 7 & 5 \\ \bullet & \bullet \end{bmatrix}} \overset{A}{\begin{bmatrix} 4 & \bullet \\ 2 & \bullet \end{bmatrix}}$$

So the element in the *first* row and the *first* column is obtained by going along the *first* row of matrix B and down the *first* column of matrix A, multiplying corresponding elements and adding them.

- Look at the top right element : $7 \times 3 + 5 \times 6$
  7 and 5 are in matrix B
  3 and 6 are in matrix A

$$\overset{B}{\begin{bmatrix} 7 & 5 \\ \bullet & \bullet \end{bmatrix}} \overset{A}{\begin{bmatrix} \bullet & 3 \\ \bullet & 6 \end{bmatrix}}$$

So the element in the *first* row and *second* column is obtained by going along the *first* row of matrix B and down the *second* column of matrix A, multiplying corresponding elements and adding them.

---

**For discussion**
- How is the element in the second row and the first column at the top of the page obtained from the elements in A and B?
- How is the element in the second row and the second column obtained from the elements in A and B?

---

You have now seen how to find the combination of the two mappings using matrices.
This method of combination of two matrices is called **matrix multiplication**.
You have found the **product** of the two matrices.

---

**B1** Find the products of these matrices:

(a) $\begin{bmatrix} 2 & 9 \\ 3 & 4 \end{bmatrix} \begin{bmatrix} 5 & 1 \\ 6 & 7 \end{bmatrix}$   (b) $\begin{bmatrix} 5 & 1 \\ 6 & 7 \end{bmatrix} \begin{bmatrix} 2 & 9 \\ 3 & 4 \end{bmatrix}$

(c) $\begin{bmatrix} 2 & -3 \\ 4 & 7 \end{bmatrix} \begin{bmatrix} 6 & 1 \\ -2 & 4 \end{bmatrix}$   (d) $\begin{bmatrix} -1 & 3 \\ -2 & 4 \end{bmatrix} \begin{bmatrix} 5 & 1 \\ 6 & 7 \end{bmatrix}$

(e) $\begin{bmatrix} 4 & 1 \\ 3 & 2 \end{bmatrix} \begin{bmatrix} 5 & -1 \\ -3 & 7 \end{bmatrix}$   (f) $\begin{bmatrix} 5 & -1 \\ -3 & 7 \end{bmatrix} \begin{bmatrix} 4 & 1 \\ 3 & 2 \end{bmatrix}$

**B2** (a) Write down the matrices for these mappings:
  (i) $(x, y) \mapsto (3x + 2y, 4x + 7y)$
  (ii) $(x, y) \mapsto (x + 5y, 8x + y)$

(b) Use the matrices to find the single mapping equivalent to doing first (i) then (ii).

(c) Find also the single mapping equivalent to doing first (ii) then (i).

> Make sure you get them the
> correct way round.
> See the panel at the bottom
> of the opposite page.

---

**For discussion**
- When multiplying two numbers *a* and *b*, *ab* gives the same result as *ba*. (For example, $3 \times 4$ is the same as $4 \times 3$.)
  Is it true that AB and BA give the same result when A and B are matrices?

# C : Area

You have seen that a matrix of the form $\begin{bmatrix} a & b \\ c & d \end{bmatrix}$ transforms the grid of squares to a grid of parallelograms (or, exceptionally, to a straight line).
*How can the area of each parallelogram be determined from the elements of the matrix?*

> **Note**
> Squares and rectangles are special cases of parallelograms.

**C1** Draw a diagram showing what happens to the unit square when transformed by the matrix $\begin{bmatrix} 4 & 0 \\ 0 & 6 \end{bmatrix}$.
What is the new area?
How can it be obtained from the elements of the matrix?

**C2** Repeat C1 for the matrix $\begin{bmatrix} 0 & 3 \\ 2 & 0 \end{bmatrix}$.

The diagram shows what happens to the unit square when it is transformed by the matrix $\begin{bmatrix} 4 & 3 \\ 2 & 6 \end{bmatrix}$.

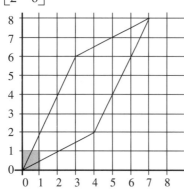

To find the area of the resulting parallelogram enclose it in a rectangle and split up the rectangle as shown into triangles and rectangles.

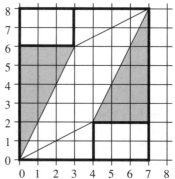

**C3** (a) What is the area of the enclosing rectangle?
(b) The two shaded triangles go together to make a rectangle. What is its area?
(c) The two unshaded triangles go together to make a rectangle. What is its area?
(d) What are the combined areas of the two rectangles at the top left and bottom right?
(e) Deduce from (a), (b), (c), (d) that the area of the parallelogram is 18 squares.
   How is the number 18 related to the areas you found in C1 and C2?
   How can 18 be obtained from the numbers in the matrix $\begin{bmatrix} 4 & 3 \\ 2 & 6 \end{bmatrix}$ using each number once and only once?

**For discussion**
• Make a conjecture about the area of the parallelograms obtained by transforming the squares using the matrix $\begin{bmatrix} a & b \\ c & d \end{bmatrix}$.

**C4** Write down the area of each of the parallelograms obtained by transforming the squares using these matrices:

(a) $\begin{bmatrix} 7 & 5 \\ 8 & 10 \end{bmatrix}$  (b) $\begin{bmatrix} 16 & 3 \\ 2 & 1 \end{bmatrix}$

(c) $\begin{bmatrix} 4 & {}^-2 \\ 5 & 3 \end{bmatrix}$  (d) $\begin{bmatrix} 6 & {}^-1 \\ {}^-4 & 2 \end{bmatrix}$

**C5** What is the area of the transformed squares for these matrices? Explain your results geometrically.

(a) $\begin{bmatrix} 1 & 0 \\ 0 & 1 \end{bmatrix}$  (b) $\begin{bmatrix} 0 & 1 \\ {}^-1 & 0 \end{bmatrix}$

(c) $\begin{bmatrix} 1 & 0 \\ 0 & {}^-1 \end{bmatrix}$  (d) $\begin{bmatrix} 6 & 2 \\ 3 & 1 \end{bmatrix}$

# D : Inverses

A natural question to ask is

*Having transformed the squares into parallelograms, how can they be transformed back? In other words, what is the matrix for the inverse transformation?*

Suppose we start with the transformation defined by the matrix $\begin{bmatrix} 4 & 3 \\ 2 & 6 \end{bmatrix}$.

Then we need to find a matrix so that $\begin{bmatrix} a & b \\ c & d \end{bmatrix}\begin{bmatrix} 4 & 3 \\ 2 & 6 \end{bmatrix}$ reduces to $\begin{bmatrix} 1 & 0 \\ 0 & 1 \end{bmatrix}$. ⟵ The 'stay-put' matrix

Here is a way to find a suitable matrix:

- Get the 0 in the top right first: $a \times 3 + b \times 6 = 0$
  This could be arranged by making the two products 'cancel'
  by putting 3 and 6 in the equation in reverse order and making
  one of them, 3 say, negative : $6 \times 3 + {}^{-}3 \times 6 = 0$
  So $a$ could be 6 and $b$ could be $^{-}3$: $\begin{bmatrix} 6 & ^{-}3 \\ c & d \end{bmatrix}\begin{bmatrix} 4 & 3 \\ 2 & 6 \end{bmatrix}$

- Next get the 0 in the bottom left corner: $c \times 4 + d \times 2 = 0$
  This could be arranged by putting 4 and 2 in the equation but in the
  reverse order and making one of them, 2 say, negative : $^{-}2 \times 4 + 4 \times 2 = 0$

  So $c$ could be $^{-}2$ and $d$ could be 4: $\begin{bmatrix} a & b \\ ^{-}2 & 4 \end{bmatrix}\begin{bmatrix} 4 & 3 \\ 2 & 6 \end{bmatrix}$.

We now have $\begin{bmatrix} 6 & ^{-}3 \\ ^{-}2 & 4 \end{bmatrix}\begin{bmatrix} 4 & 3 \\ 2 & 6 \end{bmatrix}$.

*Check that this gives* $\begin{bmatrix} 18 & 0 \\ 0 & 18 \end{bmatrix}$. ⟵ 18? Seen this number before?

But we want $\begin{bmatrix} 1 & 0 \\ 0 & 1 \end{bmatrix}$.

So divide each of the four numbers by 18:

Then $\begin{bmatrix} \frac{6}{18} & \frac{^{-}3}{18} \\ \frac{^{-}2}{18} & \frac{4}{18} \end{bmatrix}\begin{bmatrix} 4 & 3 \\ 2 & 6 \end{bmatrix} = \begin{bmatrix} 1 & 0 \\ 0 & 1 \end{bmatrix}$.

*Check also that* $\begin{bmatrix} 4 & 3 \\ 2 & 6 \end{bmatrix}\begin{bmatrix} \frac{6}{18} & \frac{^{-}3}{18} \\ \frac{^{-}2}{18} & \frac{4}{18} \end{bmatrix} = \begin{bmatrix} 1 & 0 \\ 0 & 1 \end{bmatrix}$.

---

**D1** **Apply the matrix** $\begin{bmatrix} \frac{6}{18} & \frac{^{-}3}{18} \\ \frac{^{-}2}{18} & \frac{4}{18} \end{bmatrix}$ **to the parallelogram on the previous page and**

**verify that it is transformed back to the unit square.**

On the previous page we have shown that the **inverse matrix** of $\begin{bmatrix} 4 & 3 \\ 2 & 6 \end{bmatrix}$ is $\begin{bmatrix} \frac{6}{18} & \frac{-3}{18} \\ \frac{-2}{18} & \frac{4}{18} \end{bmatrix}$.

The inverse of a matrix A is usually symbolised by $A^{-1}$.
It has the property that

$$A^{-1}A = AA^{-1} = I \ \dots\dots\dots *$$

where I is the 'stay-put' matrix $\begin{bmatrix} 1 & 0 \\ 0 & 1 \end{bmatrix}$, called the **identity** matrix.

The method on page 117 suggests that when A is $\begin{bmatrix} a & b \\ c & d \end{bmatrix}$ then $A^{-1}$ is $\begin{bmatrix} \frac{d}{ad-bc} & \frac{-b}{ad-bc} \\ \frac{-c}{ad-bc} & \frac{a}{ad-bc} \end{bmatrix}$.

Note that $A^{-1}$ is obtained from A by the following procedure:

① Interchange the elements in the diagonal from top left to bottom right.

② Multiply the other two elements by $^-1$.

③ Divide each element by $ad - bc$.

---

**D2** Apply the procedure to the following matrices. Check by calculating the matrix products that they satisfy $*$.

(a) $\begin{bmatrix} 7 & 5 \\ 8 & 10 \end{bmatrix}$   (b) $\begin{bmatrix} 3 & ^-1 \\ 2 & 4 \end{bmatrix}$   (c) $\begin{bmatrix} 8 & ^-2 \\ ^-3 & 1 \end{bmatrix}$   (d) $\begin{bmatrix} 3 & 1 \\ 5 & 2 \end{bmatrix}$

---

According to the method above the inverse of $\begin{bmatrix} 0 & 1 \\ 1 & 0 \end{bmatrix}$ is $\begin{bmatrix} \frac{0}{-1} & \frac{-1}{-1} \\ \frac{-1}{-1} & \frac{0}{-1} \end{bmatrix}$ which is $\begin{bmatrix} 0 & 1 \\ 1 & 0 \end{bmatrix}$.

So $\begin{bmatrix} 0 & 1 \\ 1 & 0 \end{bmatrix}$ is its own inverse. It is said to be **self-inverse.**

This can be interpreted geometrically:

$\begin{bmatrix} 0 & 1 \\ 1 & 0 \end{bmatrix}$ is the matrix for reflection in the line $y = x$.

The inverse of this transformation is a reflection in $y = x$!

So the inverse of $\begin{bmatrix} 0 & 1 \\ 1 & 0 \end{bmatrix}$ is $\begin{bmatrix} 0 & 1 \\ 1 & 0 \end{bmatrix}$.

---

**D3** (a) Write down the inverses of these matrices:

(i) $\begin{bmatrix} 1 & 0 \\ 0 & ^-1 \end{bmatrix}$   (ii) $\begin{bmatrix} ^-1 & 0 \\ 0 & 1 \end{bmatrix}$   (iii) $\begin{bmatrix} 0 & 1 \\ ^-1 & 0 \end{bmatrix}$   (iv) $\begin{bmatrix} ^-1 & 0 \\ 0 & ^-1 \end{bmatrix}$

(b) By considering the transformations defined by the matrices in (a) verify that the inverse matrices are correct.

**D4** (a) The matrix $\begin{bmatrix} 4 & 3 \\ 2 & 6 \end{bmatrix}$ maps $\begin{bmatrix} 2 \\ 1 \end{bmatrix}$ to $\begin{bmatrix} 11 \\ 10 \end{bmatrix}$.

Verify that the inverse matrix maps $\begin{bmatrix} 11 \\ 10 \end{bmatrix}$ back to $\begin{bmatrix} 2 \\ 1 \end{bmatrix}$.

(b) By applying the inverse matrix find the point which is mapped by $\begin{bmatrix} 4 & 3 \\ 2 & 6 \end{bmatrix}$ to $\begin{bmatrix} 8 \\ 4 \end{bmatrix}$.

(c) Find $\begin{bmatrix} x \\ y \end{bmatrix}$ such that $\begin{bmatrix} 4 & 3 \\ 2 & 6 \end{bmatrix}\begin{bmatrix} x \\ y \end{bmatrix} = \begin{bmatrix} 12 \\ 6 \end{bmatrix}$.

(d) By writing the equations $4x + 3y = 15$ in matrix form as in (c) find $x$ and $y$.
$\qquad\qquad\qquad\qquad\quad 2x + 6y = 12$

# E : Further transformations

**E1** Draw diagrams to show the result of transforming the unit square by each of these matrices:

(a) $\begin{bmatrix} 2 & 0 \\ 0 & 1 \end{bmatrix}$    (b) $\begin{bmatrix} 3 & 0 \\ 0 & 1 \end{bmatrix}$    (c) $\begin{bmatrix} {}^-2 & 0 \\ 0 & 1 \end{bmatrix}$    *The transformations defined by these matrices are called one-way stretches.*

**E2** Repeat E1 for these matrices:

(a) $\begin{bmatrix} 1 & 2 \\ 0 & 1 \end{bmatrix}$    (b) $\begin{bmatrix} 1 & 3 \\ 0 & 1 \end{bmatrix}$    (c) $\begin{bmatrix} 1 & {}^-2 \\ 0 & 1 \end{bmatrix}$

(d) $\begin{bmatrix} 1 & 0 \\ 2 & 1 \end{bmatrix}$    (e) $\begin{bmatrix} 1 & 0 \\ 3 & 1 \end{bmatrix}$    (f) $\begin{bmatrix} 1 & 0 \\ {}^-2 & 1 \end{bmatrix}$

*The transformations defined by these matrices are called shears.*

**For discussion**

- Describe the effects of the transformations defined by the matrices

$$\begin{bmatrix} k & 0 \\ 0 & 1 \end{bmatrix} \quad \begin{bmatrix} 1 & k \\ 0 & 1 \end{bmatrix} \text{ and } \begin{bmatrix} 1 & 0 \\ k & 1 \end{bmatrix}$$

- It can be shown that the matrix for any transformation in which the unit square is mapped to a parallelogram (and the origin stays fixed) can be written as a product of matrices of the form

$$\begin{bmatrix} k & 0 \\ 0 & 1 \end{bmatrix} \quad \begin{bmatrix} 0 & 1 \\ 1 & 0 \end{bmatrix} \text{ and } \begin{bmatrix} 1 & 0 \\ 1 & 1 \end{bmatrix}$$

For example,

$$\begin{bmatrix} 4 & 3 \\ 2 & 6 \end{bmatrix} = \begin{bmatrix} 2 & 0 \\ 0 & 1 \end{bmatrix}\begin{bmatrix} 1 & 0 \\ 1 & 1 \end{bmatrix}\begin{bmatrix} 0 & 1 \\ 1 & 0 \end{bmatrix}\begin{bmatrix} 3 & 0 \\ 0 & 1 \end{bmatrix}\begin{bmatrix} 1 & 0 \\ 1 & 1 \end{bmatrix}\begin{bmatrix} 1.5 & 0 \\ 0 & 1 \end{bmatrix}\begin{bmatrix} 0 & 1 \\ 1 & 0 \end{bmatrix}\begin{bmatrix} 2 & 0 \\ 0 & 1 \end{bmatrix}$$

*How can a product like this be worked out?*

Describe the transformations for each matrix in this product. Draw a sequence of diagrams showing what happens to the unit square at each stage.

All mappings of the form $\begin{bmatrix} x \\ y \end{bmatrix} \mapsto \begin{bmatrix} a & b \\ c & d \end{bmatrix}\begin{bmatrix} x \\ y \end{bmatrix}$

transform the origin to itself: $\begin{bmatrix} 0 \\ 0 \end{bmatrix} \mapsto \begin{bmatrix} a & b \\ c & d \end{bmatrix}\begin{bmatrix} 0 \\ 0 \end{bmatrix} = \begin{bmatrix} 0 \\ 0 \end{bmatrix}$

So the bottom left corner of the unit square always stays fixed.

For example, the mapping $\begin{bmatrix} x \\ y \end{bmatrix} \mapsto \begin{bmatrix} 2 & 1 \\ 1 & 3 \end{bmatrix}\begin{bmatrix} x \\ y \end{bmatrix}$ transforms

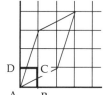

the unit square to the parallelogram shown. The point labelled A stays fixed.

To map ABCD onto A'B'C'D' a translation is also required. The parallelogram in the first diagram has been translated by 1 to the right and 2 up.

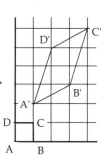

The mapping can be written $\begin{bmatrix} x \\ y \end{bmatrix} \mapsto \begin{bmatrix} 2 & 1 \\ 1 & 3 \end{bmatrix}\begin{bmatrix} x \\ y \end{bmatrix} + \begin{bmatrix} 1 \\ 2 \end{bmatrix}$

**E3** Show the effects of these mappings on the unit square ABCD:

(a) $\begin{bmatrix} x \\ y \end{bmatrix} \mapsto \begin{bmatrix} 1 & 0 \\ 1 & 1 \end{bmatrix}\begin{bmatrix} x \\ y \end{bmatrix} + \begin{bmatrix} 2 \\ 4 \end{bmatrix}$    (b) $\begin{bmatrix} x \\ y \end{bmatrix} \mapsto \begin{bmatrix} 3 & 1 \\ 1 & 2 \end{bmatrix}\begin{bmatrix} x \\ y \end{bmatrix} + \begin{bmatrix} {}^-2 \\ 1 \end{bmatrix}$

(c) $\begin{bmatrix} x \\ y \end{bmatrix} \mapsto \begin{bmatrix} {}^-1 & 0 \\ 0 & 1 \end{bmatrix}\begin{bmatrix} x \\ y \end{bmatrix} + \begin{bmatrix} 3 \\ {}^-2 \end{bmatrix}$    (d) $\begin{bmatrix} x \\ y \end{bmatrix} \mapsto \begin{bmatrix} 4 & 3 \\ 2 & 6 \end{bmatrix}\begin{bmatrix} x \\ y \end{bmatrix} + \begin{bmatrix} {}^-2 \\ {}^-4 \end{bmatrix}$

# Now try these . . .

1. (a) Show the effect of the mapping $(x, y) \mapsto (3x, 3y)$ on the unit square.
   Describe the transformation which has taken place.
   Write down the matrix for this mapping.

   (b) Write down the mapping corresponding to the matrix $\begin{bmatrix} 4 & 0 \\ 0 & 2 \end{bmatrix}$.
   Show its effect on the unit square.
   (It is called a *two-way stretch*.)

2. (a) Find the effect of each of these matrices on the unit square ABCD, labelling the
   vertices A'B'C'D'. State the geometrical transformation which has taken place in each
   case.
   (i) $P = \begin{bmatrix} 0 & 1 \\ 1 & 0 \end{bmatrix}$   (ii) $Q = \begin{bmatrix} 0 & ^-1 \\ ^-1 & 0 \end{bmatrix}$   (iii) $R = \begin{bmatrix} ^-1 & 0 \\ 0 & 1 \end{bmatrix}$

   (iv) $S = \begin{bmatrix} 0 & ^-1 \\ 1 & 0 \end{bmatrix}$   (v) $T = \begin{bmatrix} ^-1 & 0 \\ 0 & ^-1 \end{bmatrix}$

   (b) Find these matrix products and interpret the results geometrically:
   (i) PQ   (ii) QP   (iii) RS   (iv) SR

3. (a) Transform the unit square using the matrix $\begin{bmatrix} 2 & 1 \\ 1 & 3 \end{bmatrix}$.
   Without any further matrix calculations
   draw some members of the grid of parallelograms
   onto which the grid of squares is transformed.

   (b) What is the area of each parallelogram?

   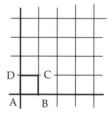

   (c) (i)   Write down the matrix which would transform the grid of
           parallelograms back to the grid of squares.
       (ii)  What point is mapped to (8,9) by the matrix $\begin{bmatrix} 2 & 1 \\ 1 & 3 \end{bmatrix}$?

       (iii) Find $\begin{bmatrix} x \\ y \end{bmatrix}$ such that $\begin{bmatrix} 2 & 1 \\ 1 & 3 \end{bmatrix}\begin{bmatrix} x \\ y \end{bmatrix} = \begin{bmatrix} 11 \\ 3 \end{bmatrix}$.

       (iv)  Use the method of (iii) to find $x$ and $y$ such that $2x + y = 7$
                                                                   $x + 3y = 1$

4. Write down two matrices (with no zeros in them) which do not change areas.

5. Find these matrix products

   (i) $\begin{bmatrix} d & ^-b \\ ^-c & a \end{bmatrix}\begin{bmatrix} a & b \\ c & d \end{bmatrix}$   (ii) $\begin{bmatrix} a & b \\ c & d \end{bmatrix}\begin{bmatrix} d & ^-b \\ ^-c & a \end{bmatrix}$

   Deduce that the inverse of $\begin{bmatrix} a & b \\ c & d \end{bmatrix}$ is $\begin{bmatrix} \dfrac{d}{ad-bc} & \dfrac{^-b}{ad-bc} \\ \dfrac{^-c}{ad-bc} & \dfrac{a}{ad-bc} \end{bmatrix}$   This proves the conjecture made about $A^{-1}$ at the top of page 118.

# Relationships

## Some experiments

Drop a 'bouncy' ball from various heights and measure the height of the first bounce.

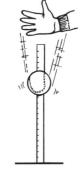

| Initial height $h$ cm | |
|---|---|
| Height of first bounce $b$ cm | |

How does $b$ depend on $h$?

Hang various masses on a spring and measure the extension.

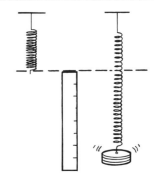

| Mass $m$ grams | |
|---|---|
| Extension $e$ cm | |

How does $e$ depend on $m$?

Find the lengths of pendulums which make complete swings ('there and back') in 1 second, 1.5 seconds, 2 seconds, etc.

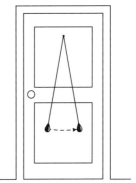

| Time $t$ seconds | |
|---|---|
| Length of pendulum $l$ metres | |

How does $l$ depend on $t$?

Roll a ball down a gentle slope (a long piece of plastic gutter or angle iron). How does the distance it travels depend on the time?

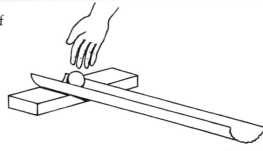

# A : Linear relationships

A car travels at a steady speed of 50 mph along a motorway.

The table shows the distances it would go in 1 hour, 2 hours, etc.

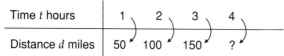

The distance can be found from the time by multiplying by 50 (look at the arrows in the table).
In symbols
$$d = 50t$$

A graph can be drawn to show the relationship:

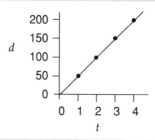

The points are on a straight line. The gradient of the line is 50.

The relationship between $t$ and $d$ in said to be *linear* (because the graph is a straight *line*).

It also useful to look *across* the table.

When the time is multiplied by 2, the distance is also multiplied by 2.

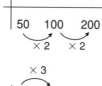

When the time is multiplied by 3, the distance is also multiplied by 3.

And so on.

The distance, $d$ miles, is said to be *directly proportional* to the time $t$ hours.

This is written $d \propto t$.

The symbol $\propto$ stands for *directly proportional to.*

*What is the distance travelled at time 2.4 hours?*

**Method 1**

Take $t$ as 2.4 in the equation $d = 50t$
Then $d = 50 \times 2.4$

**Method 2**

Multiply the time by 2.4
So multiply the distance by 2.4

|   | $\times 2.4$ | |
|---|---|---|
| $t$ | 1 | 2.4 |
| $d$ | 50 | ? |

**or**

Multiply the time by 1.2
So multiply the distance by 1.2

|   | $\times 1.2$ | |
|---|---|---|
| $t$ | 2 | 2.4 |
| $d$ | 100 | ? |

*Check that both methods give the same result.*

**A1** The mass of a cubic centimetre of iron is 8 grams.

| Volume $v$ cm³ | 1 | 2 | 3 | 4 |
|---|---|---|---|---|
| Mass $m$ g | 8 | 16 | 24 | ? |

    (a) **Copy and complete the table.**
         **Write down the relationship between $v$ and $m$: $m = \dots$**

    (b) **Draw a graph to show the relationship. Check that the points are on a straight line. What is the gradient of the line?**

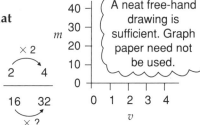

A neat free-hand drawing is sufficient. Graph paper need not be used.

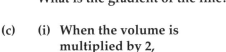

    (c)   (i) **When the volume is multiplied by 2, what happens to the mass?**

       (ii) **When the volume is multiplied by 3, what happens to the mass?**

    (d) **Copy and complete the sentence and then write it in symbols:**
         *The mass is directly . . . . . to the volume.*

**A2** A spring stretches by 0.5 cm for every 100 g of load (assuming the load is not too much for the spring!).

| Load $l$ g | 100 | 200 | 300 | 400 |
|---|---|---|---|---|
| Extension $e$ cm | 0.5 | 1.0 | 1.5 | ? |

    (a) **Copy and complete the table.**
         **Write down the equation relating $l$ and $e$ : $e = \dots$**

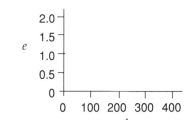

    (b) **Draw a graph (as in A1) to show the relationship. Check that the points are on a straight line. What is the gradient of the line?**

    (c)   (i) **When the load is multiplied by 2, what happens to the extension?**
       (ii) **When the load is multiplied by 3, what happens to the extension?**

    (d) **Copy and complete the sentence and then write it in symbols:**
         *The extension is . . . . . . . . to the load.*

**A3** For another spring (like the one in A2) a load of 10 g produces an extension of 0.2 cm.

    (a) **Find the extension for a load of 70 g by using the multiplier method.**

    (b) **The equation relating $l$ and $e$ is of the form**
$$e = \boxed{k} \times l$$
       **Find $k$ knowing that when $l$ is 10, $e$ is 0.2. Deduce $e$ when $l$ is 70.**

**A4** When an object is dropped its speed $v$ metres per second is directly proportional to the time $t$ seconds since it was released. At time 1.2 seconds its speed was 11.76 ms⁻¹.

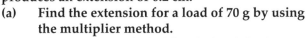

    (a) **Find the speed at time 3 seconds by using the multiplier method.**
    (b) **The relationship between $t$ and $v$ is of the form $v = \boxed{k} \times t$ Find $k$ and deduce $v$ when $t$ is 3.**

# B : Squaring relationships

The table shows the surface areas of cubes with various lengths of sides.

| Length $l$ cm | 1 | 2 | 3 | 4 |
|---|---|---|---|---|
| Surface area $s$ cm² | 6 | 24 | 54 | 96 |

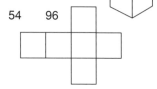

The relationship between $l$ and $s$ is $s = 6l^2$.
The surface area is proportional to the square of the side length.
In symbols $s \propto l^2$.

A graph can be drawn to show the relationship:

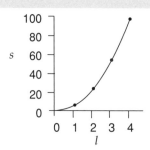

The points are not on a straight line.

It also useful to look *across* the table.

When the length is multiplied by 2, the surface area is multiplied by 4.

2 squared

When the length is multiplied by 3, the surface area is multiplied by 9.

3 squared

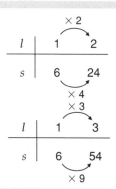

Another table can be drawn to show how the surface area depends on (Length)².

| (Length)² | 1 | 4 | 9 | 16 |
|---|---|---|---|---|
| Surface area | 6 | 24 | 54 | 96 |

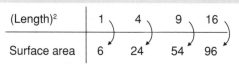

The $\times 6$ pattern down the table can now be seen.

The relationship in the table can be shown graphically.

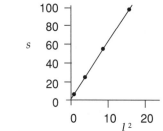

The graph is a straight line.

The gradient is 6.

$$s = 6\,l^2$$

---

*What is the surface area for a side length of 3.6 cm?*

**Method 1**
Take $l$ as 3.6 in the equation
$s = 6l^2$
Then $s = 6 \times 3.6^2$

**Method 2**
Multiply the length by 3.6
So multiply the area by $3.6^2$

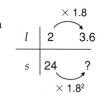

**or**

Multiply the length by 1.8
So multiply the area by $1.8^2$

*Check that both methods give the same result.*

**B1** A small ball is dropped out of a window of a tall building.
The distances it has fallen at various times are given in the table:

| Time $t$ seconds | 1 | 2 | 3 | 4 | . . . |
|---|---|---|---|---|---|
| Distance $d$ metres | 5 | 20 | 45 | 80 | . . . |

The intention is to obtain a relationship between $t$ and $d$.

(a) Draw a graph. A neat free-hand graph is sufficient.
Check that the points are not on a straight line.

(b) (i) What happens to $d$ when $t$ is multiplied by 2?

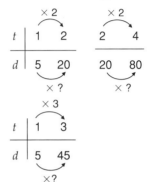

(ii) What happens to $d$ when $t$ is multiplied by 3?

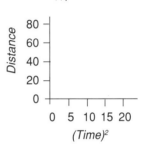

(c) What does (b) suggest about the relationship
between $t$ and $d$?

(d) Make another table
as on the right
and plot a graph.
Check that the points
are on a straight line.
What is its gradient?
What is the equation
relating $t$ and $d$?

| (Time)² | 1 | 4 | . . . . . . |
|---|---|---|---|
| Distance | 5 | 20 | 45 80 |

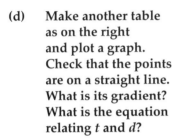

---

**B2** A small ball is thrown upwards with various initial speeds.
The height it goes to is recorded:

| Speed $v$ ms⁻¹ | 8 | 18 | 22 | 27 |
|---|---|---|---|---|
| Height $h$ m | 3.2 | 16.2 | 24.2 | 36.45 |

(a) Draw a graph. Check that the points are
not on a straight line.

(b) Find the multipliers on the right.
How can the multipliers for $h$ be obtained
from the multipliers for $v$?

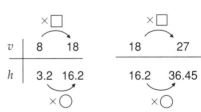

(c) What does (b) suggest about the relationship
between $v$ and $h$?

(d) Copy and complete the table (using
(c) to determine the number
represented by the question mark)
and plot a graph. Check that the
points are on a straight line.
What is its gradient?
What is the equation relating $v$ and $h$?

| (Speed)ˀ | | | | |
|---|---|---|---|---|
| Height | 3.2 | 16.2 | 24.2 | 36.45 |

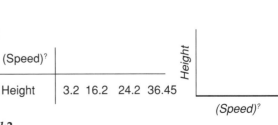

# C : Square-root relationships

The table shows the approximate times of swing of pendulums of various lengths:

| Length $l$ cm | 0.5 | 1.0 | 1.5 | 2.0 |
|---|---|---|---|---|
| Time $t$ seconds | 1.4 | 2.0 | 2.4 | 2.8 |

A graph can be drawn

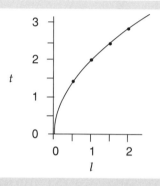

The points are not on a straight line.

When the length is multiplied by 2, the time is multiplied by 1.4 (to 1 d.p.).

When the length is multiplied by 3, the time is multiplied by 1.7 (to 1 d.p.).

This suggests that
$$\text{time} \propto \sqrt{\text{length}}$$

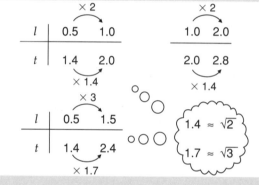

Draw up a table to show $\sqrt{l}$ and $t$:

| $\sqrt{l}$ | 0.7 | 1.0 | 1.2 | 1.4 |
|---|---|---|---|---|
| $t$ | 1.4 | 2.0 | 2.4 | 2.8 |

A $\times 2$ pattern can now be seen down the table.

The relationship can be shown graphically:

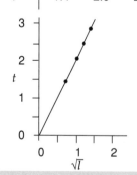

The graph is a straight line.

The gradient is 2.

$$t = 2\sqrt{l}$$

*What is the time of swing for a pendulum of length 1.8 m?*

**Method 1**
Take $l$ as 1.8 in the equation
$t = 2\sqrt{l}$
Then $t = 2\sqrt{1.8}$

**Method 2**
Multiply the length by 3.6
So multiply the time by $\sqrt{3.6}$

| $l$ | 0.5 | 1.8 |
|---|---|---|
| $t$ | 1.4 | ? |

×3.6 (top), ×$\sqrt{3.6}$ (bottom)

**or**

Multiply the length by 1.8
So multiply the time by $\sqrt{1.8}$

| $l$ | 1.0 | 1.8 |
|---|---|---|
| $t$ | 2.0 | ? |

×1.8 (top), ×$\sqrt{1.8}$ (bottom)

*Check that both methods give the same result.*

**C1** The table shows the approximate distances which can be seen from various heights when standing on the sea shore:

| Height $h$ metres | 1 | 2 | 3 |
|---|---|---|---|
| Distance $d$ km | 2.50 | 3.54 | 4.33 |

(a) Draw a graph to show the relationship.
Check that the points are not on a straight line.

(b) (i) What is the multiplier for $d$ when $h$ is multiplied by 2?
(ii) What is the multiplier for $d$ when $h$ is multiplied by 3?

(c) What does (b) suggest about the relationship between $h$ and $d$?

(d) Make another table and plot a graph.
Check that the points are on a straight line (approximately).
What is its gradient?
What is the equation relating $\sqrt{h}$ and $d$?

| $\sqrt{h}$ | |
|---|---|
| $d$ | |

(e) An alternative method to find the relationship is to write your statement in (c) as an equation: $d = k\sqrt{h}$.
Now use a pair of corresponding values of $h$ and $d$ from the table at the top of the page to find $k$.

(f) Find $d$ when $h$ is 3.6 using (i) the multiplier method (ii) the equation you found in (d) and (e).

---

**C2** The table shows the frequencies of the notes obtained from a stretched string under various tensions.

| Tension $T$ Newtons | 16 | 36 | 49 |
|---|---|---|---|
| Frequency $f$ Hertz | 200 | 300 | 350 |

(a) Find the multipliers for the tension and the corresponding multipliers for the frequency.

| $T$ | 16 | 36 |
|---|---|---|
| $f$ | 200 | 300 |

| | 16 | 49 |
|---|---|---|
| | 200 | 350 |

(b) What does this suggest about the relationship between $T$ and $f$?
(c) Find an equation connecting $T$ and $f$.
(d) What is $f$ when $T$ is 60?

# D : Cubing relationships

The table shows the masses of cubical blocks of iron with various side lengths.

| Length $l$ cm | 1 | 2 | 3 | 4 |
|---|---|---|---|---|
| Mass $m$ g | 7 | 56 | 189 | 448 |

A graph can be drawn.

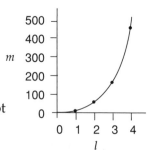

The points are not on a straight line.

Look for a relationship across the table.
When the length is multiplied by 2, the mass is multiplied by 8.

When the length is multiplied by 3, the mass is multiplied by 27.

This suggests that
$$\text{mass} \propto (\text{length})^3$$

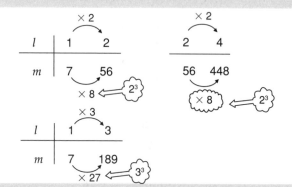

Draw up a table to show $l^3$ and $m$.

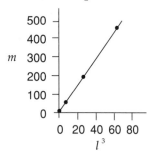

A $\times 7$ pattern can now be seen down the table.

The relationship can be shown graphically:

The graph is a straight line.

The gradient is 7.

$$m = 7\,l^3$$

*What is the mass for a side length of 3.6 cm?*

**Method 1**
Take $l$ as 3.6
in the equation
$m = 7\,l^3$
Then $m = 7 \times 3.6^3$

**Method 2**
Multiply $l$
by 3.6
So multiply
$m$ by $3.6^3$

**or**

Multiply $l$
by 1.8
So multiply
$m$ by $1.8^3$

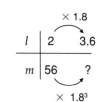

*Check that both methods give the same result.*

**D1** The table shows the volumes of spheres with various radii:

| Radius $r$ cm | 1.6 | 3.5 | 4.7 |
|---|---|---|---|
| Volume $v$ cm³ | 17.16 | 179.6 | 434.9 |

(a) (i) What are the multipliers for $r$ ?
    (ii) What are the multipliers for $v$ ?

| $r$ | 1.6 | 3.5 | 3.5 | 4.7 |
|---|---|---|---|---|
| $v$ | 17.16 | 179.6 | 179.6 | 434.9 |

(b) Check that the multipliers for $v$ are approximately the cubes of the multipliers for $r$.

(c) What does this suggest about the relationship between $r$ and $v$?

(d) What would you need to plot across the page to obtain a straight-line graph?

(e) Draw up a table which will give a straight-line graph.

(f) Find the equation relating $r$ and $v$.

**D2** The table shows the approximate masses of copper spheres of diameters 2.5 cm and 3.0 cm:

| Diameter $d$ cm | 2.5 | 3.0 |
|---|---|---|
| Mass $m$ g | 72.03 | 124.4 |

(a) Show that the table suggests that $m \propto d^3$.

(b) Find the mass of a copper sphere of diameter 4.0 cm.

(c) Find the relationship in the form $m = kd^3$.

**D3** Experiments were carried out on a small ship to measure the shaft horse-power needed to drive it at different speeds through the water. The results are shown in the table.

| Speed $s$ knots | 0 | 2 | 4 | 6 | 8 |
|---|---|---|---|---|---|
| Power $p$ h.p. | 0 | 12 | 90 | 300 | 700 |

(a) Draw a graph to show the results.

(b) What relationship between speed and power does the table suggest? (Note that the table is based on experimental results which are liable to small errors.)
Find the relationship in the form $p = ks^?$

# E : Inverse relationships

The table shows some possible lengths and widths of rectangles all with areas of 72 cm².

| Length $l$ cm | 1 | 2 | 3 | 4 | 5 |
|---|---|---|---|---|---|
| Width $w$ cm | 72 | 36 | 24 | 18 | 14.4 |

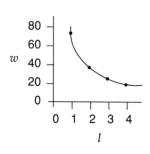

Area
72 cm²

A graph can be drawn.
The points are not on a straight line.
Note the shape of the graph: as $l$ increases, $w$ decreases.

In this case the relationship between $l$ and $w$ is obvious.

Since $l \times w = 72$ it follows that $w = \frac{72}{l}$.

So the width is proportional to $\frac{1}{l}$ .

The width is said to be *inversely proportional* to the length.

It is of interest to look at the multipliers:

When $l$ is multiplied by 2,
$w$ is multiplied by $\frac{1}{2}$ .

When $l$ is multiplied by 3,
$w$ is multiplied by $\frac{1}{3}$.

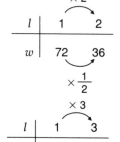

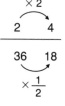

A table can be made to show $\frac{1}{l}$ and $w$.

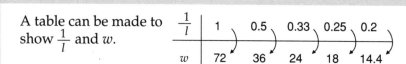

A $\times 72$ pattern can now be seen down the table.

The relationship can be shown graphically:

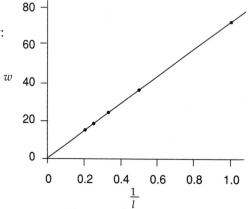

The graph is a straight line.

The gradient is 72.

$$w = 72 \times \frac{1}{l}$$

$$= \frac{72}{l}$$

E1    The table shows the time to travel a certain distance at various constant speeds.

| Speed $v$ ms⁻¹ | 10 | 20 | 25 | 30 |
|---|---|---|---|---|
| Time $t$ s | 6 | 3 | 2.4 | 2 |

(a)    Draw a graph.
Check that the points are not
on a straight line.

(b)    (i)  What happens to $t$ when
$v$ is multiplied by 2?

| $v$ | 10 | 20 |
|---|---|---|
| $t$ | 6 | 3 |

(ii)  What happens to $t$ when
$v$ is multiplied by 3?

| $v$ | 10 | 30 |
|---|---|---|
| $t$ | 6 | 2 |

(c)    What does (b) suggest about
the relationship between $v$ and $t$?

(d)    Make another table and plot a graph.
Check that the points are on a straight line.
What is its gradient?
What is the equation relating $\frac{1}{v}$ and $t$?

| $\frac{1}{v}$ | 0.1 | 0.05 | 0.04 | 0.03 |
|---|---|---|---|---|
| $t$ | 6 | 3 | 2.4 | 2 |

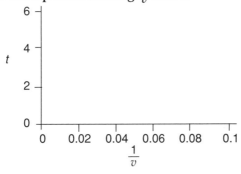

(e)    An alternative method to find the relationship is
to write your statement in (c) as an equation: $t = k \times \frac{1}{v}$ .
Now use a pair of corresponding values of $v$ and $t$
from the table at the top of the page to find $k$.

(f)    Find $t$ when $v$ is 28 using (i) the multiplier method,
(ii) the equation you found in (d) and (e).

E2    The table shows the volume of air in the tube for various pressures when the
temperature is kept constant:

| Pressure $p$ atmospheres | 1.2 | 1.6 | 2.1 |
|---|---|---|---|
| Volume $v$ cm³ | 30 | 22.5 | 17.1 |

(a)    Show that the table suggests that $v \propto \frac{1}{p}$ .

(b)    Find the volume when $p$ is 3.

(c)    Find the equation relating $p$ and $v$.

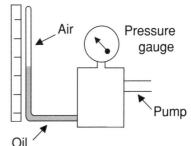

# Now try these . . .

1.  The current through the resistor was recorded
    when various cells were connected:

    | Voltage of cells $V$ volts | 1.5 | 3 | 4.5 | 6 |
    |---|---|---|---|---|
    | Current $I$ amperes | 0.3 | 0.6 | 0.9 | 1.2 |

    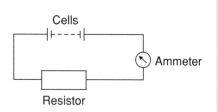

    Explain why the data suggests that $I$ is directly
    proportional to $V$. Find $I$ when $V$ is 9.

2.  The wind resistance to a cyclist is proportional to the square of the cyclist's speed.
    What is the effect on the wind resistance of doubling the speed?
    What change in speed would double the resistance?

3.  The table shows the approximate
    surface areas of spheres of various
    diameters.

    | Diameter $d$ cm | 1.6 | 3.0 | 2.4 |
    |---|---|---|---|
    | Surface area $s$ cm² | 8.04 | 28.27 | 18.10 |

    Show that the table suggests that $s \propto d^2$.
    Find the relationship in the form $s = kd^2$.

4.  The table shows the speed of a ball
    after rolling various distances down
    a slope.

    | Distance $d$ m | 2 | 2.5 | 6 |
    |---|---|---|---|
    | Speed $v$ ms⁻¹ | 11.31 | 12.65 | 19.60 |

    Find a relationship between the speed
    and the distance.

5.  The table shows the wavelengths of
    sound waves of various frequencies.
    How does the wavelength depend
    on the frequency?
    Find the missing entries.

    | Frequency $f$ (cycles per second) | 300 | 200 | 450 | 600 | ? |
    |---|---|---|---|---|---|
    | Wavelength $w$ (metres) | 1.10 | 1.65 | 0.74 | ? | 0.41 |

6.  The energy of a flywheel is proportional to the fourth power of the diameter.
    What is the effect on the energy of doubling the diameter?
    What is the effect on the energy of multiplying the diameter by 1.2?
    What must the diameter be multiplied by in order to double the energy?

7.  The force of gravity $F$ Newtons at a distance $d$ kilometres from the earth's centre is
    proportional to $\frac{1}{d^2}$ (inversely proportional to the square of the distance).

    Which of these graphs could illustrate the relationship?

    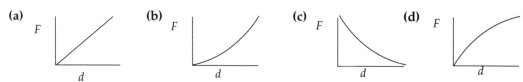

    By what is the force multiplied when $d$ is doubled?
    The radius of the earth is about 6400 km. At what distance from the centre of the earth
    would the force be half of that at the surface?

# Electric circuits

## An experiment
You will need a circuit board and the associated equipment.
Record the current and the voltage when
1.5 volt cells are connected.

| Number of cells | Current | Voltage |
|---|---|---|
| 0 | | |
| 1 | | |
| 2 | | |
| 3 | | |

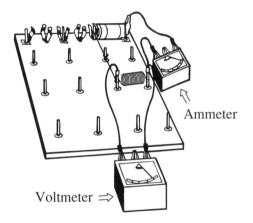

Ammeter

Voltmeter ⇒

Plot a graph :

Voltage

Current

### For discussion
• Is there a relationship between the voltage and the current?

## The cost of electricity

| TARIFF | METER READING | | UNITS | V.A.T. RATE | £ |
|---|---|---|---|---|---|
| | PRESENT | PREVIOUS | | % | |
| DOMESTIC | 9132 | 8301 | 831 | | |
| 831 @ 5.32 | | | | 0 | 44.21 |
| QUARTERLY CHARGE | | | | 0 | 8.10 |
| | | | ACCOUNT TOTAL | | 52.31 |

• What is a unit?

• Find the cost of 1 unit of electricity at the present time.

• What does it cost
    – to have a 100 watt light on all day?
    – to heat a kettle of water?
    – to iron a skirt or a shirt?

• Where does all the electricity get used in your home?
Suggest some economies.

# A : Voltage and current

You will be familiar with the idea that when an electric cell is connected to certain materials, such as a tungsten wire, the current which flows depends on the voltage of the cell.

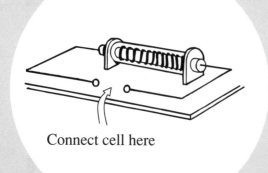

Connect cell here

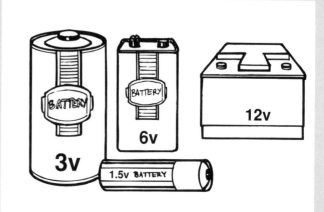

The 3 volt cell gives twice the current produced by the 1.5 volt cell, the 6 volt cell gives 4 times the current. And so on.

Thus the current in the wire is proportional to the **potential difference** caused by the cell.

This relationship between the current, $I$ amperes, and the potential difference, $V$ volts, was first noticed by a German schoolteacher, Georg Ohm, in 1826. It is called **Ohm's Law**.

Since doubling $V$ causes $I$ to double, and quadrupling $V$ causes $I$ to quadruple, etc., $\frac{V}{I}$ is always the same.

The value of $\frac{V}{I}$ is called the **resistance** of the piece of wire.

Materials, such as tungsten wire, which resist current are called **resistors**. Their resistance is measured in **ohms**.

Thus the resistance of the wire, $R$ ohms, is defined by

$$R = \frac{V}{I} \quad \dots \dots (1)$$

**Did you know?**

- The volt is named after Alessandro **Volta**, an Italian, who made the first battery in about 1800.

- The unit of current, the ampere, is named after André **Ampere**, a French physicist, who studied the magnetic effect of electric currents in about 1820.

Ohm found that for certain materials under certain conditions $\frac{V}{I}$ is constant, that is to say the resistance is constant. (There are materials and conditions for which $\frac{V}{I}$ is not constant – see Section E.)

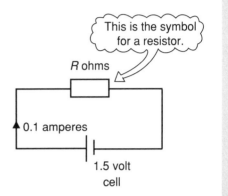

This is the symbol for a resistor.

In the circuit on the right a 1.5 volt cell produces a current of 0.1 amperes.

So $\quad R = \dfrac{1.5}{0.1} = 15.$

The resistance of the resistor is 15 ohms.

**A1** A 6 volt cell produces a current of 0.6 amperes in a circuit like the one above.
What is the resistance of the resistor?

**A2** An electric fire takes a current of 4 amperes.
The mains voltage is 240 volts.
What is the resistance of the fire?

**A3** A mains circuit (240 volts) has a 13 ampere fuse.
Find $R$ such that when the resistance in the circuit is greater than $R$ ohms the fuse will not blow.

**Note**
In the examples on this page the resistance of the battery and of the connecting wire has been ignored. It is usually small.

**To find $V$ given $I$ and $R$**

What potential difference would produce a current of 0.1 amperes in a 60 ohm resistor?

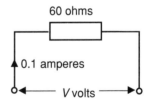

$R = \dfrac{V}{I} \quad$ gives $\quad 60 = \dfrac{V}{0.1}$

Multiply both sides by 0.1 :

$\qquad 0.1 \times 60 = V$

and so $\qquad V = 6$

A 6 volt cell would produce a current of 0.1 amperes in the circuit.

## To find *I* given *V* and *R*

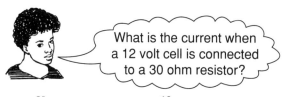

What is the current when a 12 volt cell is connected to a 30 ohm resistor?

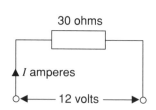

30 ohms

*I* amperes

12 volts

$$R = \frac{V}{I} \quad \text{gives} \quad 30 = \frac{12}{I}$$

Multiply both sides by *I* :

$$I \times 30 = 12$$

Divide both sides by 30 :

$$I = \frac{12}{30} = 0.4$$

With practice these two steps can be done in one – and mentally!

Thus the current is **0.4 amperes**.

---

**A4**    Find the potential difference which would cause a current of 0.2 amperes to flow through a 50 ohm resistor.

**A5**    Find the current which would flow through a 60 ohm resistor when a potential difference of 15 volts is applied.

---

**Find out**

- You might have seen resistors in TV sets looking like this :

What information is given by the coloured bands?

---

Instead of solving an equation each time it is convenient to rewrite the formula to make *V* or *I* the subject :

$$\boxed{R = \frac{V}{I}}$$

Multiply both sides by *I* :

$$I \times R = V$$

Thus    $$\boxed{V = IR} \quad \dots (2)$$

Divide both sides by *R* :

$$\frac{V}{R} = I$$

Thus    $$\boxed{I = \frac{V}{R}} \quad \dots (3)$$

Don't commit the three versions to memory.
All you need is one of them, and then rearrange it mentally.

For example,

$$V = IR$$

$$\frac{V}{\underset{I}{}} = R \qquad \frac{V}{\underset{R}{}} = I$$

---

**A6**    Find *V* when *I* is 2.1 and *R* is 40.
**A7**    Find *I* when *V* is 240 and *R* is 1000.

# B : Power in electrical circuits

When certain materials have electric currents passed through them they become hot. This heating effect is put to good use in hair driers, electric fires, immersion heaters, etc.

The rate at which heat is produced is called the **power**. It is the product of the current $I$ amperes and the potential difference, $V$ volts. Thus the power $P$ **watts** is given by

$$P = IV \ldots (i)$$

For example, in the circuit below the power developed in the resistor is $0.1 \times 6$ watts which is 0.6 watts.

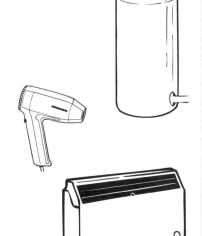

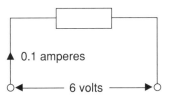

0.1 amperes

6 volts

**Find out**
• Power stations generate electricity at 25 000 volts. Why is it transformed to a higher voltage before being sent out over the National Grid?

**B1** What is the power consumed in the resistor when the current is 1.2 amperes and the potential difference is 12 volts?

**B2** Rewrite the relationship (i) to make $I$ the subject.

**B3** Rewrite (i) to make $V$ the subject.

**B4** Find $I$ when $P$ is 100 and $V$ is 240.

**B5** Find $V$ when $P$ is 50 and $I$ is 1.6.

**B6** What current does a 1 kW fire use when plugged into the mains?

The formula $P = IV$ can be rewritten
by substituting for $V$ from relationship (2)
on page 136 :
$$V = IR \text{ .................... (ii)}$$
This gives :
$$P = I \times IR$$
$$= I^2R \text{ ................ (iii)}$$
Thus the power is proportional to the
**square** of the current.
This means, for example, that doubling
the current increases the power by a
factor of 4.

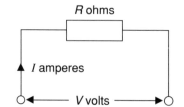

**B7**    Find the power when a current of 1.5 amperes passes through a
resistance of 200 ohms.

**B8**    Find the resistance when $P$ is 500 and $I$ is 4.

**B9**    Find the current when $P$ is 720 and $R$ is 20.

**B10**    Which of these graphs shows correctly the relationship between
$I$ and $P$ when $R$ is constant?

(a)

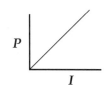

(b)

(c)

**B11**    Rewrite (iii) to make :

(a)    $R$  the subject,
(b)    $I^2$  the subject,
(c)    $I$  the subject.

# C : Combining resistors

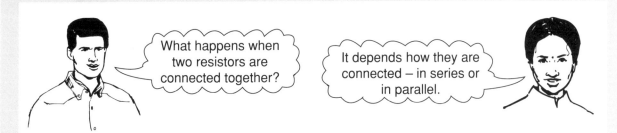

- When two resistors with resistances $R_1$ and $R_2$ ohms are connected in **series** they are equivalent to a single resistor with resistance $R_1 + R_2$ ohms.

  For example, a 15 ohm resistor and a 25 ohm resistor connected in series are equivalent to a 40 ohm resistor.

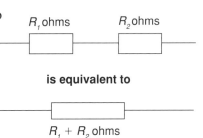

$R_1$ ohms     $R_2$ ohms

**is equivalent to**

$R_1 + R_2$ ohms

- When two resistors with resistances $R_1$ and $R_2$ ohms are connected in **parallel** they are equivalent to a single resistor with resistance $R$ ohms where

$$R = \frac{R_1 R_2}{R_1 + R_2}$$

For example, a 15 ohm resistor and a 25 ohm resistor are equivalent to a resistor with resistance

$$\frac{15 \times 25}{15 + 25} \text{ ohms}$$

which is 9.375 ohms.

Is it surprising that the equivalent resistance is less than the two single resistances?

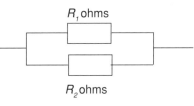

$R_1$ ohms

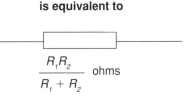

$R_2$ ohms

**is equivalent to**

$$\frac{R_1 R_2}{R_1 + R_2} \text{ ohms}$$

---

**C1** Find the single resistor equivalent to a 100 ohm resistor and a 300 ohm resistor connected **(a)** in series, **(b)** in parallel.

**C2** Find the combined resistance of a television set (500 ohms) and an iron (100 ohms) when connected in parallel.

**C3** What sizes of resistor can be made from three 10 ohm resistors?

**C4** Show that two 7 ohm resistors in parallel are equivalent to a 3.5 ohm resistor. Make a conjecture about the equivalent resistor when two equal resistors are in parallel. Can you show that your conjecture is always true?

## How the formula for resistors in parallel arises

Suppose a current $I$ amperes flows through the circuit and splits into $I_1$ amperes and $I_2$ amperes.

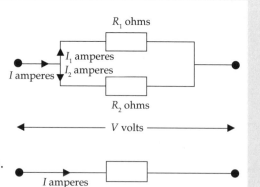

Then $\quad I = I_1 + I_2$

where $\quad I_1 = \dfrac{V}{R_1}\quad$ and $\quad I_2 = \dfrac{V}{R_2}$

Let the equivalent resistor have resistance $R$ ohms.

Then $\quad I = \dfrac{V}{R}$

So $\quad \dfrac{V}{R} = \dfrac{V}{R_1} + \dfrac{V}{R_2}$

Dividing through by $V$ gives

$$\frac{1}{R} = \frac{1}{R_1} + \frac{1}{R_2} \quad \cdots\cdots\cdots *$$

The right-hand side can be rewritten as

$$\frac{R_2}{R_1 R_2} + \frac{R_1}{R_1 R_2}$$

and then as

$$\frac{R_2 + R_1}{R_1 R_2}$$

which is the same as

$$\frac{R_1 + R_2}{R_1 R_2}$$

Hence

$$\frac{1}{R} = \frac{R_1 + R_2}{R_1 R_2}$$

and so $\quad R = \dfrac{R_1 R_2}{R_1 + R_2}$

---

To help with the algebra use a simple numerical example :

Take $R_1$ as 3 and $R_2$ as 4.

$\dfrac{1}{3} + \dfrac{1}{4}\quad$ can be rewritten as :

$$\frac{4}{3 \times 4} + \frac{3}{3 \times 4}$$

which is

$$\frac{4 + 3}{3 \times 4} \quad \text{or} \quad \frac{3 + 4}{3 \times 4}$$

So

$$\frac{1}{R} = \frac{3 + 4}{3 \times 4}$$

Hence

$$R = \frac{3 \times 4}{3 + 4} = \frac{12}{7}$$

---

**C5** Use the pattern of formula $*$ above to make a conjecture about the resistance of the single resistor equivalent to three resistors in parallel with resistances $R_1$, $R_2$, $R_3$ ohms.

Can you prove your conjecture?

**C6** Find the single resistor equivalent to three 10 ohm resistors in parallel. Make a conjecture about the equivalent resistor when three equal resistors are in parallel. Generalise for $n$ equal resistors.

Can you prove your conjecture?

**C7** Use formula $*$ to find $R$ when $R_1$ is 6.3 and $R_2$ is 8.1. Find the most efficient way to do it on a calculator.

# D : Materials for which Ohm's Law does not apply

Ohm's Law does not apply to some materials, that is to say the current and the potential difference are not directly proportional.

For example the relationship between the current $I$ amperes and the potential difference $V$ volts might be

$$V = 20\,I^{0.5} \dots\dots\dots\dots\dots (1)$$

(which could be written as $V = 20\sqrt{I}$ ).

The resistance $R$ ohms is given by

$$R = \frac{V}{I}$$

$$= \frac{20\,I^{0.5}}{I}$$

$$= \frac{20}{I^{0.5}} \dots\dots\dots\dots\dots(2)$$

Check the algebra! It might help to think of $I^{0.5}$ as $\sqrt{I}$.

**Did you know?**
- A relationship of this type applies to a thermistor in a fire-alarm. As the temperature rises the resistance of the thermistor decreases. It follows from equation (2) that $I$ then increases. The increased current then switches on an electric bell.

Thus the resistance now depends on the current whereas for materials for which Ohm's Law applies, the resistance is always the same.

When $I$ is 2, $R$ is $\dfrac{20}{2^{0.5}} = 14.1$ (to 1 d.p.).

**D1** Find $R$ for various values of $I$ between 1 and 50. Hence draw a graph to show how $R$ varies with $I$.

**D2** Using equation (1) substitute for $I^{0.5}$ in equation (2) and so show that

$$R = \frac{400}{V}\ .$$

Sketch a graph showing how $R$ varies with $V$.

A generalised form of equation (1) is

$$V = k\,I^{a}$$

where $k$ is a constant.

**D3** Show that

$$R = \frac{k}{I^{1-a}}$$

Find $R$ when $k$ is 10, $a$ is 0.7 and $I$ is 2.

**D4** Taking $a$ as 2 make sketches to show how
  (a) $V$ varies with $I$,
  (b) $R$ varies with $I$.

# Now try these . . .

The resistance $R$ ohms of a resistor when a voltage $V$ volts is applied and a current $I$ amperes flows through it is given by

$$R = \frac{V}{I}$$

1.  An electric fire takes a current of 3 amperes when used on the mains (240 volts). What is the resistance of the fire?

2.  Find the voltage across a resistor of 20 ohms when a current of 0.15 amperes flows through it.

3.  Find the current in a 160 ohm resistor when a voltage of 240 volts is applied.

The power $P$ watts developed in a resistor when the voltage across it is $V$ volts and a current $I$ amperes flows through it is given by

$$P = IV$$

4.  What is the power when a current of 1.4 amperes flows and the voltage is 240 volts?

5.  What is the current when the power is 2 kW and the voltage is 240 volts?

6.  Using the relationship between $R$, $V$ and $I$ at the top of the page write the power in terms of $V$ and $R$.
    Sketch a graph showing how the power would change as $V$ changes when $R$ is kept constant.

When two resistors with resistances $R_1$ ohms and $R_2$ ohms are connected in parallel the combined resistance is given by

$$R = \frac{R_1 R_2}{R_1 + R_2}$$

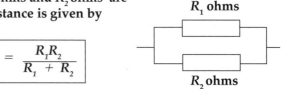

$R_1$ ohms

$R_2$ ohms

7.  What is the combined resistance when $R_1$ is 140 and $R_2$ is 180?

8.  What resistor would be needed in parallel with a 300 ohm resistor to give a combined resistance of 100 ohms?

9.  Show that the formula can be rewritten as

$$\frac{1}{R} = \frac{1}{R_1} + \frac{1}{R_2}$$

# Oscillations

A heavy object with a pen attached is oscillating up and down on a length of elastic. The pen is in contact with a piece of paper which is pulled across at a steady speed.
What would the trace on the paper look like?

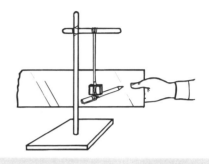

How does the horizontal displacement of a pendulum bob vary?
Think what the graph would look like.

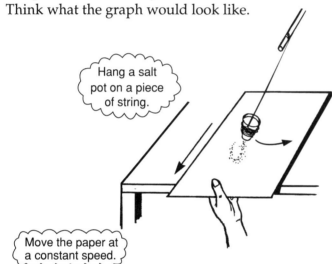

Hang a salt pot on a piece of string.

Move the paper at a constant speed.

What would the trace look like on the paper?

A disc is suspended on a string and oscillates.
A pen is used as a pointer.
Sketch a graph showing how the angle varies.

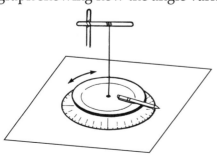

The strobe photograph shows the motion of an object on a spring.

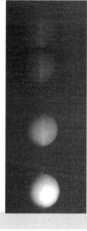

The strobe photograph shows the motion of a pendulum.

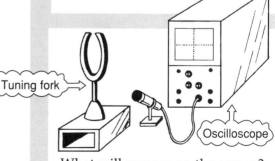

Tuning fork

Oscilloscope

What will you see on the screen?

# A : Looking at data

A1  How does the number of hours of daylight vary throughout the year?
Before going on, sketch a graph showing how you *think* it would vary.
The times of sunset and sunrise are given in some diaries for each Saturday of the year.
Obtain the times for this year and by subtraction determine the number of hours of daylight.
Plot as accurately as possible a graph to show the number of hours of daylight (number the weeks 1, 2, ..., 52).

A2  The table shows the approximate height of the tide at Milford Haven on a particular day (relative to a fixed point). Plot a graph to show the height.

| Time of day | Height of tide in metres |
|---|---|
| 06.00 | 0.0 |
| 07.00 | 1.5 |
| 08.00 | 5.2 |
| 09.00 | 10.2 |
| 10.00 | 14.8 |
| 11.00 | 18.7 |
| 12.00 | 20.0 |
| 13.00 | 18.5 |
| 14.00 | 14.6 |
| 15.00 | 10.0 |
| 16.00 | 5.5 |
| 17.00 | 1.9 |
| 18.00 | 1.0 |

What was the average height of the tide?
When was the tide rising most rapidly?

**Find out**
- Why do the times of sunset and sunrise vary throughout the year?
- What are **neap** and **spring** tides?
- What causes tides and variations in them?

**For discussion**
- Are the graphs what you expected?
- Can you account for their shape?

# B : A rotating wheel model

Put a bicycle upside down on a table. How does the height of the valve vary above and below the axle level as the back wheel rotates? Does the height change by the same amount for every 10⁰ of turn? If it was possible to take photographs showing the valve at equal intervals of time, this is what you would see (looking at the wheel edge-on from the right) :

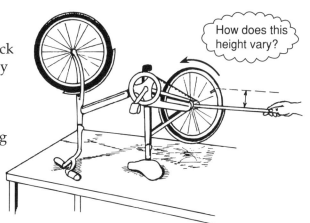

How does this height vary?

Sketch a graph to show how the height changes :

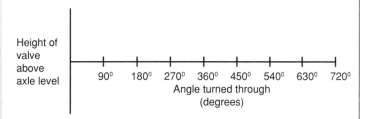

Height of valve above axle level

90⁰  180⁰  270⁰  360⁰  450⁰  540⁰  630⁰  720⁰
Angle turned through
(degrees)

**Some practical suggestions**

• Mark the tyre at 10⁰ intervals.
• Attach a plumb-line to the valve. Measure the length of the string above axle level. When the wheel has rotated through 180⁰ you will have to "reverse" gravity!

How?

**B1**  How does the distance OQ vary as the wheel rotates? Sketch a graph to show it.

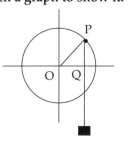

P

O  Q

**Another device**

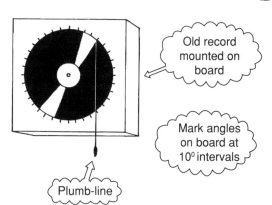

Old record mounted on board

Mark angles on board at 10⁰ intervals

Plumb-line

**B2**  Sketch graphs to show
   (a)  the height of the valve above the table
   (b)  the horizontal distance of the valve from the centre of the pedal gear wheel.

# C : Sines and cosines

The diagram shows a 'wheel' of radius 1 unit.
The distance PQ is sin 50⁰ and the distance OQ is cos 50⁰.
Thus the coordinates of P are (cos 50⁰, sin 50⁰).

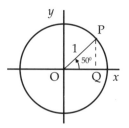

**C1**    Use a calculator to find the coordinates of P to 3
decimal places.

**C2**    Calculate the coordinates of P when the angle of
rotation (from the initial position with OP
horizontal) is 60⁰.

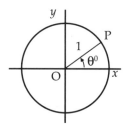

The rotating wheel idea gives a method for
defining sin $\theta^0$ and cos $\theta^0$ :

> **sin $\theta^0$ is the $y$-coordinate of P**
>
> **cos $\theta^0$ is the $x$-coordinate of P**

These definitions are valid for any value of $\theta$.

Thus when the wheel has turned through 130⁰,
the $y$-coordinate of P is  **sin 130⁰**
and the $x$-coordinate of P is  **cos 130⁰**.

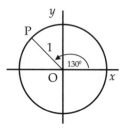

**C3**    Use a calculator to find these coordinates.

**C4**    Compare your answers to C3 with those for C1.
Explain the relationship. The diagram on the right
might help.

**C5**    Find the coordinates of P when the wheel has turned
through 120⁰. Compare the coordinates with those in
C2 and draw a diagram to explain the relationship.

**C6**    Generalise C4 and C5 to relate :

> **sin $\theta^0$        and        sin (180⁰ − $\theta^0$)**
>
> **cos $\theta^0$        and        cos (180⁰ − $\theta^0$)**

When the wheel has turned through $210^0$ the coordinates of P are ($\cos 210^0$, $\sin 210^0$).

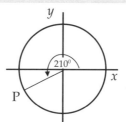

**C7** Use a calculator to find the coordinates of P.

**C8** Use a diagram to explain why :
$$\cos\ 210^0 = {}^-\cos 30^0$$
and $\sin\ 210^0 = {}^-\sin 30^0$.

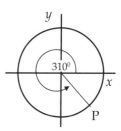

**C9** What are the coordinates of P when the wheel has turned through $310^0$?
Write the sin and cos of $310^0$ in terms of the sin and cos of $50^0$.

**C10** *Plot* as accurately as possible graphs showing how $\sin \theta^0$ and $\cos \theta^0$ change when $\theta$ goes from 0 to 360.
Compare the graphs. Explain the relationship between them.

It is a convention in mathematics that the positive direction for measurement of angles is **anticlockwise** :

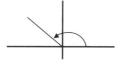

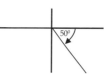

The 'clockwise' angle on the right is referred to as $^-\mathbf{50^0}$.

**C11** Use your calculator to find $\sin\ ^-50^0$ and $\cos\ ^-50^0$.
How do $\sin\ ^-50^0$ and $\cos\ ^-50^0$ relate to $\sin 50^0$ and $\cos 50^0$?

**C12** *Sketch* the graphs of sin and cos for angles between $^-720^0$ and $720^0$.

**C13** (a) Use a calculator to find
(i) $\sin^{-1} 0.5$ (ii) $\sin^{-1}\ ^-0.5$ (iii) $\sin^{-1} 1.0$
The graph of $\sin \theta^0$ suggests that for any given value of $\sin \theta^0$ there are many values of $\theta$. Which of these values does a calculator give when the inverse sine key is pressed?
(b) In the same way by using a calculator and considering the graph of $\cos \theta^0$ determine the interval used by a calculator when the inverse cos key is pressed.

**For discussion**
- $\tan \theta^0$ gives the gradient of a line making an angle $\theta^0$ with the positive $x$-axis.
- $\tan \theta^0 = \dfrac{\sin \theta^0}{\cos \theta^0}$
- What does the graph of $\tan \theta^0$ look like for $\theta$ between $^-270$ and 270?
- How does a calculator determine which value to give for $\tan^{-1}$?

# D : Graphs of sines and cosines

**You will need a computer graph plotter for this page and page 149.**

- Obtain the graph with equation

$$y = \sin x^0$$

with $x$ going from $^{-}360^0$ to $360^0$.

Check that the graph does one cycle every $360^0$.
Its **wavelength** is $360^0$.

- Now obtain the graph with equation

$$y = \sin (2x)^0.$$

What is its wavelength?

- Try $y = \sin (kx)^0$ for various values of $k$.

What is the wavelength?

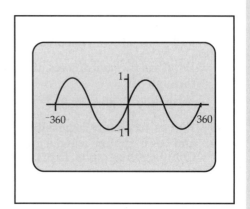

- Now obtain the graph with equation

$$y = 2 \sin x^0.$$

The *amplitude* is 2.

- Try $y = a \sin x^0$ for various values of the amplitude, $a$.

- Next try

$$y = 1 + \sin x^0$$

and $y = {}^{-}2 + \sin x^0.$

- Generalise : what does the graph with equation

$$y = c + \sin x^0$$

look like?

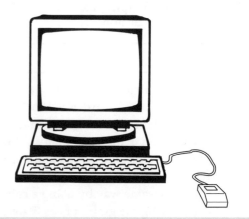

- Try some cosine graphs.

- On a particular day the height of the tide at Devonport (relative to a certain point) can be modelled by :

$$y = 5 + 12 \sin (30t)^0$$

where $t$ is the time in hours.

Obtain the graph taking $t$ from 0 to 24. (You will need to enter $x$ rather than $t$.)

What is the period of the graph?

> **Did you know?**
> - When the graph of a wave shows time along the $x$-axis, the time for one wavelength is called the **period.**

- The voltage of mains electricity at time $t$ seconds is

$$340 \sin (360 \times 50t)^0$$

Obtain its graph.

What is its period?

- A tuning fork vibrates with a frequency of 256 cycles per second. The tip has an amplitude of 2 mm.

What is the displacement at time $t$ seconds?

> **Did you know?**
> - The **frequency** of the mains is 50 cycles per second, usually written 50 Hertz.
> - Hertz was a nineteenth century physicist who discovered radio waves.

> **For discussion**
> - What is the connection between **period** and **frequency?**

- Obtain the graph of $\sin x^0$.
  Superimpose the graph of $\sin (2x)^0$.
  What do you think the graph of $\sin x^0 + \sin (2x)^0$ would look like?
  Try it on a graph plotter.

- Investigate sums of other sine waves.

Try these without the aid of a graph plotter.

**D1**   The displacement (cm) of the tip of a tuning fork from its
central position is $0.3 \sin (72000t)^0$ at time $t$ seconds.
(a)   Find the displacement when $t$ is :

(i)   $\dfrac{1}{800}$

(ii)   $\dfrac{1}{400}$

(iii)   $\dfrac{1}{200}$

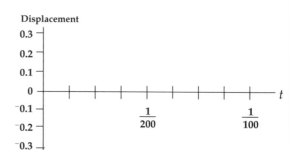

(b)   Sketch a graph to show the
displacement taking $t$
from 0 to $\dfrac{1}{100}$.

(c)   What is the greatest displacement (the amplitude)?
(d)   What is the time for a complete oscillation (the period)?
(e)   How many complete oscillations does it make in a second (the frequency)?

**D2**   The horizontal displacement (cm) of a pendulum bob from its extreme position
is $5 \cos (180t)^0$ at time $t$ seconds.
(a)   Sketch a graph to show the displacement.
(b)   What is the amplitude?
(c)   What is the period of the oscillation?
(d)   What is the frequency?

**D3**   An object attached to a spring is oscillating vertically.
The height (metres) above the floor at time $t$ seconds is $0.7 + 0.4 \sin (600t)^0$.
(a)   What is the height when $t$ is
(i)   0.1,
(ii)   0.2,
(iii) 0.4 ?
(b)   What is the greatest height?
(c)   What is the least height?
(d)   Sketch a graph to show the height.
(e)   Find (i)   the amplitude,
(ii)  the period,
(iii) the frequency.

What does the graph with equation
$y = c + a \sin (kx)^0$
look like?
Explain the significance of
$a$, $c$ and $k$.

Find formulae for the
data you graphed on
page 144.

# E : Further activities

This mechanism is called a **scotch yoke**.
Make a model of it using thick card.
What happens as the wheel rotates?
Sketch a graph showing the displacement
of the end of the T-piece.

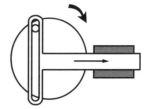

How is the rotating motion of a sewing machine drive
converted into the up-and-down motion of the needle?

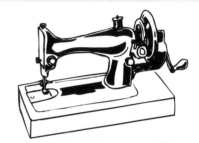

How does the height of the
piston in a car engine vary?

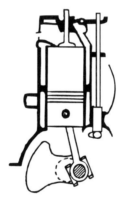

Find out about **harmonics**.

Find out about
polar coordinates
and equations of
graphs in polar
coordinates.

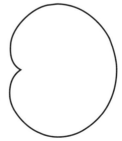

# Now try these . . .

1.  Draw a "circle diagram" to show

    $\sin 30^0$
    $\sin 150^0$
    $\sin 210^0$
    $\sin 330^0$

    Explain why   $\sin 30^0 \;=\; \sin 150^0$
    $\sin 210^0 \;=\; \sin 330^0$
    $\sin 330^0 \;=\; {}^-\sin 30^0$

2.  Using a calculator find, to 3 decimal places,

        (a)   $\sin 420^0$     (b)   $\sin 217^0$    (c)   $\cos 105^0$
        (d)   $\sin^{-1} 0.3$    (e)   $\sin^{-1} {}^-0.3$   (f)   $\cos^{-1} 0.6$
        (g)   $\cos^{-1} {}^-0.6$

3.  Draw graphs with equations $y = \sin x^0$ and $y = \cos x^0$ for $x$ from 0 to 360.
    (Use the same axes and different colours for the two graphs.)
    Find $x$ when $\sin x^0 = \cos x^0$.

4.  The distance $d$ km of a satellite from a planet at time $t$ hours is given by the formula

    $$d = 240 + 30 \cos (20t^0)$$

    (a)   What are the greatest and least distances of the satellite?
    (b)   How long does it take the satellite to make one orbit of the planet?
    (c)   Sketch the graph of $d$ with $t$ going from 0 to 18.

5.  The table shows the number $h$ of hours of daylight $t$ days after the "longest"
    day of the year. (For simplicity a year has been taken as 360 days.)

    | $t$ | $^-40$ | $^-20$ | 0 | 20 | 40 | 60 | 80 | 100 | 120 | 140 | 160 | 180 | 200 |
    |---|---|---|---|---|---|---|---|---|---|---|---|---|---|
    | $h$ | 16.8 | 17.7 | 18.0 | 17.7 | 16.8 | 15.5 | 13.9 | 12.1 | 10.5 | 9.2 | 8.3 | 8.0 | 8.3 |

    (a)   Plot a graph to show the data.
    (b)   From your graph estimate the number of days in a year which have
          12 or more hours of daylight.
    (c)   The data in the table can be modelled approximately by a relation
          of the form
    $$h = a + b \cos t^0.$$
          Find $a$ and $b$.

6.  Calculate    (a)  $(\sin 28^0)^2 + (\cos 28^0)^2$
                    (b)  $(\sin 49^0)^2 + (\cos 49^0)^2$
    Try another.
    Make a conjecture.

    Use the triangle on the right to prove your
    conjecture. (Hint : Pythagoras' Theorem)

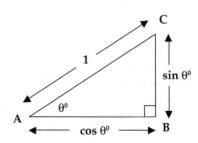

# Running a business

## What does running your own business entail?

- Accounting for assets
- Balancing the books
- Coping with credit
- Dealing with depreciation
- Interpreting invoices
- Looking for loans
- Mastering the markets
- Working out wages, income tax, National Insurance and VAT.

### For discussion
- Why are these points necessary for running a business?
- What else might be needed to be successful?

| CASH FLOW | J& S Paving plc | | 1st Year | |
|---|---|---|---|---|
| CASH OUT (£): | | Jan | Feb | Mar |
| Purchase of equipment | | 3000 | 0 | 0 |
| Rent and rates | | 0 | 0 | |
| Wages | | 1800 | 1800 | |
| Raw materials | | 700 | 300 | |
| Miscellaneous | | 800 | | |
| Bank charges | | 100 | | |

J & S
Paving
plc

**2. VAT fractions**
Normally tax is calculated at the appropriate percentage of a price which has first been decided without VAT, and the tax invoice will show these separate amounts. However, sometimes VAT has to be calculated from a price in which it is already included. To do this you need the VAT fraction.

For example, if you sell something at £2.35 and the VAT rate is 17.5%, the amount of VAT is 35p. But 35p is not 17.5% of £2.35, it is $\frac{7}{47}$ of 2.35

So with VAT at 17.5% the VAT fraction is $\frac{7}{47}$.

What is the VAT fraction for a VAT of 15%?

*From **The VAT Guide** by HM Customs & Excise*

Sylvie was looking forward to getting her first week's wages. She calculated that she had earned £130.
Why didn't Sylvie get all of the £130?
Roughly what would her 'take-home' pay be?

# A : Paving the way!

Janet and Sam run a small
business that makes paving
slabs for garden centres and
builders merchants.

The brochure
shows some of
their products.

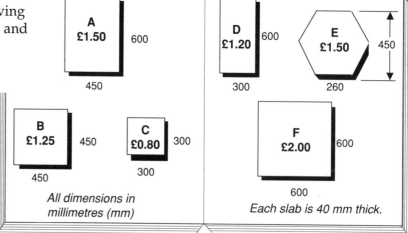

*All dimensions in
millimetres (mm)*

*Each slab is 40 mm thick.*

---

**A1**   In August Sam and Janet's sales figures were:

| Type of slab | A | B | C | D | E | F |
|---|---|---|---|---|---|---|
| Number sold | 400 | 800 | 300 | 300 | 400 | 1000 |

(a)   How many slabs did they sell altogether?
(b)   How much money did they take?
(c)   What were the average takings per slab sold?

**A2**   Calculate the volume of concrete (in cubic *metres*) required to
make slab A. (Note : the dimensions will first need to be written in
*metres*.)
In the same way find the volume of concrete required for each of
the other slabs. (Think of the hexagon as made up of 6 triangles.
The area of a triangle is (base × height)/2.)

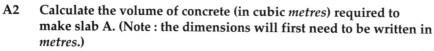

**A3**   What total volume of concrete (in m³) would be required to make
all the slabs sold in August?

---

Sam and Janet mix their own concrete using 1 part of cement to 2.5 parts of
sand to 4 parts of shingle (by volume).

---

**A4**   How much cement and shingle would
be needed for 5 m³ of sand?

**A5**   Deduce from A4 the amounts of
cement and shingle for 1 m³ of sand.
Show the amounts in a table as on the
right and find the total volume.

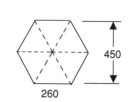

|  | Volume (m³) |
|---|---|
| Cement | |
| Sand | 1 |
| Shingle | |
| Total | |

When water is added to the mixture the resulting volume of wet concrete is reduced to about 75% of the volume of the dry mix.

**A6** What volume of the wet concrete would the dry mix in A5 produce when water is added?

**A7** (a) Copy and complete the flow-diagram to convert 'dry' volume to 'wet' volume:

(b) Underneath it draw a reversed flow diagram to convert 'wet' volume to 'dry' volume.

**A8** In busy weeks Janet and Sam use 9 m³ of 'wet' concrete.
What volume of dry mix would be required?
Use your table in A5 to find the volumes of cement, sand and shingle which would be needed.

**A9** Use your answer to A3 to find the total volume of dry mix used in August.
How much cement, sand and shingle were required?

**A10** A cubic metre of cement weighs about 1500 kg. What was the weight of the cement used in August?
Cement is supplied in 50 kg bags. How many bags did Sam and Janet need in August?

**A11** Sam and Janet buy their raw materials from a supplier at the rates shown on the right.
What was the total cost of the cement, sand and shingle in August?

**A12** Janet and Sam took £4800 in sales in August. Show that the cost of the materials was about 30% of the sales takings.

| CONCRETE SUPPLIES | |
| --- | --- |
| Cement | £3.50 per bag |
| Sand | £27 per m³ |
| Shingle | £22 per m³ |

# B : Cash flow

Using a bank loan together with their own money, Sam and Janet raised £12000 to get their business started.

The local council supplied a place on a new industrial estate which was free of rent and rates for the first three months. After that, they had to pay £400 a month.

To get the loan from the bank Sam and Janet had to show how they expected the cash to flow (in and out) during the first year. By making the prediction that their income from sales would grow at £600 per month they produced this table:

| CASH OUT (£): | Jan | Feb | Mar | Apr | May | June |
|---|---|---|---|---|---|---|
| Purchase of equipment | 3000 | 0 | 0 | 0 | 0 | 0 |
| Rent and rates | 0 | 0 | 0 | 400 | 400 | 400 |
| Wages | 1800 | 1800 | 1800 | 1800 | 1800 | 1800 |
| Raw materials | 700 | 300 | 500 | 700 | 900 | 1100 |
| Miscellaneous | 800 | 300 | 300 | 300 | 300 | 300 |
| Bank charges | 100 | 100 | 100 | 100 | 100 | 100 |
| **Total cash out** | 6400 | 2500 | ...... | ...... | ...... | ...... |
| **CASH IN :** | | | | | | |
| Loans | 12000 | 0 | 0 | 0 | 0 | 0 |
| Sales income | 0 | 600 | 1200 | 1800 | 2400 | 3000 |
| **Total cash in** | 12000 | 600 | 1200 | 1800 | 2400 | 3000 |
| Cash in − Cash out | + 5600 | − 1900 | | | | |
| Balance carried forward | —— | + 5600 | + 3700 | | | |
| **FINAL BALANCE (£) :** | + 5600 | + 3700 | | | | |

**B1**    Complete your own copy of the Cash Flow Sheet as far as the month of June. (Check : the Final Balance at the end of June should be − 1100.)

**B2**    Complete the Cash Flow Sheet for the period July to December. Note that both the cost of raw materials and the sales income are increasing at a steady rate.
(Check : the Final Balance at the end of December should be +3100.)

**B3**    Write down the increases in the Final Balance from July to August, from August to September, etc.
Continue the pattern in these increases to find the Final Balance in January, February and March of the following year.

**For discussion**

- When might Janet and Sam expect their final balance to be enough to pay off their initial £12000 loan?

# C : Make or break

In the long run Sam and Janet will have to achieve a certain level of business if they are to at least break even. They want to find out what it is likely to be.

Sam and Janet make the following approximations:

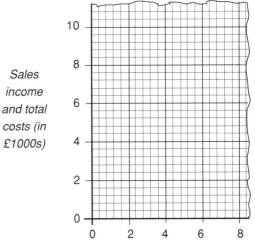

- Average takings per slab = £1.50
- Cost of materials per slab = 30% of £1.50 = £0.45
- Overheads = £3000

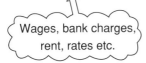

Wages, bank charges, rent, rates etc.

---

**C1** Janet makes up a table for different numbers of slabs sold per month. Copy and complete the table.

| Number sold per month | 1000 | 2000 | 3000 | 4000 | 5000 | 6000 |
|---|---|---|---|---|---|---|
| Sales income (£) | 1500 | 3000 | 4500 | ...... | ...... | ...... |
| Cost of materials (£) | 450 | 900 | ...... | ...... | ...... | |
| Overheads (£) | 3000 | 3000 | ...... | ...... | | |
| Total costs (£) | 3450 | ...... | ...... | | | |
| Profit (+) or loss(−) (£) | −1950 | ...... | | | | |

---

**C2** Draw a graph to show how the *sales income* depends on the number of slabs sold.
On the same axes draw a graph showing how the *total costs* depend on the number of slabs sold per month. Label each graph.
Based on these figures at what level of business should Sam and Janet break even?
How many slabs do they need to sell in order to make a monthly profit of
(a) £1000      (b) £2000?

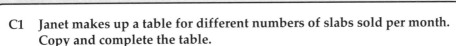

*Sales income and total costs (in £1000s)*

*Number of slabs sold per month (in 1000s)*

*Sam says that the graph in C2 does not give sufficient accuracy.*
*This is how he argues:*

Suppose we sell *s* slabs per month.

- At £1.50 per slab, the sales income is £1.50*s*.

- The cost of materials is roughly 30% of £1.50*s*
  which is £0.3 $\times$ (1.50*s*) = £0.45*s*.

- The overheads are about £3000 per month.

Break-even occurs when

Sales income    = Total costs

$$1.50s \;=\; 0.45s \;+\; 3000$$

All we have to do is solve this equation!

Subtract 0.45*s* from both sides:

$$1.50s - 0.45s \;=\; 3000$$

$$1.05s \;=\; 3000$$

Divide both sides by 1.05

$$s \;=\; \frac{3000}{1.05}$$

$$\approx\; 2857$$

This gives a break-even number of about 2860 slabs per month.

*Janet then suggests that they can use a similar method to work out the level of*
*business required to provide a monthly profit of £1000:*

A monthly profit of £1000 occurs when

Sales income $-$ Total costs        =        1000

$$1.50s - (0.45s + 3000) \;=\; 1000$$

**C3**    **Solve Janet's equation and show that they will have to sell just**
          **over 3800 slabs to make this level of profit.**

**C4**    **Formulate and solve an equation to find the level of business**
          **required to make a profit of £2000 and so check your answer to**
          **question C2 (b).**

# D : Dealing with VAT

Sam and Janet have to charge VAT (Value Added Tax) on each slab they sell.

VAT is stated as a percentage. The amount is determined by the Government. When it was first introduced in 1973 it was 10%. The rate has varied over the years first increasing to 15% and then in 1991 increasing to 17.5%.

When Janet and Sam set up in business the VAT rate was 17.5%.

They calculated the prices *with* VAT by multiplying the price *without* VAT by 1.175:

**Find out**
- What sales are exempt from VAT?
- What sales are zero-rated for VAT?
- What turnover must a firm have before they are legally bound to charge VAT?

**D1** The prices of the slabs on page 154 do not include VAT.
Find to the nearest penny the prices *with* VAT.

**D2** A customer wants enough slabs to pave her patio using the design on the right. Which three types will she require? How many of each will she need?
Find the cost of buying the slabs, including VAT.

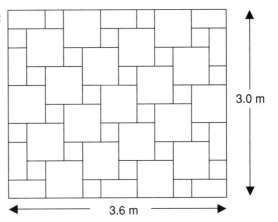

3.0 m

3.6 m

Janet and Sam extend their business to sell various accessories.
Their brochure shows the prices including VAT.
The prices excluding VAT can be found by reversing the flow diagram above.

| | Price (including VAT) |
|---|---|
| Spirit level | £9.00 |
| Concrete mixer | £300.00 |
| Wheel-barrow | £22.50 |

**D3** Find the prices without VAT for the items listed.

# E : Paying the wages

Sylvie, Winston and Nick all work for Sam and Janet's paving slab business. Sylvie works part-time as a clerk in the office.Winston and Nick work full-time as slab makers. Sylvie gets £3.20 per hour and Winston and Nick get £4.20 per hour. Sylvie comes in for three-and-a-half hours each morning, Monday to Friday. Winston and Nick work for eight hours a day, Monday to Friday.

**E1**  Calculate how much each employee earns per week.

**E2**  How much does each employee earn in a year?

*Employees* have to pay **National Insurance** contributions out of their wages. The *employers* also have to pay National Insurance contributions for their employees. The tables show how these contributions were calculated in 1992/93 for a weekly wage of £$w$.

|  | Employee's contribution |
|---|---|
| $w < 54$ | £0 |
| $54 \leq w \leq 405$ | 2% of £54 + 9% of £$(w - 54)$ |
| $w > 405$ | As for a wage of £405 |

|  | Employer's contribution |
|---|---|
| $w < 54$ | £0 |
| $54 \leq w < 90$ | 4.6% of £$w$ |
| $90 \leq w < 135$ | 6.6% of £$w$ |
| $135 \leq w < 190$ | 8.6% of £$w$ |
| $w \geq 190$ | 10.4% of £$w$ |

**E3**  How much do Sylvie, Winston and Nick each have to pay for their National Insurance contributions per week?

**E4**  How much does the firm have to pay in National Insurance contributions per week for each employee? What is the total cost per year (wages + National Insurance) of employing the three workers?
Roughly how much is this per month?
Check that it agrees with the estimate in the Cash Flow Sheet on page 156.

**E5**  An employee earns £470 per week.
How much National Insurance does the employee pay per week?
How much National Insurance does the employer have to pay each week?

**E6**  The computer program below can be used to find the employer's National Insurance contribution for any wage, £W.

```
10 INPUT W
20 IF W < 54 PRINT 0
30 IF W >=54 AND W < 90 PRINT 0.046*W
40 IF W >=90 AND W < 135 PRINT 0.066*W
50 IF W >=135 AND W < 190 PRINT 0.086*W
60 IF W >=190 PRINT 0.104*W
```

Try it out to check your results in E4.
Write a program to find the employee's weekly National Insurance contribution.

**Find out**
- What is National Insurance for?
- Obtain the latest figures for National Insurance contributions.

**You could ...**
- Improve the computer program by adding some words and by updating it for the latest National Insurance percentages.
- Draw graphs to show the National Insurance contributions for weekly wages from £0 to £500.

Employees such as Sylvie, Winston and Nick also have to pay **income tax**.
Income tax is charged on the amount earned above a certain amount, called the tax allowance.

In 1992/93 the tax allowance was £3445. So, for example, a person earning £12000 per year was charged income tax on £8555.

£12 000 − £3445

The method by which the amount of tax was calculated in 1992/93 is shown on the right.
In the table £$x$ is the taxable income, i.e. yearly income − £3445.

| Taxable income | Tax |
|---|---|
| $x \leq 2000$ | 20% of £$x$ |
| $2000 < x \leq 23\,700$ | 20% of £2000 <br> + <br> 25% of £$(x - 2000)$ |
| $x > 23\,700$ | As for a taxable income of £23 700 <br> + <br> 40% of £ $(x - 23\,700)$ |

**Note**
In some cases tax payers qualify for extra allowances. Also there is an allowance for married people.
These further allowances have been ignored here. Assume that E7 to E10 apply to single people.

**Did you know?**

- The amount earned before any deductions are made is called the **gross** pay.
  The amount after deductions is called the **net** pay.

**Find out**

- What is income tax for?
- Obtain the current tax rules and find out about the further allowances referred to above.
- Why does the tax year start on April 6th?

**You could . . .**

- Write a computer program for the tax figures above (or for the current rules).
- Draw a graph to show the amount of tax for yearly incomes from £0 to £30 000, say.
- Draw a graph to show the net yearly income for gross incomes from £0 to £30 000, say.

**E7** Use your results from E2 to find the yearly amount of tax paid by
(a) Sylvie   (b) Winston.

**E8** Income tax and National Insurance contributions are deducted by the employer and calculated on gross pay.
Use E7 and E3 to find the weekly 'take-home' pay (the net pay) of
(a) Sylvie   (b) Winston.

**E9** In 1992/93 how much income tax was paid by someone who earned
(a) £5000 per year   (b) £27 145 per year
(c) £30 000 per year?

**E10** Use the information in the table to find the yearly income of people who paid the following amounts of tax per year
(a) £300   (b) £500   (c) £6000

# Now try these . . .

1.   (a) In Janet and Sam's first year of trading the monthly overheads were £3000. In the second year they estimate that their overheads will rise by 10%. What will be the new monthly overheads?

    (b) In Janet and Sam's second year of trading the cost of materials goes up. They find that the cost of materials is 33% of their sales income. Taking the average selling price of a slab as £1.50 calculate the cost of materials for 1000 slabs.

    (c) Using the new costs found in (a) and (b) draw up a table as on page 157 to show the profit or loss for various numbers of slabs.

    (d) Using the same scales as for C2 on page 157 plot new graphs showing the sales income and the total costs.
What will be the new break-even point?

    (e) Use the information in (b) to find the sales income and the cost of the materials when $s$ slabs are sold per month.
Obtain an equation by equating the sales income to the total costs (materials + overheads). Solve this equation to find the 'break-even' number of slabs.
Check with your answer in (d).

    (f) Use the method in (e) to find the number of slabs which will need to be sold per month to make a profit of £1000.

2.   Janet and Sam put up their prices by 10%.
Calculate the new average takings per slab.
Formulate and solve the new break-even equation.

> Average takings
> per slab
> ~~£1.50~~
> Up by 10% to

3.   Chris and Jane run a pizza parlour. On average, customers spend £8 a head of which 35% goes on materials. Wages, etc. cost them about £5000 per month.
What is the income for $c$ customers?
What is the cost of the materials for $c$ customers?
Formulate and solve equations to find the number of customers needed per month to (a) break even    (b) make £1000 profit.

4.   Chris and Jane employ a chef whose gross wage in 1992/93 was £15 000.
(a) How much National Insurance did Chris and Jane have to pay for the chef?
(b) What was the chef's 'take home' pay each week?

5.   In the pizza parlour a service charge of 12.5% is added on to the bill.
(a) What is the total bill when the cost of the food is £18.50?
(b) What is the cost of the food when the total bill is £27?

# Optimising

Ann and Margaret run a small business in which they work together making blouses and skirts.

Each blouse takes 1 hour of Ann's time together with 1 hour of Margaret's time. Each skirt involves Ann for 1 hour and Margaret for an hour.
Ann has 7 hours available each day and Margaret has 5 hours each day.

They could just make blouses or they could just make skirts or they could make some of each.

Their first thought was to make the same number of each. But they get £8 profit on a blouse and only £6 on a skirt.

So what should they do?

- How can you draw rapidly graphs with equations such as

$$x + y = 5$$
$$2x + 3y = 12?$$

- Find $x + y$ at

    A, B, C

    D, E, F

    G, H, I

- Find $2x + 3y$ at

    P, Q, R

    S, T U

    V, W, X

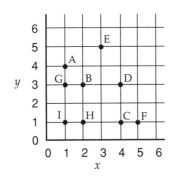

What can be said about $x + y$ for all the points below the line through A, B and C?

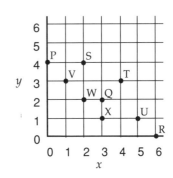

What can be said about $2x + 3y$ for all the points below the line through P, Q and R?

# A : Working in pairs

Kris and Paul have formed a partnership to make bracelets and rings.
Kris spends 1 hour on each bracelet and one-and-a-half hours on each ring.
Paul spends half an hour on each bracelet and 1 hour on each ring.
Kris can only work for 7 hours each day.
Paul can only work for 4 hours each day.

Suppose they decide to make 1 bracelet and spend the
rest of the day making rings.

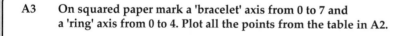

Why 4?

Kris would be able to do the work on 4 rings in one day.
Paul would be able to do the work on 3 rings in one day.

So they would only be able to complete 3 rings in one day.

> **A1**  Suppose they make *no* bracelets.
> How many rings could they complete in a day?

To help them plan their working time Kris makes up a table to show
how many of each could be completed in a working day.
It starts off like this:

| Number of bracelets | 0 | 1 | 2 | 3 | 4 | 5 | 6 | 7 |
|---|---|---|---|---|---|---|---|---|
| Number of rings |  | 3 |  |  |  |  |  |  |

> **A2**  Copy and complete Kris's table.

The information in the table can be shown on graph paper by using
the number pairs (bracelets, rings) as coordinates.

> **A3**  On squared paper mark a 'bracelet' axis from 0 to 7 and
> a 'ring' axis from 0 to 4. Plot all the points from the table in A2.
>
>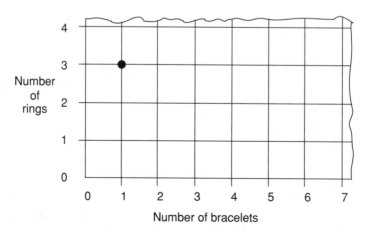

Looking at the points on the squared paper makes something apparent that was not so obvious in the table.

The points marked are those which show the *maximum* possible numbers of bracelets and rings that can be made in a day.

There are many other possibilities. For instance, 1 bracelet and 2 rings could be made. A lot of time would be wasted but it could be done.

A4     On your squared paper mark all the other points which also show a possible day's production.

Making a ring takes longer than making a bracelet and produces more profit.
The profit is £4 for each bracelet and £7 for each ring.

A5     On your squared paper decide which point would produce the greatest profit and draw a circle around it. What is the greatest profit that can be made?
What is the profit per hour worked?

A6     In an effort to make more money Kris and Paul decide that they will both work
1 hour longer each day.
Make a table and plot points on squared paper to show all the possibilities for one day's production in the longer day. Mark the point which shows the greatest profit.
Compare the profit per hour worked with that in A5.

A7     The small firm of Bladons makes garden sheds.
They make two models, the *Devon* and the *Kent*.
The *Devon* needs 2 hours of machine work and
5 hours of hand work.
The *Kent* needs 3 hours of machine work and 5 hours of hand work.
In a normal day 30 hours of machine work can be done, and there are enough workers to provide 60 hours of hand work.

(a) Make a table and plot points on squared paper to show all the possibilities for one day's production.

(b) The profit is £20 on a *Devon* and £28 on a *Kent*. Explain how Bladons should operate in order to produce the maximum profit.

A8     Use the same method to find the greatest profit in the problem on page 163.

# B : Solving by algebra

Here is a way to solve the problem on page 164 using algebra.

Suppose Kris and Paul together make $x$ bracelets and $y$ rings each day.

Kris spends 1 hour on each bracelet and one-and-a-half hours on each ring.
So for $x$ bracelets and $y$ rings Kris takes $1 \times x + 1.5 \times y$ hours.
Since Kris has 7 hours available each day

$$1 \times x + 1.5 \times y \leq 7$$

So   $x + 1.5y \leq 7$   . . . . . . . . . . (1)

Paul spends half an hour on each bracelet and 1 hour on each ring.
So for $x$ bracelets and $y$ rings he takes $0.5 \times x + 1 \times y$ hours.
Since he has 4 hours available each day

$$0.5x + y \leq 4 \quad \ldots\ldots\ldots\ldots(2)$$

These *inequalities* can be shown graphically.

---

**1**   Draw the line with equation

$$x + 1.5y = 7$$

Then shade the region which is not wanted.

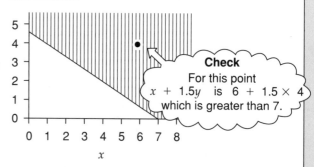

When $y$ is 0, $x$ is 7
When $x$ is 1, $y$ is 4

**Check**
For this point
$x + 1.5y$ is $6 + 1.5 \times 4$
which is greater than 7.

*Choose a point below the line and check that it satisfies the inequality $x + 1.5y \leq 7$*

---

**2**   Draw the line with equation

$$0.5x + y = 4$$

Then shade the region which is not wanted.

**Check**
For this point
$0.5x + y$ is $0.5 \times 8 + 2$
which is greater than 4.

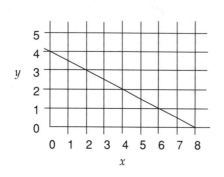
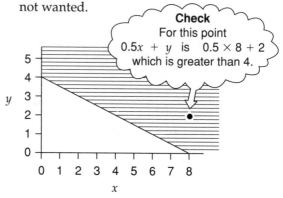

*Choose a point below the line and check that it satisfies the inequality $0.5x + y \leq 4$*

On the opposite page the lines and regions were drawn separately for clarity of explanation, but to solve the problem they are both needed on the same diagram as shown on the right.

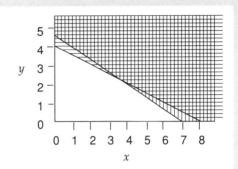

Now all the points which are either on or under both lines show a possible day's production.
There are 23 possibilities as shown by the black dots in the second diagram.

The profit on a bracelet is £4 and on a ring is £7.
*Which point gives the greatest profit?*

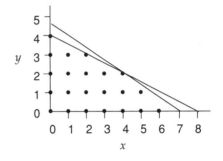

**For discussion**
- The point where the lines cross offers the "best" solution to arranging their day's production.

**B1** Kris and Paul both decide to work 1 hour longer each day. (See A6 on page 165.)
  (a) Write out the new inequalities for both of them.
  (b) On squared paper show both inequalities, and mark each point which represents a possible day's production.
  (c) Which point gives the greatest profit? Check that this agrees with your answer to A6.

**B2** For the garden shed problem in A7 suppose Bladons make
  $x$ *Devon* sheds and $y$ *Kent* sheds.
  (a) How many hours of machine work are needed for making
    $x$ *Devon* sheds?
    How many hours of machine work are needed for making
    $y$ *Kent* sheds?
    Explain how the inequality $2x + 3y \leq 30$ arises.
  (b) Make another inequality relating to hand work.
  (c) On squared paper show both inequalities and mark each point which represents a possible day's production.
  (d) Which point gives the greatest profit? Check that this agrees with your answer to A7.

**B3** For the problem on page 163 suppose that $x$ blouses and $y$ skirts are made.
  (a) How many hours of Ann's time will this take?
    Write down an inequality relating to Ann's time.
  (b) Make another inequality relating to Margaret's time.
  (c) On squared paper show both inequalities and find the numbers of blouses and skirts to obtain the greatest profit.

# C : More constraints

*A factory employs unskilled workers earning £90 per week and skilled workers earning £180 per week. The owners do not want the weekly wage bill to exceed £16 200.*

*The machines need a minimum of 110 operators, of whom at least 40 must be skilled. Regulations require that the number of skilled workers should be half or more of the number of unskilled workers.*

*Find the possible numbers of skilled and unskilled workers that could be employed.*

The statements can be turned into algebra.
Let the number of unskilled workers be $x$ and the number of skilled workers be $y$.

From the first two sentences we have that
$$90x + 180y \leq 16\,200$$
Dividing by 90 gives
$$x + 2y \leq 180 \quad \ldots\ldots (i)$$

The third sentence says that the number of operators $(x + y)$ has to be at least 110.

So $\qquad\qquad x + y \geq 110 \quad \ldots\ldots (ii)$

The two inequalities (i) and (ii) can be shown on a single diagram.

Notice that (i) allows all the points *on and below* the line $x + 2y = 180$ to be accepted. So the unwanted region is *above* the line.

In (ii) the acceptable points are *on and above* the line $x + y = 110$. So the unwanted region is *below* the line.

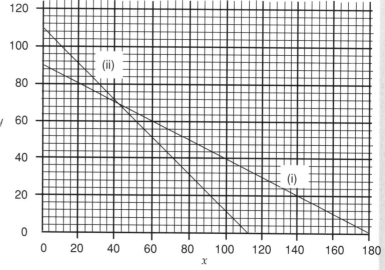

The third sentence also says that "at least 40 must be skilled". So $y \geq 40 \quad \ldots\ldots (iii)$

Finally, the fourth sentence produces this inequality $\qquad y \geq \tfrac{1}{2}x \quad \ldots\ldots (iv)$

---

**C1** **(a)** Copy the diagram onto 2 mm graph paper. Shade the region *above* line (i) and the region *below* line (ii).
Draw the line representing $y = 40$ and shade in the unwanted region from the inequality in (iii).
Draw the line representing $y = \tfrac{1}{2}x$ and shade in the unwanted region from the inequality in (iv).
All possible solutions are now shown by the unshaded area.

**(b)** What is the *least* number of unskilled workers that could be employed?
How many skilled workers would then be required?

**(c)** What is the *greatest* number of unskilled workers that could be employed?
How many skilled workers would then be required?

**(d)** What is the greatest *total* number of workers that could be employed?

**C2** A farmer grows two crops: barley and swedes.
The farmer has 20 hectares of land available.
Planting barley costs £30 a hectare and swedes £20 a hectare.
The farmer does not want to spend more than £480 on planting.
Working on barley needs 1 day per hectare and working on swedes needs 2 days per hectare.
There are 36 working days available.
Suppose the farmer plants $x$ hectares of barley and $y$ hectares of swedes.
(a) Explain why $x + y \leq 20$.
(b) Explain how the third and fourth sentences produce $3x + 2y \leq 48$.
(c) Make a third inequality showing the relationship between $x$ and $y$ and the number of working days.
(d) On graph paper show these three inequalities and shade the regions which do *not* satisfy them.
(e) The profit on barley is £100 per hectare, and on swedes £120 per hectare.
Determine the amount of each crop which needs to be planted to maximise the profit.

**C3** A distribution firm has to transport 1200 packages using large vans which can take 200 packages each and small vans which can take 80 packages each.
The cost of running each large van is £40 and of each small van is £20.
Not more than £300 is to be spent on the job.

Suppose $x$ large vans and $y$ small vans are used.
(a) Explain how the inequality $200x + 80y \geq 1200$ arises.
Simplify this inequality by dividing through by 40.
(b) Show how the statement about the cost leads to the inequality $2x + y \leq 15$.
(c) A further restriction is made : the number of large vans must not exceed the number of small vans. Write this statement as an inequality.
(d) On graph paper show these three inequalities and shade the regions which do not satisfy them.
(e) How many ways are there of doing the job? Which is the cheapest?

> Is it true that the 'best' point is always at or near an intersection of the lines?

**C4** A firm manufactures wood screws and metal screws. All the screws have to pass through a threading machine and a slotting machine. A box of *wood* screws requires 3 minutes on the slotting machine and 2 minutes on the threading machine. A box of *metal* screws requires 2 minutes on the slotting machine and 8 minutes on the threading machine. In a week, each machine is available for 60 hours.

There is a profit of £10 per box on wood screws and £17 per box on metal screws.
It is required to find how many boxes of each type should be made to maximise the profit.

Suppose $x$ boxes of wood screws and $y$ boxes of metal screws are made each week.

(a) Show how the inequalities $3x + 2y \leq 3600$ and $x + 4y \leq 1800$ arise.
(b) On graph paper show these two inequalities.
(c) Determine the maximum profit as closely as you can (at the point where the two lines cross).

# D : Towards greater accuracy

In C4 it was difficult to find the intersection point with any accuracy because the scale was so small. Here we look at another method of finding where the lines cross.
On page 166 there were equations

$$x + 1.5y = 7 \quad \ldots \ldots \text{ (i)}$$

$$0.5x + y = 4 \quad \ldots \ldots \text{ (ii)}$$

Why double?

Double both sides of equation (ii) to give $x + 2y = 8 \ldots \ldots$ (iii)
and write equation (i) underneath $\quad x + 1.5y = 7 \ldots \ldots$ (i)

It is apparent that the left-hand side of (iii) is bigger than the left-hand side of (i) by $0.5y$ and the right-hand side of (iii) is bigger than the right-hand side of (i) by 1.
So $0.5y$ must equal 1.
From which it follows that $y$ must equal 2.

Using this value of $y$ in equation (ii) gives $0.5x + 2 = 4$.
From which it follows that $0.5x = 2$ and so $x = 4$.

Looking back at the graph on page 167 it can be seen that the two lines do indeed cross at the point where $x$ is 4 and $y$ is 2.

Next look at the equations of the lines in the garden shed problem (B2 on page 167).

$$2x + 3y = 30 \quad \ldots \ldots \text{ (i)}$$
$$x + y = 12 \quad \ldots \ldots \text{ (ii)}$$

Compare these two equations:
This $\implies 2x + 3y = 30 \impliedby$ This
exceeds                                    exceeds
this $\implies x + y = 12 \impliedby$ this
by $x + 2y$.                              by 18.

In effect, it amounts to subtracting the left-hand sides and subtracting the right-hand sides.

So $\quad x + 2y = 18 \quad \ldots \ldots$ (iii)

Now when equations (iii) and (ii) are compared it can be seen that the left-hand side of (iii) exceeds the left-hand side of (ii) by $y$, and the right-hand side of (iii) exceeds the right-hand side of (ii) by 6.

Again, in effect, subtracting.

So $\quad\quad\quad y = 6$

Then from equation (ii)
$$x = 12 - y$$
$$= 6$$

Check in equation (i) :
Left-hand side $= 2x + 3y$
$\quad\quad\quad = 2 \times 6 + 3 \times 6$
$\quad\quad\quad = 30$
Right-hand side $= 30 \ \checkmark$

**D1**    Solve these pairs of equations

(a) $\quad x + 1\frac{1}{2}y = 12$
$\quad\quad \frac{1}{2}x + y = 7$

(b) $\quad 2x + 3y = 44$
$\quad\quad x + y = 17$

(c) $\quad x + \frac{1}{2}y = 19$
$\quad\quad 2x + \frac{1}{2}y = 34$

(d) $\quad 3x + 2y = 31$
$\quad\quad 4x + 4y = 52$

(e) $\quad 2\frac{1}{2}x + 2y = 31$
$\quad\quad \frac{1}{2}x + y = 8$

(f) $\quad 6x + 4y = 74$
$\quad\quad 4x + 3y = 51$

Solving equations by this method usually requires some manipulation to make the two equations alike in either the $x$ or the $y$ term.

The way to do this is to multiply one (or sometimes both) of the equations by a suitable number.

This method can be used on the equations in C4 where it was not easy to find the intersection point accurately:

$$3x + 2y = 3600 \quad \ldots \ldots \text{(i)}$$

$$x + 4y = 1800 \quad \ldots \ldots \text{(ii)}$$

Looking at the coefficients on the left-hand sides it can be seen that if equation (i) is multiplied by 2 then the $y$ terms are the same and can be eliminated by subtraction:

(i) $\times$ 2 gives $\qquad 6x + 4y = 7200 \quad \ldots \ldots \text{(iii)}$

(iii) $-$ (ii) gives $\qquad 5x = 5400$
and so $\qquad\qquad\quad x = 1080$

Then from equation (i) $\qquad 2y = 3600 - 3x$
$\qquad\qquad\qquad\qquad\quad = 3600 - 3240$
$\qquad\qquad\qquad\qquad\quad = 360$
and so $\qquad\qquad\qquad y = 180$

> Check in (ii):
> LHS $= 1080 + 4 \times 180$
> $\qquad\quad = 1800$
> RHS $= 1800 \ \checkmark$

Thus the lines meet at (1080, 180).
*Compare this with the answer from your graph.*

---

**D2**    (a) **Find the maximum profit in problem C4.**
           **Compare it with your previous answer.**
      (b) **Another way to solve the equations would be to arrange for the $x$ terms to be made alike. Find the appropriate multiplier and do it that way.**

---

In some cases both equations might need a multiplier.
For example: $\qquad\qquad 5x + 3y = 19 \ \ldots \ldots \text{(i)}$
$\qquad\qquad\qquad\qquad\quad 2x + 7y = 25 \ \ldots \ldots \text{(ii)}$
To make the $y$ terms the same, both sides of equation (i) could be multiplied by 7 and both sides of equation (ii) by 3:

(i) $\times$ 7 gives $\qquad 35x + 21y = 133$
(ii) $\times$ 3 gives $\qquad 6x + 21y = 75$
Then by subtraction the $y$ terms are eliminated:
$\qquad\qquad\qquad\qquad\qquad 29x = 58$
and so $\qquad\qquad\qquad\qquad x = 2$
From equation (i) $\qquad 10 + 3y = 19$
and so $\qquad\qquad\qquad\qquad y = 3$

> Why were these multipliers chosen?

> Check in (ii):
> LHS $= 2 \times 2 + 7 \times 3$
> $\qquad\quad = 25$
> RHS $= 25 \ \checkmark$

---

**D3**    **Alternatively, the $x$ terms in (i) and (ii) could be made the same. Choose appropriate multipliers and do it that way.**

**D4**    **Find the points of intersection of the lines with the following equations. There are various ways of doing them. Choose the way you think is easiest. They do not all have whole number solutions.**

     (a) $2x + y = 4$         (b) $5x + y = 23$        (c) $7x + 6y = 16$
          $x + 3y = 7$             $3x + 2y = 18$          $x + 2y = 2$

     (d) $13x + 9y = 36$     (e) $3x + 4y = 1$        (f) $4x + 3y = 11$
          $2x + 3y = 6$           $2x + y = 4$           $x + 5y = 24$

> Don't forget to check your solutions!

# E : Further methods

With equations such as
$$2x - y = 4 \quad \dots \text{(i)}$$
$$x + y = 5 \quad \dots \text{(ii)}$$

it is convenient to **add** the left hand sides so that the $y$ terms are eliminated.

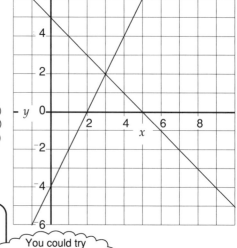

Then $\qquad\qquad 3x = 9$

and so $\qquad\qquad\quad x = 3$

From (ii) $\qquad\qquad y = 5 - x$
$$= 2$$

Check in (i) :
LHS $= 2 \times 3 - 2$
$= 4$
RHS $= 4 \checkmark$

For some equations it might be necessary to use an appropriate multiplier as well.

---

**E1** Find the point of intersection of the lines with the following equations.
Choose the method you think is easiest.

(a) $\quad 2x + y = 10$
$\qquad\quad x - y = 2$

(b) $\quad 2x + 3y = 16$
$\qquad\quad 3x - y = 3$

(c) $\quad 5x + 3y = 41$
$\qquad\quad x - 2y = 3$

(d) $\quad 2x + 5y = 19$
$\qquad\quad x - 3y = 4$

You could try multiplying the second equation by 3.

Always remember to check your solutions to see that they do work.

---

Consider the equations :
$$x + y = 105 \qquad \dots \text{(i)}$$
$$y = \tfrac{1}{2}x \qquad \dots \text{(ii)}$$

The graphs for these equations are shown on the right. The simplest way to find their point of intersection is to replace $y$ in equation (i) by $\tfrac{1}{2}x$ from equation (ii).
Then (i) becomes
$$x + \tfrac{1}{2}x = 105$$

and so $\qquad\qquad \tfrac{3}{2}x = 105$

and $\qquad\qquad x = \tfrac{2}{3} \times 105 = 70$

From equation (ii)
$$y = 35$$

Check in (i) :
LHS $= 70 + 35$
$= 105$
RHS $= 105 \checkmark$

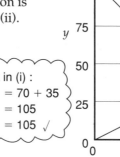
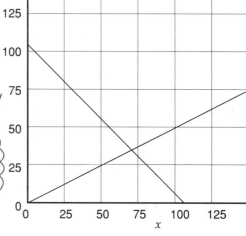

---

**E2** Find the point of intersection of the lines with equations :

(a) $\quad x + 2y = 180$
$\qquad\qquad y = \tfrac{1}{2}x$

(b) $\quad 2x + 3y = 28$
$\qquad\qquad y = x + 1$

(c) $\quad 3x + 4y = 36$
$\qquad\qquad x = y + 5$

---

**E3** Use either of the above methods to find the point of intersection of the lines with the following equations :

(a) $\quad 2x + 3y = 40$
$\qquad\qquad y = 2x$

(b) $\quad 5x + 4y = 51$
$\qquad\qquad y = 2x + 3$

(c) $\quad 2x + y = 18$
$\qquad\quad 3x - y = 17$

(d) $\quad 3x + 4y = 47$
$\qquad\quad 4x - 3y = 21$

(e) $\quad 8x - 3y = 5$
$\qquad\qquad y = 2x$

(f) $\quad 7x - 2y = 24$
$\qquad\qquad y = 3x - 1$

When both equations are in the form $"y = mx + c"$ it is easiest to proceed as shown below.

Consider the equations

$$y = 3x - 1 \quad \ldots \ldots \text{(i)}$$
$$y = 2x + 3 \quad \ldots \ldots \text{(ii)}$$

The lines represented by these equations are shown on the right.

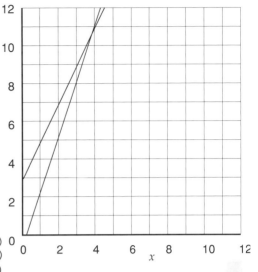

At the point where the lines intersect the $y$ values are equal. So
$$3x - 1 = 2x + 3$$

Subtracting $2x$ from both sides gives
$$x - 1 = 3$$

and then adding 1 to both sides gives
$$x = 4$$

From equation (i)
$$y = 3 \times 4 - 1$$
$$= 11$$

> Check in (ii) :
> LHS $= 11$
> RHS $= 2 \times 4 + 3$
> $= 11 \checkmark$

---

**E4    Find the point of intersection of the lines with the following equations :**

| | | | |
|---|---|---|---|
| **(a)** $y = 5x + 1$ | **(b)** $y = 2x - 3$ | **(c)** $y = 7x + 5$ | **(d)** $y = 3x - 4$ |
| $\phantom{(a)} y = 3x + 7$ | $\phantom{(b)} y = \frac{1}{2}x - 1$ | $\phantom{(c)} y = 3 - 4x$ | $\phantom{(d)} y = 7x + 8$ |

---

The method above can be applied to equations of the form $ax + by = d$ by rewriting them as $y = mx + c$. For example $2x + 3y = 7$ can be rewritten as

$$3y = {}^-2x + 7$$

and then as

$$y = \tfrac{{}^-2}{3}x + \tfrac{7}{3} \quad \ldots \ldots \text{(i)}$$

Similarly $5x + 2y = 12$ can be rewritten as

$$y = \tfrac{{}^-5}{2}x + 6 \quad \ldots \ldots \text{(ii)}$$

At the point of intersection of the two lines represented by the equations (i) and (ii) the $y$ values are equal and so

$$\tfrac{{}^-2}{3}x + \tfrac{7}{3} = \tfrac{{}^-5}{2}x + 6$$

Adding $\tfrac{5}{2}x$ to both sides and subtracting $\tfrac{7}{3}$ from both sides gives

$$\tfrac{5}{2}x - \tfrac{2}{3}x = 6 - \tfrac{7}{3}$$

From which
$$\tfrac{11}{6}x = \tfrac{11}{3}$$

and
$$x = 2$$

Hence from (ii)
$$y = 1$$

> Check in (i) :
> LHS $= 1$
> RHS $= \tfrac{{}^-2}{3} \times 2 + \tfrac{7}{3}$
> $= 1 \checkmark$

---

**E5    Try the method above for these equations**

| | | | |
|---|---|---|---|
| **(a)** $2x + y = 10$ | **(b)** $2x + 3y = 16$ | **(c)** $2x + y = 4$ | **(d)** $5x + y = 23$ |
| $\phantom{(a)} x - y = 2$ | $\phantom{(b)} 3x - y = 3$ | $\phantom{(c)} x + 3y = 7$ | $\phantom{(d)} 3x + 2y = 18$ |

**Check your answers with E1 (a), (b) and D4 (a), (b) where you solved the equations by a different method.**

# F : More problems

The method of optimisation which you have been using is called *linear programming*. (Linear because the graphs you have drawn have been straight lines.)

The methods of linear programming were originally developed between 1945 and 1955 by American mathematicians to solve problems arising in industry and economic planning. Many such problems involve constraints on the size of the workforce, the quantities of raw materials, the number of machines available and so on. The problems on the previous pages have two variables in them and can be solved graphically, but the problems occurring in industry have many more variables and have to be solved by computer. For example, in oil refineries problems arise with hundreds of variables and tens of thousands of constraints.

Another application is in determining the best diet for farm animals such as pigs. In order to maximise the profit a pig farmer needs to ensure that the pigs are fed appropriate food and sufficient quantities of it to produce lean meat. The pigs require a daily allocation of carbohydrate, protein, amino acids, minerals and vitamins. Each of these involves various components. For example, the mineral content includes calcium, phosphorus, salt, potassium, iron, magnesium, zinc, copper, manganese, iodine, selenium. There are therefore many constituents in the diet.

Here is a simplified diet problem.
- Each day a sow requires 50 megajoules of energy and 1 kilogram of protein.
- The sow is to be fed on barley and soya. Each kilogram of barley provides 13 megajoules of energy and contains 0.1 kg of protein. Each kilogram of soya provides 11 megajoules of energy and contains 0.4 kg of protein.
- A diet consisting of more than 2.5k g of barley per day may cause digestive problems.
- Barley costs £110 per tonne and soya costs £160 per tonne.
*Find the cheapest diet.*

Let the amounts of barley and soya be $x$ kg and $y$ kg respectively.
Then the energy constraint leads to the inequality
$$13x + 11y \geq 50 \quad \ldots \ldots (i)$$
and the weight constraint gives
$$0.1x + 0.4y \geq 1$$
which can be rewritten by multiplying through by 10 as
$$1x + 4y \geq 10 \quad \ldots \ldots (ii)$$
Also
$$x \leq 2.5 \quad \ldots \ldots (iii)$$

These inequalities are shown graphically on the opposite page.

The coordinates of A can be found by solving the equations
$$x = 2.5$$
$$x + 4y = 10$$

> **F1** Substitute $x = 2.5$ in the second equation to find $y$.

The coordinates of B can be found by solving the equations
$$13x + 11y = 50$$
$$x + 4y = 10$$

> **F2** Solve these equations (to 3 decimal places).
>
> **F3** Which point A, B or C gives the cheapest diet?

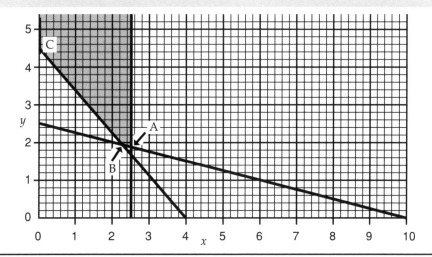

---

F4  A firm manufactures two types of box, each requiring the same amount of material. They both go through a folding machine and a stapling machine.

Type A boxes require 4 seconds on the folding machine and 3 seconds on the stapling machine.

Type B boxes require 2 seconds on the folding machine and 7 seconds on the stapling machine.

Each machine is available for 1 hour.

Suppose the number of Type A boxes made is $x$ and the number of Type B boxes is $y$. Write down two inequalities and represent them graphically. Shade out the regions which do *not* satisfy them.

There is a profit of 40p on Type A boxes and 30p on Type B boxes. How many of each type should be made to maximise the profit?

---

F5  A landscape designer has £200 to spend on planting trees and shrubs to landscape an area of 1000 m². For a tree he plans to allow 25 m² and for a shrub 10 m². Planting a tree will cost £2 and a shrub £5.

Set up appropriate inequalities and represent them graphically.

(a)  If the designer plants 30 shrubs what is the maximum number of trees which can be planted?

(b)  If the designer plants 3 shrubs for every tree, what is the maximum number of trees which can be planted?

---

F6  A contractor hiring earth-moving equipment has the choice of two machines. Type A costs £25 per day to hire, needs one man to operate it and moves 30 tonnes of earth per day. Type B costs £10 per day to hire, needs four men to operate it and moves 70 tonnes of earth per day.

The contractor can spend up to £500 per day, has a labour force of 64 men available and can use a maximum of 25 machines on the site.

Set up appropriate inequalities and represent them graphically.

Find the maximum weight of earth that the contractor can move in one day.

# G : For discussion

Solve these equations.
Choose the most convenient method each time.

(a)  $7a + 3b = 54$
     $5a + 2b = 34$

(b)  $2m + 6n = 9$
          $n = 2m - 3$

(c)      $q = 7p - 2$
          $q = 2p - 5$

(d)  $8r - 5v = 22$
     $3r + 7v = 26$

> Letters other than $x$ or $y$ can be used in equations!

Try to solve these equations:

(a)  $2x + 3y = 5$
     $4x + 6y = 12$

(b)  $2x + 3y = 5$
     $4x + 6y = 10$

By drawing graphs explain what is going on.

What does the graph with equation

$$y = mx + c$$

look like when

(a)  $m > 0, c > 0$
(b)  $m < 0, c > 0$ ?
     etc.

What does the graph with equation

$$ax + by = c$$

look like when

(a)  $a > 0, b > 0, c > 0$
(b)  $a > 0, b < 0, c > 0$ ?
     etc.

What is the equation of this line?

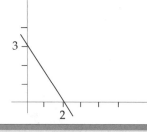

Generalise :

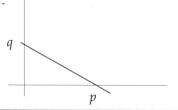

$2x + 3y = 5$ is the equation of a line.

Is there a geometrical interpretation of the equation

$2x + 3y + 6z = 12$ ?

Solve the equations

$2x + 3y + z = 13$
$4x - 2y + 3z = 15$
$7x + 5y - 2z = 7$

Is there a general formula for solving equations of the form

$$ax + by = p$$
$$cx + dy = q ?$$

What about exceptional cases?
A computer program?

The greatest profit, etc. seems to occur at or near a vertex of the appropriate polygon.
Is this always so?
Is there a way to find out where the maximum profit occurs without having to try various points?

# Now try these . . .

1. On half-centimetre squared paper draw the lines with equations
$$x + 2y = 8$$
$$2x + y = 10$$

By shading out the regions not required find regions such that
$$x + 2y \leq 8$$
$$\text{and} \quad 2x + y \geq 10$$

2. Solve the equations and illustrate graphically:

(a) $5x + 2y = 20$
    $x + y = 7$

(b) $4x - 6y = 12$
    $2x + y = 14$

(c) $7x - 8y = 12$
    $y = \frac{1}{2}x$

3. A camp site for caravans and tents has an area of 1800 m² and is subject to the following regulations :

- The number of caravans must not exceed 6.
- Reckoning on 4 persons per caravan and 3 per tent, the total number of persons must not exceed 48.
- At least 200 m² must be available for each caravan and 90 m² for each tent.

The nightly charges are £2 for a caravan and £1 for a tent.

Suppose there are $x$ caravans and $y$ tents. Write the three regulations as inequalities. Show the inequalities on graph paper.

Find the greatest possible nightly takings.

How many caravans and tents should be admitted if the site owner wants to make the maximum profit and have
(a) as many caravans as possible,
(b) as many tents as possible?

4. A small firm which produces radios employs both skilled workers and apprentices. Its workforce must not exceed 30 people and it must make at least 360 radios per week to satisfy demand. On average a skilled worker can assemble 24 radios and an apprentice 10 radios per week.

Union regulations state that the number of apprentices must be less than the number of skilled workers but more than half of the number of skilled workers.

Set up appropriate inequalities and find graphically the greatest number of skilled workers that can be employed.

Skilled workers are paid £300 a week, and apprentices £100 a week.

How many of each should be employed to keep the wage bill as low as possible?

Note the wording : "less than" not "less than or equal to". Therefore points on the line are not included. Show this by drawing a dotted line for this statement. Similarly use a dotted line for the "more than" statement.

5. The annual subscription for a tennis club is £20 for adults and £8 for juniors. The club needs to raise at least £800 in subscriptions to cover its expenses. The total number of members is to be restricted to 50. The number of junior members is to be between one quarter and one third of the number of adult members.

Represent the information graphically and find the numbers of adult and junior members which will bring in the largest amount of money in subscriptions.

Find also the least total membership which will satisfy the conditions.

6. The numbers of units of vitamins $A$, $B$ and $C$ in each kilogram of two foods $X$ and $Y$ are as follows:

|          | Vitamin A | Vitamin B | Vitamin C |
|----------|-----------|-----------|-----------|
| Food $X$ | 5         | 2         | 6         |
| Food $Y$ | 4         | 6         | 2         |

A mixture of the two foods is made which has to contain at least 20 units of vitamin $A$, at least 24 units of vitamin $B$ and at least 12 units of vitamin $C$ .

Represent the information graphically and find the smallest total amount to satisfy these constraints.

Food $Y$ is three times as expensive as Food $X$. Find the amounts of each to minimise the cost and satisfy the constraints.

7. In laying out a car park it is decided, in the hope of making the best use of the available parking space (7200 sq. ft.), to have some spaces for small cars, the rest for large cars. For each small space 90 sq. ft. is allowed and for each large space 120 sq. ft. Every car must occupy a space of the appropriate size. It is reliably estimated that, of the cars wishing to park at any given time, the ratio of small to large will be neither less than 2 : 3 nor greater than 2 : 1.

Represent the information graphically and find the number of spaces of each type in order to maximise the number of cars that can be parked.

# Making comparisons

Some sixteen year olds who had part-time jobs were asked how much money they had earned in the previous week.
Here are the results in £ to the nearest ten pence:

| | | | | | | | | | |
|---|---|---|---|---|---|---|---|---|---|
| *Female :* | 9.10 | 16.40 | 7.60 | 13.20 | 5.20 | 20.50 | 23.20 | 17.60 | 8.70 |
| *Male:* | 11.70 | 14.20 | 8.10 | 24.80 | 19.90 | 6.00 | 12.90 | 27.60 | 15.00 |
| | 18.30 | 10.30 | 22.60 | | | | | | |

Compare the earnings of males and females.

Compare the sentence lengths from contrasting newspapers such as The Times and the Daily Mirror.
You might be able to find articles from the two papers on the same subject.

Are the weights of Brand X more variable than the weights of Brand Y? With the cooperation of the school shop (or some other shop) weigh packets of crisps of two different makes.

Compare the times taken to deliver first- and second-class mail.
You might be able to get the school office to save discarded envelopes for you.

# A : Position and spread

It is not easy to compare the wages for females and males from the lists on the previous page.
One way to make the data visual is to show it on number lines:

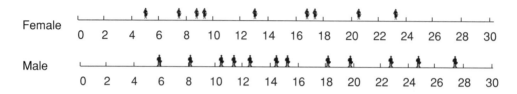

These number line pictures then suggest two questions:
- **Where roughly are the numbers 'centred' on each number line?**
- **How are the numbers spread out on each number line?**

- The first question is asking for an average position.
One possible average is the **median average** (the half-way number).
There were 9 female students. The median wage is therefore the wage of the 5th student, when arranged in increasing order.

*Check that this is £13.20*

> **Reminder**
> When there is an even number of items the median is taken as half-way between the two middle items.

**A1** Find the median average for the male students.
Compare the two medians.

The median is easy to find and gives a central position unaffected by 'freak' numbers, large or small. But it does not take into account all the information.
Another average is the **mean average.**
For the female students the mean average is $\dfrac{\text{total wage of the 9 female students}}{9}$.

*Check that this is £13.50*

**A2** Find the mean average for the male students.
Compare the two means.

- The second question is asking for a measure of spread.
An obvious measure of spread is the **range:**
    largest wage − smallest wage

*Check that the range for the wages of the female students is £18.*

**A3** Find the range for the wages of the male students.
Compare the two ranges.

The range is influenced by 'freak' numbers at the ends and might therefore be unfairly large when most of the data might be more compact. Sometimes the lower and upper quarters of the data are ignored and the *inter-quartile range* is used. But this is not worth bothering with when there are such small sets of data as here.

Another way to describe the spread is to see how the wages deviate from a central position such as the mean.

The diagram shows the deviations of four of the wages of the females from the mean (£13.50).

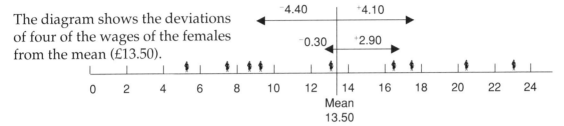

The deviations are more conveniently shown in a table:

*Check that the sum of the deviations is 0.*
*Explain why this must be so.*

In finding the spread it is irrelevant whether a deviation is to the left or to the right. The negative numbers therefore need to be made positive. An obvious way to do this is to ignore the sign. However, for reasons which become apparent in more advanced study, it is not usual to do this. An alternative way to make numbers positive is to *square them.* (A negative number squared is positive!) The next table shows the squares of all the deviations.

| Wage (£) | Deviation from mean |
|---|---|
| 5.20 | ⁻8.30 |
| 7.60 | ⁻5.90 |
| 8.70 | ⁻4.80 |
| 9.10 | ⁻4.40 |
| 13.20 | ⁻0.30 |
| 16.40 | ⁺2.90 |
| 17.60 | ⁺4.10 |
| 20.50 | ⁺7.00 |
| 23.20 | ⁺9.70 |
| | |

The right-hand column has been added up to find the total of the squared deviations. For comparison purposes it is sensible to divide this total by the number of female students (9): $\dfrac{314.50}{9}$

The result will be in square pounds! So finally take the square root to return to the original units (£): $\sqrt{\dfrac{314.50}{9}}$

*Check that this gives 5.91 (to 2 dp).*

The resulting number is called the **standard deviation**.

Clearly, if the original wages were very spread out the result of the calculation will be large. On the other hand if the original wages were close together the result of the calculation will be small. The standard deviation does therefore give us a measure of how spread out the numbers are.

| Wage (£) | Deviation from mean | (Deviation from mean)² |
|---|---|---|
| 5.20 | ⁻8.30 | 68.89 |
| 7.60 | ⁻5.90 | 34.81 |
| 8.70 | ⁻4.80 | 23.04 |
| 9.10 | ⁻4.40 | 19.36 |
| 13.20 | ⁻0.30 | 0.09 |
| 16.40 | ⁺2.90 | 8.41 |
| 17.60 | ⁺4.10 | 16.81 |
| 20.50 | ⁺7.00 | 49.00 |
| 23.20 | ⁺9.70 | 94.09 |
| | | |
| | | 314.50 |

**Did you know?**
- In many situations the data clusters fairly closely around the mean. Most of it is within two standard deviations of the mean. Very rarely is data more than three standard deviations from the mean.

The method on the previous page can be written in one sentence like this:

$$\text{Standard deviation} = \sqrt{\frac{\text{sum of squared deviations from the mean}}{\text{number of items}}}$$

The stages of the calculation were as follows:

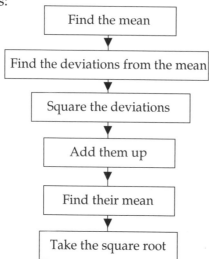

Find the mean

Find the deviations from the mean

Square the deviations

Add them up

Find their mean

Take the square root

**For discussion**
- Calculate the mean and the standard deviation of the numbers
    1, 4, 8, 9

  Deduce the mean and the standard deviation of

  (a)   21, 24, 28, 29

  (b)   3.01, 3.04, 3.08, 3.09

**A4**   **Find the standard deviation of the wages of the male students, setting out your calculation as on the previous page. See A2 for the mean.**
**Compare it with the standard deviation of the wages of the female students.**

**A5**   **The weights in grams of packets of sugar from two packing machines were recorded:**

**Machine A** 1043  1014  1065  1052  1027  1071  1038  1026

**Machine B** 1026  1037  1015  1046  1009  1024  1051  1024

**Compare the outputs of the two machines by calculating the means and standard deviations.**

**A6**   **The house prices (£ thousands) in two districts of a town were recorded from an estate agent's advertisement:**

**District A**   79      56      134    91      127    83

**District B**   68      115    150    105    86      139    128

**Compare the prices in the two districts.**

**You could ...**
- Collect data as suggested on page 179 and make comparisons.

# B : Using calculators and computers

The table shows the monthly unemployment figures in millions for the UK from 1986 to 1991.

| | 1986 | 1987 | 1988 | 1989 | 1990 | 1991 |
|---|---|---|---|---|---|---|
| Jan | 3.41 | 3.30 | 2.72 | 2.07 | 1.69 | 1.96 |
| Feb | 3.34 | 3.23 | 2.67 | 2.02 | 1.68 | 2.05 |
| Mar | 3.32 | 3.14 | 2.59 | 1.96 | 1.65 | 2.14 |
| Apr | 3.33 | 3.11 | 2.54 | 1.88 | 1.63 | 2.20 |
| May | 3.27 | 2.99 | 2.43 | 1.80 | 1.58 | 2.21 |
| Jun | 3.23 | 2.91 | 2.34 | 1.74 | 1.56 | 2.24 |
| Jul | 3.28 | 2.91 | 2.33 | 1.77 | 1.62 | 2.37 |
| Aug | 3.28 | 2.87 | 2.29 | 1.74 | 1.66 | 2.44 |
| Sep | 3.33 | 2.87 | 2.31 | 1.70 | 1.67 | 2.45 |
| Oct | 3.24 | 2.75 | 2.12 | 1.64 | 1.67 | 2.43 |
| Nov | 3.22 | 2.69 | 2.07 | 1.61 | 1.73 | 2.47 |
| Dec | 3.23 | 2.70 | 2.05 | 1.64 | 1.85 | 2.55 |

In order to compare the data the mean and standard deviations for each year could be found.
This would involve a large amount of computation if it was done by hand in a table as on the previous three pages.
It is therefore sensible to use a 'machine' to do the computations.

- Many scientific calculators have keys for finding the mean and the standard deviation of a set of numbers.
  You will need to find out how *your* calculator can be used for these statistical calculations.
  A word of warning: there might be two keys on your calculator which give standard deviation. The one which coresponds to the process in this chapter is often labelled $\sigma_n$ or $s_n$.

- It is also possible to use a computer to find means and standard deviations either with appropriate software or by writing your own program.

**B1** Use a calculator or computer to find the mean and standard deviation of the data above
(a) for each year
(b) for each month.
Write a brief report comparing the data.

**B2** To show any trends in data of this type it is useful to calculate quarterly moving averages.
Use a calculator or computer to find the moving averages and plot them on graph paper.
Make some comments about your results.
(The first moving average is
$$\frac{3.41 + 3.34 + 3.32}{3}$$
The second is $\frac{3.34 + 3.32 + 3.33}{3}$ )

**You could ...**
- Calculate the mean and standard deviation of
  0, 1, 2, 3, 4, 5, 6, 7, 8, 9
  Random digits from a computer or a calculator should occur with equal frequencies. So their mean and standard deviation should be as you have just calculated.
  Generate a sample of random digits and calculate their mean and standard deviation. Compare with the theoretical values.

# Facts and formulas

| | | |
|---|---|---|
| **Triangle** | Area | $= \frac{1}{2} \times$ base $\times$ perpendicular height |
| **Trapezium** | Area | $= \frac{1}{2} \times$ sum of parallel sides $\times$ distance between them |
| **Circle** | Circumference | $= \pi \times$ diameter $\qquad = \pi d$ |
| | Area | $= \pi \times$ (radius)$^2$ $\qquad = \pi r^2$ |
| **Prism** | Volume | $=$ area of cross-section $\times$ length |
| **Cylinder** | Volume | $=$ area of circular end $\times$ height $= \pi \times$ (radius)$^2 \times$ height $= \pi r^2 h$ |
| | Curved surface area | $=$ circumference of circular end $\times$ height $\qquad = \pi d h$ |
| **Pyramid** | Volume | $= \frac{1}{3} \times$ area of base $\times$ perpendicular height |
| **Cone** | Volume | $= \frac{1}{3} \times$ area of base $\times$ perpendicular height $\qquad = \frac{1}{3}\pi r^2 h$ |
| | Curved surface area | $= \pi \times$ base radius $\times$ slant height $\qquad = \pi r l$ |
| **Sphere** | Volume | $= \frac{4}{3} \times \pi \times$ (radius)$^3$ $\qquad = \frac{4}{3}\pi r^3$ |
| | Surface area | $= 4 \times \pi \times$ (radius)$^2$ $\qquad = 4\pi r^2$ |

| | | |
|---|---|---|
| 1 hectare (ha) | $=$ 10000 | square metres (m$^2$) |
| 1 litre (l) | $=$ 1000 | cubic centimetres (cm$^3$) |
| 1 cubic metre (m$^3$) | $=$ 1000 | litres (l) |
| 1 tonne (t) | $=$ 1000 | kilograms (kg) |
| 1 kilowatt (kW) | $=$ 1000 | watts (W) |

| | | |
|---|---|---|
| 1 metre | *is about* | 39.37 inches |
| 2.54 centimetres | *is about* | 1 inch |
| 1.61 kilometres | *is about* | 1 mile |
| 1 kilometre | *is about* | 0.621 miles |
| 1 hectare | *is about* | 2.47 acres |
| 4.55 litres | *is about* | 1 gallon |
| 1 kilogram | *is about* | 2.20 pounds |
| 28.3 grams | *is about* | 1 ounce |

**Pythagoras' Theorem**

$$c^2 = a^2 + b^2$$

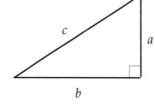

**Trigonometry**

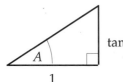

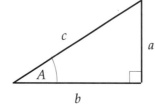

$a = b \times \tan A$

$\tan A = \dfrac{a}{b} = \dfrac{\text{opposite}}{\text{adjacent}}$

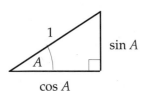

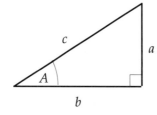

$a = c \times \sin A$

$\sin A = \dfrac{a}{c} = \dfrac{\text{opposite}}{\text{hypotenuse}}$

$b = c \times \cos A$

$\cos A = \dfrac{b}{c} = \dfrac{\text{adjacent}}{\text{hypotenuse}}$